HOW
TO IMPROVE
PERFORMANCE
THROUGH
APPRAISAL AND
COACHING

HOW TO IMPROVE PERFORMANCE THROUGH APPRAISAL AND COACHING

Donald L. Kirkpatrick

Foreword by James L. Hayes
FORMER PRESIDENT AND CHIEF EXECUTIVE OFFICER

AMERICAN MANAGEMENT ASSOCIATION

amacom

American Management Association

Library of Congress Cataloging in Publication Data
Kirkpatrick, Donald L.
    How to improve performance through appraisal and coaching.

    Includes index.
    1. Employees, Rating of.   I. Title.
HF5549.5.R3K54   658.3'125   81-66221
ISBN 0-8144-5719-3   AACR2

Ninth Printing

Foreword

There are some ideas in management whose time comes and goes and comes again, depending on circumstances of economy or fashion. I have in mind such things as direct costing, the most profitable means of inventory valuation, and the eternal shift between centralization and decentralization of authority. There are other ideas whose time is ever present and whose demands for effective practice are immutable. Of these perhaps the most pertinent for all managers anywhere in no matter what type of operation—whether in the public or the private sector, whether in a market or a socialist economy—is the need for effective performance appraisal.

The end result of any proper appraisal system, according to Donald L. Kirkpatrick in this extensive treatment of the subject, is to improve performance through a combination of on-the-job coaching, appraisals, counseling sessions, interviews, and performance improvement plans jointly developed by manager and subordinate. Effective communication of expectations and achievements is also necessary. All well and good; few would argue with this philosophy. Why then, we may ask, do good intentions go awry, and why is the system itself so often feared by employees and managers alike?

Kirkpatrick guides us step by step through all the elements of a workable performance improvement program, from both the standpoint of the practicing manager and that of the program's overall administrator. He shows conclusively at each step, the logic of the process and the reasons that it will ultimately lead to success. By building up the process in this logical, well-reasoned fashion, he removes the manager's uneasiness about conducting appraisals, and this in turn goes a long way toward relieving the subordinate's apprehensiveness about the whole question of performance improvement. Rather than something to be dreaded and faced up to once a year or so, or a disagreeable duty that must be rushed through by all parties as quickly as possible, performance appraisal and employee coaching are strong, very positive actions. They are perhaps the most important tools that managers can use in their job of getting things done through others.

Kirkpatrick points up some fresh techniques in performance appraisal and improvement. One of the most important is what he calls "significant job segments'' and their role in appraisal. He also includes advice and comments from successful athletic coaches and points out the similarities in approach between coaching professional athletes and coaching employees.

Significant job segments are those seven or eight major factors that must be evaluated by the manager in any appraisal interview. They have the virtue of focusing attention on results rather than on some such irrelevancy as personality. They also serve to eliminate the less crucial or repetitive elements in a job so that the manager and employee can concentrate on achievement and improvement, not isolated instances of superior or mediocre performance.

The significant job segments describe *what* is done. And so they lead to standards of performance, which describe for the boss and the employee *how well* the job must be done. By describing the proper use of performance standards, Kirkpatrick achieves possibly his greatest contribution in his valid and forceful presentation. For it is through standards of performance that the employee understands what he or she is expected to accomplish. Standards also permit the manager to evaluate performance—not hearsay—and plot a path for the employee's improvement and development. As few other ideas or systems have done, performance standards help the manager to eliminate bias and prejudice in evaluating performance. What a powerful managerial tool these standards are, benefiting both the organization and the individual. Kirkpatrick shows us exactly how they are developed and administered.

But despite all the correct form and procedures, a mechanical, routinized, robotlike approach can rob even the best evaluation programs of their effectiveness. Performance appraisal as described in this book extends beyond the formal interview. When most productive and decisive, it is really a day-to-day concern with people. It is helping people set their goals and then helping them to achieve those goals. It is being available when needed. It is daily communication of expectations and feedback on results. It is on-the-job coaching in new areas of endeavor and counseling in weak areas of performance. It is concern with people and helping them grow. Helping people improve their performance and watching them develop are the rewards that effective managers cherish most. This book will provide some practical ideas and approaches to help managers improve their effectiveness in these areas.

James L. Hayes
*Former President
and Chief Executive Officer
American Management Association*

Preface

If you are a manager who conducts performance appraisals with subordinates, you may find this book somewhat frustrating because you are probably locked into a program with forms and procedures. However, regardless of the forms and approaches you are required to use, you will find some practical help in such areas as clarifying what's expected, appraising performance, self-appraisal, conducting the appraisal interview, developing a performance improvement plan, and on-the-job coaching. You'll be particularly interested in the comments from some nationally known athletic coaches, and you'll be amazed by how much of their advice will apply directly to you on your job.

Part II includes sample forms, case studies, and research conducted by General Electric. This material will be of practical use as you evaluate your own philosophy, forms, and procedures.

Also, this book may help you discover why your program isn't working as well as you'd like it to. If you have any suggestions that you think will help improve your performance review program, pass them along to those in your organization who are responsible for the program's administration.

If you have an overall responsibility for an effective performance appraisal and review program in your organization, this book will have special benefit for you. If you already have a program, you can compare it with the ideas, examples, and case studies presented here. Of particular interest and benefit to you will be Chapter 6, which describes the five requirements for effective programs and gives some specific ideas for improving them.

If you have no program at all and are about to establish one, the book will be of maximum benefit. Study the principles and approaches suggested here, and read the listed references describing the philosophies and recommendations of other writers. Also, study the case studies presented in Part II. After this study and analysis, develop and implement your own program as described in Chapter 6.

Whether you are appraising and coaching employees, administering an existing program, or establishing a new one, I hope this book will give you ideas that will make your job more rewarding and your program more successful.

Donald L. Kirkpatrick

Contents

PART I
EMPLOYEE PERFORMANCE, APPRAISAL, AND COACHING

A Conceptual Framework for the
Appraisal/Coaching Process   **3**

Pretest   **4**

1 **Introduction and Overview**   **7**
How to Get Maximum Performance from Subordinates
The Performance Review Program

2 **The Basis for Appraisal**   **26**
Significant Job Segments
Standards of Performance

3 **The Appraisal and the Interview**   **45**
The Appraisal Process
Preparing for the Appraisal Interview
Conducting the Appraisal Interview

4 **The Performance Improvement Plan**   **61**
Preparing an Effective Plan

5 **On-the-Job Coaching**   **73**
The Effective Coach
Coaching Approaches and Techniques

6 **Five Program Requirements**   **92**
An Effective Performance Review Program

Posttest   **100**

Test Answers and Reasons for Them   **103**

PART II
APPLICATIONS: EXAMPLES FROM VARIOUS ORGANIZATIONS

7 Sample Forms   109

8 Case Study: A Large Midwestern
    Heavy Manufacturing Organization   174

9 Case Study: General Motors Corporation   207

10 Case Study: Kimberly-Clark Corporation   240

11 Research at General Electric Company   253

Index   260

Part I
Employee Performance, Appraisal, and Coaching

A Conceptual Framework for the Appraisal/Coaching Process

In order to get improved performance from appraisal and coaching, a continuous process is necessary. It can be illustrated by the following diagram.

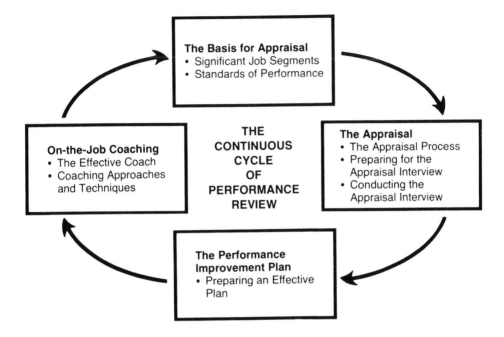

The first step is to clarify what's expected of the subordinate. This can be done by identifying significant job segments and developing standards of performance. The second step is to appraise performance and discuss it in an appraisal interview. At the conclusion of the interview, a performance review plan can be developed. On-the-job coaching is necessary to help the subordinate improve the performance. The first step is repeated on whatever time schedule is established by the organization.

On the next page is a pretest dealing with the philosophy and principles discussed in this book. Complete it to see what you know before you begin to read. The same test is included on page 100 as a posttest to complete *after* you read Part I of this book. My suggested answers, and the reasons for them, follow the posttest. I suggest that you not look at the answers until after you have finished both tests. Then you can compare your two scores to see what you learned.

Pretest

Write "yes" in front of each statement if you agree and "no" if you disagree.

_____   1. Every employee has responsibility for his or her own development.

_____   2. Every manager has responsibility for the growth and development of all subordinates.

_____   3. Every organization has responsibility for the growth and development of all employees.

_____   4. Most people want to know how they are doing their job as the boss sees it.

_____   5. Most employees would like to improve their performance.

_____   6. Less than maximum performance of an employee is often due to factors over which the employee has no control.

_____   7. The same performance review program (forms, procedures, interview) should be used both for improved performance and for salary administration.

_____   8. Performance appraisals and reviews should be voluntary on the part of managers.

_____   9. The more writing required of the boss on the appraisal form, the more effective the program.

_____   10. The less paperwork required in a performance appraisal program, the more effective the program.

_____   11. Appraisal forms should include about a 50-50 balance between items dealing with performance and those dealing with personality.

_____   12. Agreement on significant job segments and standards of performance is an important prerequisite to the appraisal of job performance.

_____   13. The word "appraisal" connotes both judgment and communication.

_____   14. A group appraisal of a person's performance is better than having an appraisal just by the boss.

_____   15. A self-appraisal by the subordinate is a good idea.

_____   16. The main objective of the appraisal interview is for the boss to explain and sell his or her prepared appraisal to the subordinate.

_____   17. In the interview discussing the performance of the subordinate, there should be no surprises.

_____   18. In an appraisal interview, it's a good idea to have at least three people present (for example, the boss, the subordinate, and a neutral party such as a representative of the personnel department).

_____   19. Appraisal interviews should be a pleasant experience for both boss and subordinate.

_____ 20. In the appraisal interview, the boss should not show his or her completed form to the subordinate.

_____ 21. An organization can be assured that an effective appraisal interview has been conducted if the employee is required to sign the form.

_____ 22. In an appraisal interview, the boss should always give his or her appraisal of the subordinate and then ask the subordinate for reactions and comments.

_____ 23. It's a good idea to divide the appraisal interview into two or three separate interviews.

_____ 24. An appraisal interview should always end on a positive note.

_____ 25. A specific written performance improvement plan is an important part of a performance review program.

_____ 26. A performance improvement plan should include what should be done, by whom, and when.

_____ 27. It's a good idea for employees to work toward performance improvement in several areas at once.

_____ 28. Coaching means the same as counseling.

_____ 29. Coaching a group of employees is similar to coaching a team of athletes.

_____ 30. On-the-job coaching is necessary to be sure that the performance improvement plan is implemented.

_____ 31. Coaching on the job should include praise for good work as well as constructive criticism and help to improve poor work.

_____ 32. Improvement in performance should be immediately rewarded by the boss.

_____ 33. Rewards should be based on performance rather than seniority.

_____ 34. Both the boss and subordinate should have a copy of all completed forms.

_____ 35. A copy of the completed appraisal forms should be put in the personnel file of the subordinate.

_____ 36. A standard of performance should be:

_____   a.   Established for a job.

_____   b.   Established for an individual.

_____   c.   An "acceptable" level of performance.

_____   d.   A "well done" level of performance.

_____   e.   Challenging (requires stretch but can be reached).

_____   f.   Unattainable (requires stretch and can't be reached).

_____   g.   Agreed on between boss and subordinate.

_____   h.   Determined solely by the boss.

_____   i.   Determined solely by the subordinate.

_____   j.   Jointly determined by boss and subordinate.

_____   k. Clear to boss and subordinate.
_____   l. Written.
_____   m. Time-oriented.
_____   n. Specific (numbers, percentages, dollars, wherever possible).
_____   o. The basis for performance appraisal.
_____   p. Subject to change.
_____ 37. The same appraisal forms and procedures can be effectively used by any kind of organization.
_____ 38. The people supervising a performance appraisal program must do more than simply oversee paperwork. They must communicate the program and sell it to those involved.
_____ 39. It takes no real training to conduct performance reviews effectively.
_____ 40. Administrative controls must be established for performance review programs.

1
Introduction and Overview

How to Get Maximum Performance
_____from Subordinates _____

The major challenge that faces managers in all types of organizations is how to get maximum performance from their subordinates. First, they need to motivate their subordinates—to get maximum effort from them. This means ensuring that people will try their best to do the job, and it can be measured by the energy and time subordinates expend. If only motivation would guarantee maximum results! Unfortunately, much of this energy and time is wasted. Therefore, the second requirement is for managers to get maximum accomplishments and achievements from their subordinates. This twofold challenge—effort plus results—faces every manager.

Ways to Improve Employee Performance

On a recent visit to India, I was asked by the manager of a small clothing shop in the Chola Hotel in Madras, "What is the one thing that managers can do to get their employees to do their best?" I replied that it isn't as simple as "just one thing." He repeated the question, "What is the *one thing* that managers can do to get their employees to do their best?" I hemmed and hawed and started to tell him that there are eight things.

He interrupted and said, "Don't tell me eight, tell me *one!*" I said, "I can't." He replied, "Then I'll tell you!" I answered, "O.K., you tell me."

And he did. "You have to give your people encouragement. It doesn't mean just money, although that's one of the ways to encourage your people. It also means a pat on the back when they do a good job. If you rub them into the

7

ground with your heel, you won't get the best work from them, and they won't like you besides.''

I was supposed to be the expert who was conducting seminars on leadership for managers in business and government in India. And I received a good lesson in motivation from a shopkeeper in the basement of a hotel.

It isn't quite as simple as encouragement, but that's a good start. Here are the eight conditions I was going to describe to the shop owner that will get maximum effort and results from employees:

1. Make the job important in the eyes of the employee.
2. Select a person who has the potential to perform the job.
3. Clarify what's expected of the employee in the job.
4. Train the employee in the necessary knowledge, skills, and attitudes.
5. Evaluate performance, and communicate results and expectations to the employee.
6. Help him or her improve performance.
7. Maintain rapport with the employee.
8. Reward for performance.

These eight conditions will be developed further in the following paragraphs.

Make the Job Important

People who feel their jobs are important are more apt to try their best, because they realize that it does make a difference how well the job is done.

In his research, Frederick Herzberg[1] found that the major factors leading to motivation and satisfaction had to do with the job itself and not with policies, the boss, salary, and working conditions. To be specific, he found that the following factors were most important in creating satisfaction:

> Feeling of achievement for doing a good job.
> Being recognized for good work.
> The actual work being done.
> Being given broader responsibility.
> Growth on the job.

On the basis of his research he formulated a theory called motivation through job enrichment. When the manager increases the scope and importance of the job, people are more apt to put forth maximum effort.

Select the Right Person

The well-known Peter Principle states that people tend to rise to their level of incompetence.[2] One reason for incompetence is that people are promoted on the basis of performance. Where the old job and the new ones are alike, performance is a valid basis for promotion. But where the jobs are different, performance may be a poor criterion for promotion. This is especially true where the promotion is from a "doer" to management. Management, according to Lawrence A. Appley, past president of the American Management Associations, is "getting things done through others" rather than doing them yourself.

When considering a person for a job, whether it is an entry-level job or a promotion, the problem is to match the person to the job. Usually the match is not a perfect one because the candidates have never done that exact job before. Therefore, the potential of the person must be determined. In other words, the question should be asked, "With the proper training, would this person be able to perform the job successfully?"

Potential is a difficult thing to measure. Typically, the candidates' backgrounds are analyzed with special emphasis on education and experience. Next, interviews are conducted, and the candidates are evaluated on the basis of their answers to questions as well as their appearance and the impression they make on the interviewer. Often references are checked to find out from former supervisors or acquaintances how the people performed in previous jobs. Some organizations also use testing and assessment centers. The higher the job level, the more time and money an organization should spend to determine potential.

There is good evidence that many people are promoted to supervisory positions who never should have been. The typical selection process places undue emphasis on performance, years of service, and cooperative attitude. A more systematic approach has been recommended by Kirkpatrick, Coverdale, and Olsen-Tjensvold in their manual, *Selecting and Training First-Line Supervisors*.[3] They stress the importance of desire—*wanting* to be a supervisor—as well as leadership qualities.

Clarify What's Expected

Many frustrations and failures occur because employees don't understand exactly what's expected of them by their supervisors. They put forth much effort doing what they *think* is wanted, rather than what *is* wanted.

When I worked for a large chemical corporation, my friend Bill worked for Joe, a vice president. One day Bill and I had this conversation:

Bill: I think I'm in trouble with Joe, my boss.
Don: What do you mean?
Bill: I don't think Joe is happy with my performance.
Don: What makes you think so?
Bill: I just have a feeling.
Don: Has he told you he's unhappy with your performance?
Bill: No, he hasn't told me anything about my performance since I started working here nine months ago.

Don: Then why do you think he's unhappy?

Bill: Well, he gave me a three-page job description when I came, and I can't do everything that he expects.

Don: What are you doing?

Bill: I'm doing the things I think are most important.

Don: And?

Bill: I'm not sure *he* thinks they are the most important.

Don: I have a suggestion.

Bill: What?

Don: Go and see Joe and tell him your problem. Take the job description with you, and show him the things you are doing and the things you aren't doing. And see if he agrees.

Bill: I can't.

Don: Why not?

Bill: Because he's not available. He's either up in the president's office or else he's out of town or busy entertaining some important people.

Don: Then the only suggestion I have for you is to try to do the things that *he* thinks are important instead of those *you* think are important.

About three months later, I learned that Bill had been terminated for "poor performance." Because of our conversation, I was most interested in learning more about the termination. I got my chance one noon when I saw Joe sitting alone in the company dining room.

Don: Joe, can I talk with you for a few minutes?

Joe: Sure, have a chair.

Don: I understand that you terminated Bill a couple of weeks ago.

Joe: That's right.

Don: Would you mind telling me why?

Joe: Not at all. He just wasn't doing his job.

Don: Can you be more specific?

Joe: Sure. He was spending his time and energy on the unimportant parts of his job and wasn't getting the most important things done.

Don: Did you ever tell him what the most important parts of his job were?

Joe: I gave him a job description. I expected him to be smart enough to know which things were most important!

Then I related to Joe the conversation that Bill and I had had several months earlier. Joe replied, "Well, that's life. If he wasn't smart enough to separate the important things from the unimportant things, that's his problem!"

I was very disappointed in Joe, not so much for actually terminating Bill, but for his attitude toward it. I had hoped that Joe would have felt some guilt and would have learned something from the incident.

There are many Joes in management who do not clarify what is expected of subordinates. And there are many Bills who suffer the consequences even if they have the necessary qualifications and try their best. I only hope that most of the Joes who read this book will look at their own situations and either take the initiative in clarifying what's expected or at least make themselves available to subordinates who have the courage to ask for clarification themselves.

Train the Person

No matter how well the person matches the job, some training is always necessary. Training includes the teaching of knowledge, skills, and attitudes. The first step is to decide who will be the trainer. The qualifications are:

Knowledge and skill in doing the job.
A desire to teach.
Communication skills.
Patience.
A positive attitude toward the organization and the job to be learned.
A knowledge of teaching methods and procedures.
Time to train.

Many supervisors like to do the training personally. They are usually the best ones if they meet the other requirements listed above. But some are too busy or lack one or more of the qualifications, so they delegate the training to someone else. If this is done, the supervisor should be sure that the chosen trainer is qualified, and even then, some checking is necessary to be sure that an effective job has been done. The supervisor may delegate the task to another person, but the supervisor has final responsibility and must live with the results.

If the person being trained is a supervisor, the training should emphasize management knowledge, skills, and attitudes. This means that the boss usually has to call on outside help for the training, such as in-house management courses or those presented by outside organizations. And it's a good idea to begin the management training as soon as the new supervisor is appointed. As an example, a one-day conference at the Management Institute of the University of Wisconsin—Extension is called "Basics of Management for New Supervisors," and it is designed for organizations that do not have a similar in-house program. Other universities, associations, and consultants offer similar training programs.

In addition to courses, a management library should be available for new supervisors. The books should be carefully selected so that they are readable and practical for the supervisor.

The jump from "doer" to manager is a big one. Great care must be taken to ensure that the new supervisor not only knows the difference between a "doer" and a manager, but also has the knowledge, skills, and attitudes necessary for success.

Evaluate Performance and Communicate the Appraisal

People want to know how they are doing on the job, and it is the responsibility of the boss to tell them. This requires the boss to evaluate their performance and communicate the appraisal to them. This process of appraisal and communication should be regular and ongoing; bosses should not wait until the annual appraisal interview to do it. Nor should they rely entirely on informal day-to-day coaching. Instead, both formal and informal appraisals are necessary. This book will cover in detail the process as well as the forms and procedures for an effective performance appraisal program.

Help the Person Improve

The appraisal should measure how well the various parts of the job are being performed. It should identify the employee's strengths as well as the aspects of the job where improved performance is needed. When these have been identified and agreed on between boss and subordinate, a performance improvement plan should be developed and implemented. Methods for doing this will be covered in detail in this book.

Build and Maintain Rapport

Rapport can be defined as a good working relationship or a climate of mutual trust and respect between boss and subordinate. To build rapport, the manager must try to understand and meet the employee's needs and wants, not just the organization's. Only when both are met has the manager really succeeded.

There are many ways to build rapport. An obvious one is for the boss to praise good work and give credit when due. Another is for the boss to take a personal interest in the hobbies, family, problems, and other things that are dear to the heart of the subordinate. Perhaps the most important thing that a boss can do is to make clear that he or she is interested in the successful performance of the subordinate on the present job. Also, the boss must show an interest in the future of the subordinate with the organization.

This consideration for the future presents a real challenge to a boss. Many organizations have developed formal approaches to career planning and development. They have found there are some advantages and some drawbacks to the formal approach. On the positive side, it demonstrates a concerted effort to see that employees move ahead in a systematic fashion. It shows that the organization is willing to spend time and money to be sure that promotions are made fairly. On the negative side, employees might get the impression that the promotions are going to come in a planned progression. The organization might give false hopes to those who aren't going to be promoted or to those whose promotion opportunity is far in the future.

Advancement in an organization usually depends on three separate and distinct factors:

The interests, desires, and aspirations of the employee.
The potential of the employee as determined by management.
Openings.

Some organizations ask employees to indicate their ambitions and goals. Sometimes this is done formally at the conclusion of a performance appraisal interview. Sometimes it is done informally in conversations between boss and subordinate. And some organizations do it as a separate project by sending forms for employees to complete. All these approaches can be effective in gathering this important information.

In addition to determining interests, aspirations, ambitions, and goals of employees, management must determine potential for advancement. At best, the process requires some subjectivity and comes down to an educated guess. The attitudes of many unions, for example, is that you can't really tell whether a person can perform a higher-level job unless you give the person a chance to try. And in some cases they may be right. But management must determine potential with as much objectivity as possible. The assessment center approach is one of the best ways.

The final factor that determines advancement is the number of promotional opportunities that will occur. In most organizations, large and small, people can't advance unless an opening is created by retirement, promotion, death, transfer, quitting, or growth. In some organizations, these openings occur frequently. In others, they occur infrequently.

Career planning and development must consider all three of these factors. There are eight possible combinations of these three factors that a manager could face. In the examples below, the term "management" is used to mean whoever inside or outside the organization assesses potential.

Situation 1: Mary wants to be promoted, management doesn't feel she has the potential to do a higher-level job, and a promotional opportunity exists.

Situation 2: Tom wants to be promoted, management feels he is promotable, but no openings exist.

Situation 3: Kathy has no desire to be promoted, management feels she has the potential for promotion, and no openings exist.

Situation 4: Barbara has no desire to be promoted, management feels she has the potential, and an opening exists.

Situation 5: Jim wants to be promoted, management feels he has the potential, and an opening exists.

Situation 6: Ted has no desire to be promoted, management feels he has no potential, and no openings exist.

Situation 7: Colleen has a desire to be promoted, management doesn't feel she's promotable, and no openings exist.

Situation 8: Bryan has no desire to be promoted, management doesn't feel he's promotable, and an opening exists.

These situations can be depicted in a table, as shown below. Quick reference to the table will show that situations 6 (Ted) and 8 (Bryan) are easy to handle. In both cases, the desire of the employee agrees with the analysis of potential by management. Neither Ted nor Bryan wants to be promoted, so no problem exists.

At first glance, situation 5 (Jim) also seems to be an easy one. Jim wants to be promoted, management feels he can handle the job, and an opening exists. However, complications arise because Jim is a white male. Situation 1 (Mary) must also be considered. Even though management doesn't think she has the potential, she wants the job. And potential is subject to debate. Besides, upgrading minorities may be part of management's obligation under its Affirmative Action Program.

Also, situation 4 (Barbara) must be considered when we consider Jim and Mary. Management has stamped her promotable even though she has no desire to be promoted. Perhaps she doesn't realize that she can do the job or hasn't really thought too much about it. Isn't it the obligation of management—as well as a sign of good judgment—to persuade her that she can handle the job? So now the organization has three people to consider in filling the opening.

Situation 2 (Tom) presents an interesting challenge to management. Tom wants to be promoted and is considered qualified, but no openings exist. Can you keep him, or will he become impatient and leave? Possible approaches for keeping him would include job enrichment, special assignments, delegated tasks, and other types of challenges and rewards until an opening occurs.

Situation 7 (Colleen) presents another challenge to management. Colleen wants to be promoted, but management doesn't feel she has the potential to be successful. No immediate problem exists because there are no openings. But as

	Desire for Promotion	*Potential for Promotion*	*Openings*
1. Mary	Yes	No	Yes
2. Tom	Yes	Yes	No
3. Kathy	No	Yes	No
4. Barbara	No	Yes	Yes
5. Jim	Yes	Yes	Yes
6. Ted	No	No	No
7. Colleen	Yes	No	No
8. Bryan	No	No	Yes

soon as an opening occurs, the organization will have the same problem it currently has with situation 1 (Mary).

Situation 3 (Kathy) offers a pleasant problem for management with no particular time pressures. Kathy has no desire to move up, but management feels she has potential. This allows management time to persuade her that she is promotable or to wait until an opening occurs and treat her like situation 4 (Barbara).

These eight situations illustrate the problems of career planning and development. The planning must be less than scientific, and plans must be flexible instead of firm. According to Dr. Walter Storey of General Electric, the best approach is for managers and subordinates to engage in "career conversations."[4] The word "conversation" connotes an informal discussion concerning the future of the employee. Goals and aspirations as well as potential should be frankly discussed. Also, the existence or possibility of openings should be made clear. These conversations should result in a realistic understanding of the employee's future in the organization, and the entire process should demonstrate clearly that the boss is sincerely interested in the employee and his or her future success and happiness. These conversations can help to develop rapport between boss and subordinate and help achieve maximum effort and performance.

As stated earlier, many organizations have formalized their approach to career planning and development. An example is the Crocker National Bank of California.[5] During the first two and a half years of the program, over 200 employees were involved, ranging from senior vice presidents to bank tellers, with a majority in lower exempt professional positions. In San Francisco, Los Angeles, and San Diego, the program was made available to any of the 14,000 employees whose supervisors or employee relations representatives recommended them. The following steps were taken in developing the program:

1. Obtained the support, cooperation, and participation of senior management.
2. Integrated career counseling into the performance appraisal system.
3. Obtained adequate professional staff to initiate a system for career counseling.
4. Developed a communications network of resource people and a centralized job information and education resource center.
5. Established clear referral procedures for career counseling.
6. Initiated individual career counseling services.
   a. Counseled employees on self-analysis, diagnosis of the organization, and action plans.
   b. Educated managers in career planning techniques and the bank's career opportunities.
7. Evaluated the program every six months.

   8. Reviewed progress of counseled employees every six months.
   9. Updated information files regularly.
   10. Planned and presented career planning workshops on a pilot basis.
   11. Trained and certified employee relations representatives in career counseling techniques and knowledge of the bank.
   12. Presented career planning workshops on a continual basis.

An extensive research project was implemented to evaluate the career counseling program. Here are one-year results for 1978:

> Turnover was reduced by 65 percent.
> Performance was improved by 85 percent.
> Promotability was increased by 75 percent.
> Savings of $1,950,000 were realized.

Reward for Performance

The eighth and last requirement for getting maximum effort and performance from employees is to reward for performance, not on the basis of years of service, favoritism, or anything else. Rewards can be monetary, such as wage incentives, merit salary increases, bonuses, profit sharing, and prizes. Or they can be nonmonetary, such as praise, special job assignments, more responsibility, delegated tasks, asking for ideas, better working conditions, status symbols, and authority.

Probably the most effective and least recognized of the nonmonetary rewards is authority, or freedom to act. There are four degrees of authority:

   1. Do what the boss says—no more and no less.
   2. Suggest and recommend to the boss, but take no action until the boss approves.
   3. Act, but tell the boss afterward.
   4. Act.

In the first two degrees, the subordinate has been given no authority. The second degree is more pleasant than the first, but there is no freedom to act until the boss says O.K.

The third and fourth degrees give the subordinate the authority to act. In the third, the boss wants to know about the action after it has been done. There are several reasons why this may be. Many bosses want to know what goes on in their departments, either because they feel they should know or because their bosses expect them to know. Also, if the action causes problems, the boss should know so that corrective action can be taken and future problems avoided.

There is also a different kind of reason for knowing what action the subordinate has taken, one related to rewards for performance. If the subordinate consistently makes poor decisions, the boss should move the subordinate back to degree 2, in which the subordinate checks with the boss *before* action is taken. If the action in degree 3 is consistently good, the subordinate can be moved to degree 4. In other words, performance is rewarded with more authority. And this type of reward is very significant to many people.

Promotion has not been mentioned as a reward. Obviously, past performance should be considered when a person is a candidate for promotion. Where the new job is entirely different from the present job, performance should carry very little weight. As was stated earlier, this is especially true when a person is promoted from a "doer" to a first-line supervisor or foreman. Where the new job is similar to the present job, performance should carry much more weight as one of the criteria for selection. For example, when a person is promoted from one level of management to another, promotion is an important reward for performance.

Summary

Managers must depend on the performance of their subordinates. As one manager put it, "When they're doing their jobs, I'm doing mine!" This chapter has described the eight requirements for getting maximum effort and performance from subordinates. The rest of the book will deal in detail with three of these eight factors: clarifying what's expected, appraising and communicating quality of performance, and coaching for improved performance. It is important to put these three factors in the proper context and recognize that other things can also be done to improve performance.

_____ The Performance Review Program _____

Before we go any further, let's define some important terms that will be used throughout the book. Then four aspects of a performance review program will be discussed in detail: program objectives, forms and procedures, frequency of reviews, and equal employment opportunity and Affirmative Action considerations.

Definition of Terms

The term "performance review" will be used in this book to include significant job segments, standards of performance, appraisal, appraisal interview, and on-the-job coaching. These terms will be used with the following meanings:

Significant job segments. These are the most important parts of the job. Dale McConkey refers to them as key result areas.[6] Not every detailed duty and responsibility should be evaluated. The word "significant" is a subjective term, and each organization (and even each manager) should determine its exact meaning. Chapter 2 will cover this.

Standards of performance. These are the conditions that will exist when the work has been done in an acceptable manner. They explain *how well* the job should be done, while significant job segments describe *what* should be done. These standards become the basis on which performance is judged, and are discussed in Chapter 2 as well.

Appraisal. This is the evaluation or judgment of how well the job has been done. It is always done by the boss with or without input from other people.

A self-appraisal is an evaluation by the subordinate. Some organizations require it in their performance review programs. Other organizations do not include it, or leave it up to the boss whether or not to ask the subordinate for a self-appraisal. Chapter 3 will deal with this.

Appraisal interview. The appraisal interview is the discussion of the appraisal between the boss (reviewer) and the subordinate (person being reviewed). As described in this book, it consists of the following aspects:

Communication of the boss's appraisal to the subordinate.
Communication of the subordinate's appraisal to the boss.
Agreement on a fair appraisal.
Agreement on the strengths of the subordinate.
Agreement on the job segments needing improvement.
Agreement on a performance improvement plan that spells out the specific things to be done to improve performance.

The length of interview time to cover all these items varies greatly. In most cases, the boss should conduct two or even three interviews instead of trying to discuss all of them in one interview. Chapter 3 will cover the appraisal interview, and Chapter 4 will discuss the performance improvement plan.

On-the-job coaching. After the formal performance appraisal interview has been conducted, both the boss and subordinate go back to their day-to-day activities. Part of the boss's activity should be the on-the-job coaching of the subordinate. This coaching should be a direct follow-up to be sure the agreed-on performance improvement plan is carried out. It should serve as a regular means for praising good performance and correcting mistakes. It should be the vehicle for updating significant job segments and standards of performance. In short, it should be a method for following up on an interview and avoiding surprises in the next formal performance appraisal interview. Chapter 5 will cover coaching.

Program Objectives

There are three basic reasons why organizations have performance appraisal programs: to provide information for salary administration, to provide information for promotion, and to improve performance on the present job. The next three subsections deal with each of these objectives and its relationship to performance appraisal.

To Provide Information for Salary Administration

Many factors should be considered to determine salary increases. They include:

1. The employee's performance. This can be measured by actual results or by results compared to objectives if the organization has a program of management by objectives.
2. The amount of improvement in performance since the last salary increase.
3. The minimum and maximum salary range for the job and where the employee's salary is presently located in the range.
4. A comparison of the employee's performance with the performance of others doing the same or similar jobs.
5. A comparison of the employee's salary with salaries of others doing the same or similar jobs.
6. Length of service. Some increase is usually given for being on the job another year.
7. Education. In some organizations, additional education, particularly if a degree is granted, is rewarded with a salary increase.
8. The rate of inflation since the last salary increase. A raise given for this reason is usually called a cost-of-living increase.
9. Established guidelines. These could be established by outside sources, such as the President of the United States, or by company policy. For example, a maximum salary increase amount can be set.
10. The salary that other organizations are paying people in the same or similar jobs.

Performance appraisal systems can provide information relating to factors 1, 2, and 4. It is important to recognize that many other factors must also be considered in determining salary adjustments.

To Provide Information for Promotion

Many performance review programs include the appraisal of potential as well as performance. Usually, the boss will consider past performance as one indication of the potential of the individual to do higher-level jobs. Past performance is probably the best predictor of future performance if the present job and the future job are pretty much the same. Other factors to be considered are desire, intelligence, personality, emotional stability, leadership skills, and other characteristics related to the job to be filled. An individual may be an outstanding performer and not be promotable because the requirements for success on the present job are different from those for the higher-level job. Likewise, an employee can be performing a job at a mediocre or even unsatisfactory level and be promotable because the necessary knowledge and skills are entirely different.

To Improve Performance on the Present Job

The third objective of performance review is to improve performance on the present job. To achieve this, past performance is reviewed, and steps are taken to improve future performance. This book provides philosophy, principles, approaches, and specific forms and techniques for accomplishing this objective.

One Program for All Three Objectives?

Some organizations have one program that is designed to accomplish all three objectives. Usually such programs fail to accomplish the third one, which is to improve performance on the present job. The main reason is that there is so much emotion involved in the discussion of salary and promotion that it is not possible to be objective about ways to improve performance. For example, a person may be doing an outstanding job, have substantially improved performance since the last review, and still not receive a large salary increase. Also, a person may be an outstanding performer and deemed not promotable. These situations don't lend themselves to encouraging and helping employees improve their performance.

Table 1 reveals a number of significant differences between performance reviews for improved performance and those for salary administration purposes. Because of these differences, performance review for improved performance should be separated from performance review for determination and discussion of salary increase and promotability. This recommendation is shared by Marion Kellogg. She states:

> The manager needs to tell the employee in a general way, and briefly, why he or she did or did not recommend a salary increase. If, however, the question is whether the manager should discuss how the employee can improve performance

Table 1. Comparison of two kinds of performance reviews.

	Performance Reviews for Salary Administration	*Performance Reviews for Improved Performance*
Looking	Backward	Forward
Considering	Overall performance	Detailed performance
Comparing with	Other people	Job standards and objectives
Determined by	Boss, higher management, personnel department	Boss and subordinate together
Interview climate	Subjective, emotional	Objective, unemotional
Factors to consider	Salary range, total money available, inflation, seniority, performance, education	Performance

at the same time he or she discusses salary, the answer, generally speaking, is no. It is better to reserve this discussion for another time, one more conducive to constructive thinking.[7]

In an extensive study on performance reviews, researchers at General Electric came to the following conclusion:

> Implicit in performance appraisal programs as now structured are two distinct objectives: (1) letting a person know where he or she stands via ratings and salary actions, and (2) motivating him or her to improve. The results of this study showed that attempts to achieve the first objective frequently produce threat and defensiveness, and these reactions, in turn, interfere with the achievement of the second objective.
>
> A merit-pay type of salary plan makes some variety of summary judgment or rating of performance necessary, or at least desirable; but this rating should *not* be expected to serve also as a primary medium for changing performance. Quite separate from this rating activity, the manager can use goal planning discussions, special assignments, and other techniques to achieve improved performance on the part of subordinates.[8]

Clearly, then, the two kinds of performance reviews should be separate. One approach is to have separate annual reviews for salary administration and for improved performance, and to schedule them approximately six months apart.

Forms and Procedures

Many different types of performance review forms have been developed and used by organizations. They vary all the way from a blank piece of paper to a 22-page form used by a general sales manager for five regional sales managers. Some forms are very simple with a list of factors to be rated and a few boxes to check. Others require the boss to work with the subordinate to develop the factors on which the appraisal will be based. There is no right or wrong form. The important factor is that the form accomplishes the objectives of the program.

To achieve improved job performance, a form should be designed to accomplish this objective and not necessarily to accomplish the objectives of determining salary increases or potential for promotion. If the form provides information that is helpful in determining potential or salary increases, so much the better.

In addition to accomplishing program objectives, the form should fit the organization or department that is using it. For example, the form for appraising a production foreman may be quite different from one for an office supervisor or an engineer. Or one form may be designed to apply to all types of jobs.

Another consideration in designing a form is that it should be effectively used by the managers. For example, if an organization has limited clerical help, poor facilities in which to conduct interviews, and managers who hate paperwork, common sense tells us to keep it simple. On the other hand, if the managers are sophisticated and oriented to paperwork, a more complicated form can be used.

As nearly as possible, the form should be self-explanatory. A manager should not have to study a manual to understand how the form should be completed. Also, the words used should be as clear as possible. Words like "dependability," "responsibility," or even "quality" have different meanings to different people. The manager might think "quality, accurate work" meant perfect work, or work with no scrap, while the subordinate might think it meant work without too many mistakes or without too much scrap.

All forms should include not only what should be done but also how well it should be done. This combination will clarify what is expected so that the boss's and the subordinate's appraisals will be based on the same understanding of the job.

Examples of various types of forms are provided in Chapter 7. Comments are included on the positive and negative aspects of each form.

Frequency of Reviews

Formal performance reviews covering the entire job of a subordinate should be conducted at least once a year by the boss, and twice a year would be preferable. The frequency would be influenced by five main factors:

1. *How complicated is the program?* If the forms and procedures are complicated and involve much time and paperwork, the review should be done only once a year. If they are relatively simple and take little time, it can be done semiannually.

2. *How enthusiastic are the managers about the program?* If managers are enthusiastic about reviewing performance and feel it helps both relationships and productivity, it can be done twice a year. If it becomes a chore they dread and complain about, once a year is probably sufficient. It is better to start on a once-a-year basis and move to twice a year than to start with twice-a-year reviews and have the managers become discouraged and sour on the program.

3. *How much staff help is available to coordinate the program?* A coordinator and secretarial help are required to keep up with forms, schedules, and other paperwork. If enough such staff help is available, then twice a year might be advisable.

4. *How many people are going to be appraised by the boss?* This is related to the first factor because it influences the total time needed for performance reviews. In general, the more people that must be reviewed, the less frequently it can be done.

5. *How skilled are the appraisers?* If a new program is being integrated, it would be better to require a formal appraisal only once a year while the appraisers learn the approach. This would not put too much demand on the managers' time and would get the program off to a good start. As the managers become trained and effective in conducting the reviews, the frequency might be increased to semiannual reviews, depending on the four factors described above.

Equal Employment Opportunity and Affirmative Action Considerations

Contract compliance regulations have been developed by the Office of Federal Contract Compliance Programs (OFCCP) of the Department of Labor.[9] It is the policy of most companies—large and small—to have employment and personnel policies that are nondiscriminatory with regard to race, creed, color, sex, religion, or age. Such policies determine practices in recruiting and hiring, promotion, pay, training, layoff and recall, and reviewing employee performance.

An Affirmative Action Program is a set of specific, results-oriented procedures by which an employer makes a commitment to apply every effort, in good faith, toward equal employment opportunity. Procedures without effort to make them work are meaningless, and effort undirected by specific and meaningful procedures is inadequate.

An acceptable Affirmative Action Plan must include an analysis of areas within which the employer is deficient in the employment of minority groups and women. It must also include goals and timetables to which the employer's good-faith efforts will be directed to correct the deficiencies. The employer does this to achieve prompt and full utilization of minorities and women at all levels and in all segments of the workforce where deficiencies may exist.

A formal Affirmative Action Plan is implemented as follows:

1. The employer should validate worker specifications by division, department, location, or other organizational units and by job title using job performance criteria.

2. All personnel involved in the recruiting, screening, selection, promotion, disciplinary, and related processes should be carefully selected and trained to ensure elimination of bias in all personnel actions.

3. The employer should ensure that minority and female employees are given equal opportunity for promotion. Suggestions for achieving this result include:

(a) Develop and implement formal performance appraisal programs.

(b) Establish valid requirements for promotion, directly related to the job. These should be used exclusively when deciding on promotions.

(c) Review the qualifications of all employees to ensure that minorities and women are given full opportunities for transfers and promotions.

(d) Establish formal career counseling programs to include attitude development, education aid, job rotation, a buddy system, and similar programs.

(e) Provide full opportunity for minority and female employees. Encourage them to participate in all company-sponsored educational, training, recreational, and social activities, and provide them with the same benefits as other employees. Apply all personnel programs uniformly to all employees without exception.

(f) Evaluate the work performance of supervisors on the basis of their equal employment opportunity efforts and results, as well as other criteria.

Summary

This chapter first defined the various terms connected with performance review. Next, the three major objectives of a program were described. Emphasis was placed on the fact that different approaches must be used for the different objectives.

Forms and procedures were then discussed with guidelines for selecting the right ones for a particular organization. The section on frequency of reviews described the considerations for deciding whether to do them annually or semi-annually. Finally, guidelines for equal employment opportunity and Affirmative Action programs were presented.

References

1. Frederick Herzberg, *Work and the Nature of Man*. Cleveland: World Publishing, 1966.
2. Laurence J. Peter and Raymond Hull, *The Peter Principle: Why Things Always Go Wrong*. New York: Bantam, 1970.
3. Donald Kirkpatrick, Dave Coverdale, and Reynolds Olsen-Tjensvold, *Selecting and Training First-Line Supervisors*. Chicago: Dartnell, 1980.
4. Walter Storey, "Career Dimensions." Croton-on-Hudson, N. Y.: General Electric, 1976.
5. Karen R. Kobrosky, "Approach to Career Management." Copyright © by Karen R. Kobrosky. Published by Crocker National Bank, San Francisco, 1979. All rights reserved.
6. Dale McConkey, *How to Manage by Results*. New York: AMACOM, 1979.
7. Marion Kellogg, *What to Do About Performance Appraisal*. New York: AMACOM, 1975.
8. E. Kay, J. P. French, Jr., and H. H. Meyer, "A Study of the Performance Appraisal Interview." Lynn, Mass.: Behavioral Research Service at General Electric, 1962.
9. "Compliance Responsibility for Equal Employment Opportunity." Washington, D.C.: Department of Labor, 1978.

2
The Basis for Appraisal

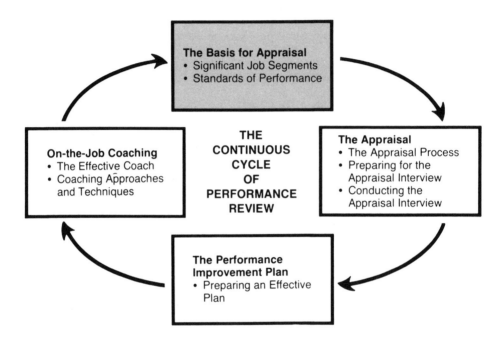

_____ Significant Job Segments _____

The first step in the appraisal process is to select the significant segments of the job. Most organizations have job descriptions that cover the duties and responsibilities of jobs, and these can provide a good basis for selecting the significant job segments.

There is no hard-and-fast rule about the number of significant job segments to identify. It depends more on the wishes of the manager than it does on the nature of the job. Some managers consider nearly all aspects of a subordinate's job significant. Others prefer to select the four to six most significant aspects of the job. As a general rule, from six to eight segments are recommended.

Sample Lists of Significant Job Segments

Here are some actual examples taken from different types of organizations. They illustrate job descriptions and the significant job segments derived from them.

Position Title: SECRETARY

Duties and Responsibilities
1. Take dictation in shorthand.
2. Compose routine letters.
3. Type letters and reports.
4. Answer telephone and place calls.
5. Schedule appointments.
6. Screen visitors.
7. Open and screen incoming mail.
8. Maintain correspondence and subject files.
9. Make travel arrangements.
10. Maintain confidential personnel files.
11. Maintain a follow-up system for correspondence.
12. Maintain a reminder system for appointments, telephone calls, and correspondence to be answered by supervisor.

Significant Job Segments
1. Dictation
2. Typing
3. Telephone
4. Visitors
5. Mail
6. Files

Position Title: SYSTEMS ANALYST

Duties and Responsibilities
1. Research and analyze current systems.
2. Analyze current problems related to systems.
3. Conduct meetings with users to determine problems and/or suggested improvements.
4. Recommend equipment modifications or additions.
5. Design and develop new systems.
6. Implement new or modified systems.
7. Coordinate efforts with senior programmers and/or programmer analysts.
8. Train and develop assigned personnel in systems techniques.
9. Serve as project leader.

Significant Job Segments
1. Problem analysis
2. Meetings with users
3. Systems design
4. Systems implementation
5. Coordination with programmers
6. Training and development of personnel
7. Project leadership

Position Title: SALES REPRESENTATIVE

Duties and Responsibilities

1. Maintain current product, product application and capability, and product justification knowledge. Know enough to be accepted and recognized as an expert in your field.
2. Establish friendly business and personal relationships with all potential customers for all assigned product lines in the assigned territory.
3. Get to know potential customers' organization and personnel. Know intimately their responsibilities, products, economics, problems, requirements, methods, and so on.
4. Conduct all activities in a manner contributory to maintenance of optimum corporate image, as defined in our sales and services policies.
5. Organize, plan, and schedule utilization of time to provide optimum effective account and territory coverage. Plan each specific sales call for most effective use of time.
6. Creatively sell an optimum volume of all assigned products to all potential users in the assigned territory, commensurate with the potential for each product line.
7. Conduct after-order follow-up in recognition of the fact that we are in a repeat business.
8. Maintain knowledge of and adhere to company organizational procedures and policies regarding pricing, deliveries, warranty service, sales terms, forecasts, work hours, records, reports, vacation scheduling, use of company car, and so on.
9. Identify, keep informed about, and report on customers' present and future requirements, problems, and desires. This will facilitate adapting our product lines and your efforts to these requirements.
10. Keep informed about and report on all competitive products and developments.
11. Utilize home office assistance, advice, and guidance as required or offered.
12. Cooperate with home office, other territories, and other sales and service personnel as required to accomplish overall sales objectives.
13. Perform other specific assignments as required or requested.

Significant Job Segments

1. Product knowledge
2. Customer relations
3. Customer knowledge
4. Time utilization
5. Sales volume
6. Company knowledge
7. Reports

Position Title: PAYROLL SUPERVISOR

Duties and Responsibilities

1. Supervises the following:

    a. Compiling of data.
    b. Tabulation of data.
    c. Computing of detail.
    d. Preparation of summaries and control figures.
    e. Preparation of tax reports.
2. Assigns work to subordinates.
3. Interviews, selects, and trains employees.
4. Evaluates and counsels subordinates.
5. Recommends people for promotion.
6. Recommends salary increases.

Significant Job Segments

1. Data compilation, tabulation, and computing
2. Preparation of reports
3. Work assignment
4. Personnel
5. Promotion and salary increases

Position Title: MACHINE SHOP SUPERVISOR

Duties and Responsibilities
1. Plans and coordinates precision machining of standardized components involving diversified operations and machine setups.
2. Interprets and directs compliance with the union contract and labor relations policies.
3. Enforces compliance with administrative practices and procedures.
4. Establishes budgets.
5. Maintains surveillance to ensure timely production that meets quality standards.
6. Keeps costs within established budget.
7. Interviews, selects, trains, counsels, promotes, evaluates, and assigns work to nonsalaried personnel.
8. Acts as liaison with other divisions.

Significant Job Segments

1. Planning
2. Union contract and policies
3. Practices and procedures
4. Budgets
5. Schedules
6. Quality
7. Personnel

Position Title: MARKETING ANALYST

Duties and Responsibilities
1. Conduct market surveys.
2. Gather data on business activity trends.
3. Gather data on economic conditions.
4. Prepare data for analysis by computer.
5. Monitor computer output.
6. Prepare reports.

7. Participate in development of new company sales programs.
8. Assist in implementation of new or modified management information systems.

Significant Job Segments
1. Market research
2. Computer interface
3. Reports
4. Sales programs
5. Systems

Position Title: HEAD NURSE

Duties and Responsibilities

TO PATIENTS
1. Plan safe, economical, and efficient nursing care.
2. See that quality patient care is given to each patient in accordance with quality standards.
3. Formulate and utilize patient care plan to assist in resolving patient problems.
4. Act as liaison between patient, physician, and family.

TO MEDICAL STAFF
5. Act as liason between physician and patient care team.

TO OWN NURSE MANAGER
6. Share appropriate communications with unit personnel.
7. Ensure adequate staffing.
8. Make out patient care assignments.
9. Help with budget planning; operate unit within budget.

TO DEPARTMENT PERSONNEL
10. Hold regular unit personnel meetings.
11. Promote an environment in which the patient care team can work co-operatively toward objectives.
12. Provide an opportunity for personnel staff development.
13. Counsel personnel when necessary.

TO COMMITTEES
14. Participate actively in selected committee activities.

TO OTHER ORGANIZATIONS
15. Maintain membership in appropriate professional organizations.

TO SELF
16. Participate in continuing education programs.

Significant Job Segments
1. Patient care
2. Medical staff
3. Staffing
4. Budget
5. Meetings
6. Subordinate development
7. Self-development

Position Title: DATA PROCESSING MANAGER

Duties and Responsibilities
 1. Establish departmental objectives.
 2. Schedule operations.
 3. Protect and maintain present equipment.
 4. Recommend new or modified equipment.
 5. Provide timely and pertinent reports.
 6. Administer tape library.
 7. Conduct departmental meetings.
 8. Administer company personnel policies.
 9. Hire, orient, and train new personnel.
10. Train and develop subordinates.
11. Handle employee suggestions and problems.
12. Evaluate employee performance.

Significant Job Segments

1. Objectives	5. Tape library
2. Operations	6. Meetings
3. Equipment	7. Personnel
4. Reports	

Position Title: SALES MANAGER, CUSTOMER SERVICE PARTS

Duties and Responsibilities
 1. Supervise repair parts order analysts to ensure the expeditious writing and processing of parts orders.
 2. Provide instructions and guidance on difficult parts identification problems.
 3. Oversee warrantee parts activities to ensure proper crediting of return parts and fulfillment of vendor warranty obligations, and to alleviate problems regarding warrantee claims and related billings.
 4. Monitor correspondence procedures required to acknowledge parts and orders.
 5. Advise customers of order and price changes.
 6. Monitor the inventory and replenishment of parts at the company's bonded warehouses.
 7. Organize and expedite the maintenance of up-to-date references, price lists, and files essential to service customers.
 8. Interview, select, train, counsel, evaluate, and assign work to clerical and technical personnel.
 9. Prepare reports.
10. Help develop objectives and budget.
11. Operate within budget.

Significant Job Segments
1. Orders
2. Warrantees
3. Customer contacts
4. Personnel
5. Reports
6. Budget

Position Title: MANAGER, MANUFACTURING ENGINEERING

Duties and Responsibilities
1. Document all manufacturing engineering procedures, including routing cards, CRT update, engineering change notices, form design and modification, and any other required new procedures that are repeatable and necessary for future reference.
2. Develop and implement procedures for an effective bonus incentive system.
3. Direct the Idea Action Program in analyzing suggestions and computing awards.
4. Oversee the packaging function which is responsibile for the design and purchase specification of packaging material and the procedures for the actual packaging operation.
5. Manage a waste and scrap program to include sales of scrap material, recycling scrap where possible, and solution of scrap and waste problems.
6. Conduct special projects on plant operations and functions.
7. Handle employee relations function for the department.

Significant Job Segments
1. Documentation
2. Bonus system
3. Idea Action Program
4. Packaging function
5. Scrap program
6. Employee relations

Determining Job Segments Without Job Descriptions

In organizations that do not have up-to-date job descriptions, the boss should sit down with the subordinate and discuss the job. The first step is to list all the duties and responsibilities that would apply to any person doing the job. If more than one person is doing the same job, the boss should conduct a meeting with all the subordinates to agree on duties and responsibilities. If the number of people is too large for a meeting, it would be advisable to meet with a representative sample of the group.

When agreement has been reached on all the duties and responsibilities, the next step is to agree on the significant job segments. Again the group approach should be used if more than one person is doing the same job.

In agreeing on the significant job segments, there are three different approaches that might be used:

1. The boss and subordinate(s) independently list the significant job segments and then get together and discuss them to reach understanding and agreement.
2. The boss makes a tentative list and presents it to the subordinate(s) for reaction, modification, and agreement.
3. The subordinate(s) makes a tentative list and presents it to the boss for reaction, modification, and agreement.

It doesn't make much difference which of the three approaches is used as long as understanding and agreement are reached. There is a possibility that the second choice will not be as effective as the other two because subordinates may be reluctant to challenge the "tentative" list made by the boss. Also, the involvement of the subordinate in choices 1 and 3 will probably create a climate in which the subordinate is more highly motivated toward the entire performance review process.

Summary

The first step in the performance review process is to clarify what's expected of the subordinate. The first part of this is for boss and subordinate to agree on the significant job segments that should be appraised. Typically, from six to eight segments should be identified. If job descriptions are available, they should be used as a basis for selecting the significant job segments. If not, a list of duties and responsibilities should be prepared. In order to be sure that the significant job segments are clear and agreed on, they should be jointly determined by boss and subordinate(s). The next step in the process of clarifying what's expected is to develop standards of performance for each significant job segment.

Standards of Performance

Standards of performance are an important and often neglected element in the performance review process. While significant job segments describe what needs to be done, standards of performance describe how well it must be done. The two of them together clarify what's expected of the subordinate. This clarification is necessary to guide the behavior of the subordinate as well as to provide a basis for appraisal.

Defining Standards of Performance

There is a difference of opinion among performance appraisal experts on the exact meaning of standards of performance. Some use the definition, "the conditions that will exist when the job segment is well done." Others use the definition, "the conditions that will exist when the job segment is done in an acceptable manner." Although the difference between "well done" and "acceptable" seems to be slight, the difference is very significant. The following two examples will illustrate the difference:

Example 1

Here are some facts about the percentage of manufactured parts that were classified as scrap in a manufacturing plant. The figures refer to the past six months.

1. The best it has been is 2 percent for a one-week period. This happened on two occasions.
2. It went as high as 15 percent for a one-week period. This is considered uncontrolled.
3. Except for these three one-week periods, it has varied from 3 percent to 10 percent on a weekly basis. The 3 percent figure occurred three times, and the 10 percent occurred twice.
4. The average weekly figure for the last six months has been 7 percent.
5. From 3 to 4 percent is considered excellent.

At what level should the standard be set? Mark your estimate before reading further.

2%   3%   4%   5%   6%   7%   8%   9%   10%

Example 2

Here are some facts about a daily report in an office. The figures are for the last six months.

1. Ideally, there should be no errors such as miscalculations and wrong entries, because this causes extra work and delay.
2. The best record for a week was one error. This occurred only once.
3. The report is sufficiently complex and frequent that as many as four errors are usually made per week even by people thoroughly experienced. This you can live with.
4. When errors reach the level of six per week, the finance department complains because of the excessive amount of time needed to correct the errors.

5. The worst record for one week by an experienced employee was seven. This occurred only once. Six errors were made twice during the last six months.
6. There has been an average of 4.1 errors per week for the past six months.

At what level of errors per week do you think the standard should be set? Mark your estimate before reading further.

0   1   2   3   4   5   6

If standard of performance is defined as the conditions that will exist when the job is *well done,* the standards would probably be set at 4 percent scrap for Example 1, and 2 errors per week for Example 2. If standard of performance is defined as the conditions that will exist when the job is done in an acceptable manner, the standards would be set at 7 percent scrap for Example 1, and 4 errors per week for Example 2.

This book will use the definition "the conditions that will exist when the job segment is done in an *acceptable* manner." This means that the answers to the examples are 7 percent scrap and 4 errors per week.

The reason for this definition is that it provides a great deal of opportunity for the employee to exceed the standard and be recognized for it. It also means that performance is unsatisfactory if the standard is not met. If the other definition is used and the standard is met only when the job is well done, many satisfactory employees would not meet the standard, and it might have a negative effect on their attitude and desire to improve.

Characteristics of Standards

There are eight characteristics of effective standards:

1. *They are based on the job and not the person(s) in the job.* Standards of performance should be established for the job itself regardless of who occupies the job. For example, the job of administrative secretary or production foreman may be a job that a number of people perform. There should be one set of standards for the job, not one set for every person doing that particular job.

Standards of performance are different from objectives. Objectives should be set for an individual rather than for a job. And a typical characteristic of an objective or goal is that it should be challenging. Therefore, a manager who has several subordinates doing the same job will have one set of standards for the job but may have different objectives for each person, based on that person's experience, skills, and past performance. For example, the objective for a mediocre performer may be the same as the standard, while the objective for an outstanding employee may be much higher than standard.

2. *They are achievable*. This characteristic is directly related to the definition described earlier. It means that practically all employees on the job should be able to reach the standard. (An exception would be a new employee who is learning the job. The standard may not apply until the employee has passed the probationary period.) Most production standards are set so that practically everyone can meet the standard and many employees can reach 125 percent of standard.

In the 1980 Winter Olympics at Lake Placid, there were two ski hills. One was called the 70-Meter Hill and the other was called the 90-Meter Hill. The distance referred to the length of the jump by the skiers. Nearly all the competing skiers exceeded the 70 meters and the 90 meters, and many of them jumped from 20 to 30 meters beyond. The standard (70 meters or 90 meters) was much less than the objective as well as the performance of the competitors.

3. *They are understood*. It almost goes without saying that the standard should be clear to boss and subordinate alike. Unfortunately, there is often confusion between the two parties on the exact meaning of a standard.

4. *They are agreed on*. Both boss and subordinate should agree that the standard is fair. This is very important in motivating an employee. It is also important because it becomes the basis for evaluation.

5. *They are as specific and measurable as possible*. Some people feel that standards *must be* specific and measurable. They insist that they must be stated in numbers, percentages, dollars, or some other form that can be quantifiably measured. Every effort should be made to do this, but if it can't be done, the standard *should be* stated as specifically as possible even if subjective judgment must be used to evaluate performance against it. Early in a performance review program, it might seem impossible to state standards in measurable terms. With practice and experience, it may be possible to be specific on all or nearly all standards.

6. *They are time-oriented*. It should be clear whether the standard is to be accomplished by a specific date or whether it is ongoing.

7. *They are written*. Both boss and subordinate should have a written copy of the standards that are agreed on. In this way, they won't have to rely on memory, and the standard can be a constant reminder to both parties.

8. *They are subject to change*. Because standards should be achievable and agreed on, they should be periodically evaluated and changed if necessary. The need to change could be caused by new methods, new equipment, new materials, or changes in other significant job factors. But they should not be changed just because a performer is not meeting the standard.

Who Should Set Standards?

Because standards are to be clear and agreed on, there is good reason to involve subordinates in setting their own standards. Another reason for this involvement is to motivate the employee to put forth maximum effort to achieve and even exceed the standard. Helping to set the standards will probably result in a higher degree of commitment.

If there is only one person doing a particular job, the boss and subordinate should jointly set the standards. If there is more than one person doing the same job, all the people on that job, or at least a representative group, should be involved. (In this respect setting standards is just like determining significant job segments.) Where differences of opinion exist, the boss must have the final say. The boss should make every effort, however, to get the subordinates to agree that the standard is fair.

There are three ways of getting subordinate involvment in setting standards.

1. The boss considers all factors, prepares tentative standards, and discusses them with subordinates to get agreement. The boss must listen to them and be willing to change the standards if the subordinates' suggestions warrant a change.
2. The subordinates set their own tentative standards and bring them to the boss for agreement. Subordinates should be told in advance that their recommendations are not necessarily final.
3. The boss and subordinates independently set standards for significant job segments. These standards are compared and discussed to reach agreement.

The first approach is probably the least effective because subordinates might be reluctant to disagree with the tentative standards set by the boss. Often a boss who develops tentative standards becomes defensive and impatient with subordinates who challenge them. If this first approach is to be effective, the boss must be sure to create a climate in which subordinates feel free to disagree and in which the tentative standards are subject to change.

The second approach can be effective if the boss is knowledgeable enough to judge the standards suggested by the subordinate. It puts the major part of the responsibility on the subordinate, which is apt to create a commitment to achieve or exceed the standards.

The third approach is probably the best because each party has given some time and effort to establish fair standards. Their discussion should result in the best standards.

Sometimes an outside person such as a consultant or personnel director can effectively conduct a meeting between boss and subordinates to establish standards. This neutral party can keep the discussion objective so that good standards are developed and rapport is maintained between boss and subordinates.

How Many Standards?

This question is similar to "How many significant job segments?" There is no magic number, nor is there any rule of thumb that says it all depends on the job. The main factor that determines the number of standards is the boss. How many standards does he or she feel are needed to clarify what is expected of a subordinate? If two standards will do it (say, quantity and quality), then that should be sufficient. If it takes 10 or 20 pages to do it, then that's how many there should be. There is an advantage to many rather than few. It not only gives a subordinate a clearer understanding of the total job, but it also allows the boss to appraise many different facets of the job and pinpoint an employee's areas of strength as well as those needing improvement. Therefore, an organization should not put a limit on the number of standards that should be developed for a job.

Following are samples of standards of performance that have been developed for segments of different jobs in a variety of organizations.

Position: SECRETARY

Significant Job Segments	Standards of Performance
1. Typing A. General	1. Typing is done from dictation or longhand. 2. No visible erasures on typed work. 3. No errors in spelling or grammar. 4. Work is completed by time requested.
B. Letters, memos, reports	1. Writer always gets 1 yellow carbon, and 1 green carbon always goes to chronological file. 2. As requested, white carbons are typed for others.
C. Materials to be reproduced	1. Supervisor proofreads these before they are reproduced. 2. Requisition form is typed.

D. Forms,   1. These are typed as directed.
   handouts, 2. Requisitions are personally taken to
   requisitions   Purchasing, and any questions about what is
                   needed and when are answered clearly.

Position: PRODUCTION FOREMAN

Significant Job Segments	*Standards of Performance*
1. Safety	1. Monthly safety meetings are conducted in accordance with company schedules. 2. Safe operating procedures are followed by all employees. 3. Regular monthly inspections are held in the department in accordance with the approved checklist. 4. Action is taken within five days to correct any unsafe condition. 5. Monthly safety reports are submitted by the 5th of the following month.
2. Controlling costs	1. Waste and scrap are kept below 2% of total production. 2. One cost-saving improvement per month is initiated and put into operation. 3. Overtime costs are held to a maximum of 3% of direct labor costs. 4. All purchases are made in the most economical manner according to a buying plan. 5. Overhead costs are kept within budget limitations. 6. Salary controls are exercised in accordance with the salary administration plan. 7. The ratio of productivity to costs is improved by 1% every 6 months.
3. Developing subordinates	1. New subordinates are inducted and trained in accordance with a definite plan. 2. Performance reviews are held with all subordinates on an annual basis. 3. The appraisal and performance improvement plan aspects of the performance review program are reviewed with superior.

4. Discussions are held with subordinates at least quarterly to see that performance improvement takes place according to plan.
5. Responsibilities and authority are delegated to subordinates on a planned basis.

Position: EMPLOYMENT SUPERVISOR

Significant Job Segments	*Standards of Performance*
1. Recruiting	1. 90% of requisitions for qualified employees are filled within three weeks of date of requisition. 2. Each employee is recruited at a cost lower than the cost of hiring one employee through a commercial placement agency. 3. Current file of qualified applicants is maintained to fill recurring job openings. 4. Job inquiries are answered within 2 working days of receipt.

Position: OFFICE SUPERVISOR

Significant Job Segments	*Standards of Performance*
1. Written communication	1. All correspondence is answered, and a carbon filed, within one week of receiving it. 2. All written communication is handled so that there is minimal misunderstanding. 3. All interdepartmental and intradepartmental memorandums are answered within 2 working days of receipt. 4. All official memorandums are posted and/or circulated, initialed, dated, and returned to department head within one week of receiving them. 5. Minutes of officially called meetings are distributed to participants within five days after the meeting.

Position: REGIONAL SALES MANAGER

Significant Job Segments	*Standards of Performance*
1. Developing subordinates A. Conducts performance reviews	1. Performance reviews are conducted with all subordinates according to the procedure approved by the sales manager. 2. For new employees, job duties and standards are clarified within the first three months of employment. 3. A complete performance review is conducted within nine months of hire of each new employee.
B. Coaches	1. Subordinates are coached and worked with on a day-to-day basis to help them perform better on their present jobs. 2. Follow-up is conducted to ensure implementation of performance improvement plan. 3. Selected assignments are delegated to subordinates to help develop them for greater responsibilities.
C. Trains in products	1. Subordinates understand the products, procedures, programs, and policies that are pertinent to their work. 2. District sales managers know how to use these items. 3. District sales managers put pertinent items into operation.
D. Counsels	1. Subordinates feel that regional sales managers are readily available and glad to discuss problems with them. 2. All personal conversations are kept confidential.
E. General	1. Subordinates clearly understand their jobs. 2. Subordinates are qualified and skilled to perform their jobs. 3. Subordinates know how well they are doing and what improvement needs to be made.

4. Subordinates are consistently improving performance on their present jobs.

Position: COORDINATOR OF MANAGEMENT DEVELOPMENT

Significant Job Segments	*Standards of Performance*

1. Training classes	1. Training needs are determined by using one or more of the following:
	  a. Surveys of potential participants.
	  b. Advisory committee meetings.
	  c. Discussion and/or correspondence with key people.
	2. Program objectives are established on the basis of needs.
	3. Program content is developed on the basis of objectives.
	4. Speakers are selected and coached.
	  a. Teachers have knowledge and teaching skills.
	  b. Teachers are oriented on program objectives and participants.
	5. Coordination.
	  a. A minimum of 45 program days are held per year.
	  b. Facilities, introduction of leaders, visual aids, and materials are effectively coordinated.
	6. Evaluation.
	  a. Standard reaction sheet is used for each program.
	  b. Standard of 3.7 on a 4.0 scale is achieved in 90% of the programs.

2. Performance review	1. All salaried personnel are reviewed annually. 2. All reviewers receive 14 hours of training on performance reviews by January 1. 3. All completed performance improvement plans are received by February 15. 4. Confidential files are maintained on all performance reviews and made available only to authorized persons.

Position: DEPARTMENT HEAD

Significant Job Segments	*Standards of Performance*
1. Planning	1. Suggested items for next year's expense budget are submitted by September 15.
	2. Suggested capital expenditures for next year are submitted by September 15.
	3. Specific annual objectives are established for next year by December 1.
	4. A report on specific accomplishments for the past year is submitted by January 20.
	5. Long-range plans covering a 5-year period are prepared by December 15 and updated yearly.
	6. Daily assignments are given to accomplish a minimum of 85% of established schedules.

Position: DIVISION MANAGER

Significant Job Segments	*Standards of Performance*
1. Communications	1. Superior and functional staff are kept informed of all important or unusual conditions or trends that have a bearing on the company's interests, so that no such matters come first to their attention from outside sources.
	2. All regularly scheduled managers' conferences are attended by division manager unless ill or away. Pertinent information based on field experience is relayed to other managers and staff members in attendance, and appropriate opinions are expressed to contribute to the discussion of subjects under consideration.
	3. Meetings are held with division staff and district supervisory personnel within 10 days following each managers' conference to relay items of information from the conference and to discuss pertinent topics of local interest.
	4. Similar meetings are held within one week in each of the districts in the division.
	5. New developments and pertinent information

such as company plans and policy changes are relayed to all division personnel involved within one week of receiving such information.

6. Employees feel that division manager is personally available to them to discuss problems or ideas.

Summary

Standards of performance are defined as conditions that will exist when the job has been done in an acceptable manner. They have two purposes. First, they guide the behavior of a subordinate to accomplish the standards that have been established. According to James L. Hayes, president of the American Management Associations and an internationally known expert on standards of performance,

> If you go through the exercise of establishing standards of performance with your subordinates and clarify what your expectations are, it is a worthwhile exercise even if you never appraise their performance. This is because most people want to do an acceptable job.

The second reason for standards of performance is to provide a basis against which the performance of an individual can be effectively and fairly appraised. Unless clear standards of performance are established, appraisals are too often biased by feelings and subjective evaluation. Regardless of the approach and forms that are used in a program on performance appraisal and review, the process of clarifying what's expected is essential if the program is going to be effective. Standards of performance are the best way to do this.

Effective standards of performance are based on the job and are achievable, understood, agreed on, specific and measurable, time-oriented, written, and subject to change.

So that the standards can be properly set and subordinates are motivated to meet or exceed them, subordinates should be involved in setting their own standards. In case of disagreement, the boss must make the final decision.

There is no minimum or maximum number of standards that should be set for a job. Having many standards helps the subordinate understand more clearly what is expected, and also helps the boss pinpoint specific strengths and areas needing improvement. The boss and subordinate should decide how many are appropriate and practical.

3
The Appraisal and the Interview

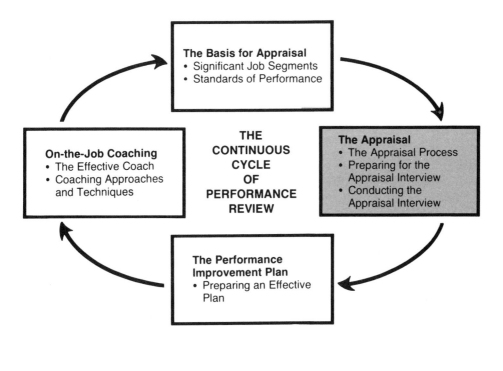

The Basis for Appraisal
- Significant Job Segments
- Standards of Performance

On-the-Job Coaching
- The Effective Coach
- Coaching Approaches and Techniques

THE CONTINUOUS CYCLE OF PERFORMANCE REVIEW

The Appraisal
- The Appraisal Process
- Preparing for the Appraisal Interview
- Conducting the Appraisal Interview

The Performance Improvement Plan
- Preparing an Effective Plan

The Appraisal Process

If an effective job is done in clarifying what's expected in terms of significant job segments and standards of performance, the appraisal by the boss becomes quite easy and objective. It is a matter of comparing actual performance with definite standards. And the more specific and measurable the standards, the more objective the appraisal.

Two Traps to Avoid

In the book *Management by Objectives,* George Odiorne warns that two kinds of flaws may exist in a performance appraisal if the standards are vague: the halo effect and the horns effect.[1]

The Halo Effect

The halo effect is the tendency of the boss to overrate a favored employee. This can happen for a variety of reasons:

1. *Effect of past record.* Because the person has done good work in the distant past, performance is assumed to be O.K. in the recent past too. Good work tends to carry over into the current rating period.

2. *Compatibility.* There's a tendency to rate people whom we find pleasing of manner and personality more highly than they deserve. Those who agree with us, who nod their heads when we talk, or who—even better—make notes of our words: these people get better ratings than their performance justifies.

3. *Effect of recency.* The person who did an outstanding job last week or yesterday can offset a mediocre performance over the rest of the year by this single act.

4. *The one-asset person.* The glib talker, the person with an impressive appearance or an advanced degree, or the graduate of the boss's own alma mater gets a more favorable rating than the person lacking these often irrelevant attributes.

5. *The blind-spot effect.* This is the case where the boss doesn't see certain types of defects because they are just like his or her own. For example, the boss who loves accounting may overrate another detail person.

6. *The high-potential effect.* We sometimes judge the person's paper record rather than the accomplishment for the organization.

7. *The no-complaints bias.* Here the appraiser treats no news as good news. The subordinate who has no complaints and says that everything is terrific is likely to go over well.

The Horns Effect

This is the reverse of the halo effect—the tendency to rate a person lower than the circumstances justify. Some specific causes of this are:

1. *The boss is a perfectionist.* Because the expectations of the boss are so high, he or she is more often disappointed and rates a subordinate lower than deserved.

2. *The subordinate is contrary.* Here the boss vents private irritation with the subordinate's tendency to disagree too often on too many issues.

3. *The oddball effect.* Despite all the lip-service to noncomformity, it seldom finds its way into practice when appraisal time comes around. The oddball,

the maverick, the nonconformist get low ratings simply because of being different.

4. *Membership in a weak team.* A good player on a weak team ends up with lower ratings than he or she would have gotten if playing on a winning one.

5. *The guilt-by-association effect.* The person who isn't really known well by the boss is often judged by the company he or she keeps.

6. *The dramatic-incident effect.* A recent goof can wipe out the effect of months of good work and give a person a lower rating than deserved.

7. *The personality-trait effect.* The subordinate who is too cocky, too brash, too meek, too passive, or otherwise lacks some trait the boss associates with good employees suffers in the appraisal.

8. *The self-comparison effect.* The person who does the job differently than the boss did it when he or she was back on that job suffers more than a person whose job the boss has never done.

If standards of performance have been effectively established, both the halo and horns effects can be eliminated or at least drastically reduced.

Gathering Information

From one appraisal time to the next, a manager should be gathering information that will make the appraisal fair and accurate. If this is not done, the appraisal may be based on hazy memory or on only the most recent behavior and accomplishments of the subordinate.

J. C. Flanagan developed an objective approach for gathering data for the appraisal. He called it the critical incident method.[2] This technique relies on the collection of specific observable job incidents that are judged to be critical because they are related directly to either good or poor job performance. After the incidents are collected and tabulated, components are grouped under one of the headings in a specially designed performance record.

The performance record is accompanied by a manual that describes and illustrates each of the 16 critical requirements. The supervisor records each incident on either the effective (blue) or the ineffective (red) half of the page for the employee involved. The manual states that to be critical, an incident must be directly observed by the supervisor and must clearly show either outstanding or less than satisfactory performance.

In his experience with Delco-Remy Division of General Motors, he found that most of the recorded incidents were positive. There was speculation that the manager would be much more apt to record the negative incidents, but this was not true.

The critical incident method involves three basic steps: (1) completion of the performance record as critical incidents occur; (2) summarizing them for the rating period; and (3) conducting a performance review interview with the employee. Flanagan recommends that this three-phase program be carried out at six-month intervals, and he suggests further that the performance review interview should take the average supervisor from half an hour to an hour. Summarizing his method, he says:

> A performance record is not a yardstick. It is not a rating method. It is a procedure for collecting significant facts about employee performance. These facts are gathered in such a way that they will be of maximum use to supervisors and management, both in improving the employee's understanding of the requirements of his present job and in developing his potential for more responsible positions. It is not simply a new form but a new approach.

If the critical incident method is used, managers should be sure to look for both positive and negative incidents. Otherwise, the appraisal will become biased and the subordinate will be unfairly appraised.

In gathering information, the manager should have one objective: to make an accurate appraisal of performance. He or she can get this information from two major sources:

1. Performance records such as quantity of production, quality of work, meeting deadlines and schedules, safety, actual costs versus budget costs, absenteeism, and the number of complaints from customers or co-workers.

2. Other people who have had dealings with the subordinate. This could include the boss, staff personnel, people served by the subordinate, and even people in other departments with whom the subordinate worked. If the organization uses project teams on which the subordinate has served, the project leader should be contacted. This should be as objective as possible. Instead of asking, "How do you feel about Harry?" it's better to ask, "What kind of service has Harry given you?" or, "How would you evaluate Harry's performance in regard to this issue?"

In other words, the more sources used, the better. But each source should be carefully selected to provide objective data. All these data should then be analyzed and compared with the standards of performance to arrive at the most accurate appraisal.

Appraisal Categories and Scales

The appraisal process requires some type of scale to allow the manager to differentiate between different levels of performance. Perhaps the simplest and best approach would be to use the following four categories to appraise performance on each standard:

DNMS   Does not meet standard
MS   Meets standard
ES   Exceeds standard
O   Outstanding

The appraisal form would look like this:

Significant Job Segments	Standards of Performance	DNMS	MS	ES	O	Comments

Some organizations use such words as *unsatisfactory, satisfactory, outstanding,* and *superior.* Other organizations prefer such terms as *unacceptable, acceptable, good, very good,* and *excellent.*

Some military units use such words as *good, excellent, outstanding,* and *superior.* Here there are two words that mean something better than *excellent,* so *excellent* becomes a term that means about the same as *marginal* or *acceptable.*

Some organizations prefer a 5- or 10-point scale with 1 at the low end of the scale meaning *poor* or *unsatisfactory* and 5 or 10 at the top level of the scale to mean *outstanding* or *superior.*

Still other organizations try to describe the gradations by saying such things as:

Poor: Consistently unsatisfactory. Doesn't come close to meeting standard.
Fair: Occasionally meets standard. Usually is slightly below standard.
Good: Consistently meets standard. Rarely exceeds standard.
Very Good: Consistently above standard. Occasionally doesn't meet standard. Occasionally far above standard.
Excellent: Consistently far above standard.

Other categories and scales are used in the examples in Part II of this book.

If the purpose of performance appraisal is to improve performance, the word *average* should not be used. This word invites comparison with other people rather than with the standard. In order to improve performance, it is important to identify, for each person, the level of performance for each standard. This will reveal strengths as well as areas that need improvement. If the purpose of the appraisal is to determine salary increases, instead of to improve performance, then the word *average* may be used. In this context, individuals' performances are compared with each other.

Self-Appraisal

The concept of self-appraisal is required in some programs, left optional in some, and discouraged or prohibited in others. In a situation where the subordinate does not complete a self-appraisal, the boss makes out the appraisal form, calls in the subordinate for the appraisal interview, and tries to get both understanding and acceptance of the appraisal from the subordinate. The subordinate usually comes to the interview without any specific preparation and is perhaps fearful that it will be an unpleasant experience. He or she may have made an informal self-appraisal, but not one in writing. The subordinate is apt to be on the defensive because the boss will read off the appraisal and ask him or her to agree or to substantiate any disagreement. Many subordinates will not speak freely because of lack of information to substantiate their judgments of themselves or because they are afraid to disagree with the boss. Therefore, they might very well express agreement—or rather, refrain from expressing disagreement—even though they don't really agree. And the boss will naively feel that both understanding and agreement have been reached.

If the subordinate completes a self-appraisal, preferably on the same form the boss uses, the two of them can sit side by side and compare their appraisals. This can create a relaxed climate in which the objective is to arrive at an accurate appraisal. If both of them have honestly tried to be as objective as possible, and if the significant job segments and standards of performance have been clearly stated, the appraisals shouldn't be far apart.

The concept of self-appraisal says to the subordinate: "Your input is important. Maybe you know some things about your performance I don't know. I want to be sure that you have a chance to communicate them to me. And I'll listen to you and consider your input before arriving at a final appraisal."

Several factors should be kept in mind if self-appraisals are going to be used:

1. Subordinates should be given enough advance notice so that a fair self-appraisal can be made. A minimum of three weeks should be allowed.
2. Subordinates should be told the reasons for the self-appraisal and how it will be used in the interview.
3. Specific instructions should be given subordinates on the form to use and what to do.
4. Subordinates should be urged to make an objective appraisal and not to

be overly aggressive (rating themselves higher than justified) or shy (rating themselves lower than justified).

5. Managers should assure subordinates that the self-appraisal will be used to help arrive at a fair appraisal.

Summary

The appraisal process must be done in a systematic and objective manner, by first gathering data from various sources and then comparing performance with standards that have been previously set. It is important for the subordinate to accept the appraisal as fair. The best way to accomplish this is to have the subordinate prepare a self-appraisal that can then be compared with the appraisal by the boss. Free and open discussion will also help to arrive at a fair appraisal agreed on and accepted by both parties. In case of disagreement, the boss must make the final appraisal, but in most cases agreement can be reached without the boss exercising this authority.

————— Preparing for the Appraisal Interview —————

If the interview is going to be effective, the appraiser must prepare. The first step is to determine the objectives to accomplish, and the second is to make preparations to accomplish them.

Objectives to Accomplish

In the appraisal interview, there are five major objectives to accomplish:

1. To reach agreement on the performance of the subordinate.
2. To identify strengths.
3. To identify performance areas that need to be improved.
4. To agree on a performance improvement plan for one area needing improvement.
5. To agree on what's expected (that is, significant job segments and standards of performance) for the next appraisal period.

Because there are so many objectives, it is very difficult to accomplish all of them in one interview. As suggested earlier, it is usually better to plan for two or three interviews. For example, the first interview would cover objectives 1, 2, and 3. The second interview would accomplish objective 4, and a third interview would accomplish objective 5. It probably wouldn't take any more time than if it were done in one interview. And both parties could adequately prepare for each interview.

Preparation by the Boss

Before the interview takes place, the boss should make the following preparations:

1. *Decide on the best time*. The best time is when both parties are able to spend time together without interruption, so it is a good idea for the boss to suggest a time and get approval from the subordinate.

2. *Decide on the best place*. A private office is the best place. It may be the office of the boss or a neutral place. It should be a private place where the door can be closed and people can't look in and see what's going on. Also, it should be a comfortable place where both parties can relax.

3. *Prepare the facilities*. Arrange the furniture so that the subordinate will feel at ease. Perhaps the chairs should be side by side instead of across the desk from each other. If possible, have coffee or water available.

4. *Gather information and materials*. Make a complete and objective appraisal as described earlier in this chapter. Have the forms and information on hand so that they are readily available during the interview.

5. *Plan the opening*. Decide whether to talk about a current event—such as sports, politics, or weather—or to begin by stating the purpose of the interview. Use whatever approach is most natural and will create the best climate for the interview.

6. *Plan the approach*. Here are some alternatives to consider:

(a) Begin with strengths and then discuss job segments needing improvement.

(b) Go straight through the form, give your appraisal, and discuss one item at a time to get agreement before going ahead to the next item.

(c) Ask the subordinate for his or her appraisal before giving your own. You could do this for the entire form or on each item.

(d) Alternate between yourself and the subordinate as to who gives the appraisal first.

There is no right or wrong approach. Your approach might depend on whether or not the subordinate has made a self-appraisal. Remember that the objective is to get agreement, so use whatever approach is best for you.

7. *Give the subordinate appropriate advance notice*. The subordinate should have enough time to prepare for the interview and should clearly understand the time, place, objectives, and probable length of the interview.

8. *Plan the conclusion*. Know how and when you want to end the interview. For example, you may want to agree on the total appraisal, three strengths, three areas needing improvement, and one performance area to improve. Then you may want to summarize and describe what will happen next. For example, you may want to close the interview by saying, "Joe, before we get together again, I'd like you to think about this one area of improvement that you and I think is most important. Jot down some things that you can do. Also, jot down some things that I can do to help you. I'll do the same. Let's get together to develop a specific performance improvement plan that we both think will work. How about two weeks from today at the same time and place? Does that sound O.K. to you?"

In some instances, all the objectives may be accomplished in one interview. In other cases, the first interview may end with an agreement on the final appraisal. The second interview would accomplish the objectives of agreeing on three strengths, three areas requiring improvement, and the one area to be covered in the performance improvement plan. A third interview would develop the performance improvement plan and agree on significant job segments and standards of performance for the next period of time.

Any of these approaches can be effective. The important factor is that the boss should decide in advance what should be accomplished in the interview and should prepare to conclude accordingly.

9. *Guarantee no interruptions*. Be sure that there are no interruptions by phone calls or visitors.

10. *Avoid inappropriate preparation*. When I worked for a large mineral and chemical corporation in the early 1960s, my first job was to develop a corporate performance review program. The program was first introduced and implemented at the Carlsbad, New Mexico, plant. After that, we implemented it in a plant at Bartow, Florida, and one in San José, California, as well as in the sales department at Skokie, Illinois. It was based on some of the principles and approaches described in this book. Emphasis was on the boss and subordinate working together to improve job performance.

A near-disaster occurred when a firm of consulting psychologists tried to sell its services to management. The psychologists wanted to coach every manager before the manager conducted the appraisal interview with a subordinate. Their philosophy was to describe to the manager the personality and other characteristics of the subordinate. Then, according to the psychologists, the manager would be able to conduct an effective interview on the basis of this knowledge.

The approach would have been detrimental for two reasons. First, it would have bogged down the entire program because every manager would have had to be counseled before every interview. Second, the managers would not have been able to conduct straightforward performance appraisal interviews. Rather, they would have been required (or at least encouraged) to conduct interviews the way they had been told by the psychologists. This would probably have been contrary to the practical approach we built into the program, where manager and subordinate sat down side by side and discussed openly and frankly the past and future performance of the subordinate.

Fortunately, top management decided not to hire the psychologists, and the program was implemented as planned with frank and open job-oriented interviews.

Another type of inappropriate preparation would be for the boss to prepare to define his or her own appraisal and convince the subordinate that it is right. This would create a negative interview climate in which the subordinate would be inhibited from being honest and open. Also, if the critical incident method is used for appraisal as described earlier, the boss should avoid using lots of examples of negative behavior to prove a point. This would seriously hamper the interview's effectiveness by placing too much emphasis on past performance rather than looking toward the future.

Preparation by the Subordinate

The subordinate must be given enough advance notice, as stated in item 7 above. In preparing for the interview, the subordinate should do the following:

1. Gather information related to past performance. This would include specific data on activities and accomplishments as well as reasons why certain things weren't done or were done incorrectly.
2. Complete a self-appraisal if requested by the boss.
3. Arrange for work coverage while he or she is absent from the department. This is important so that the subordinate can concentrate on the interview and not worry about whether or not the job is being done properly.

Preparation Time

The amount of time required for preparation depends on various factors, including the forms that must be completed and discussed, the relationship and rapport that exist between boss and subordinate, previous performance review interviews between them, and whether or not they have jointly developed significant job segments and standards of performance.

Summary

Preparation for the appraisal interview should be made by both boss and subordinate. The boss should determine the objectives to accomplish, arrange for proper facilities, notify the subordinate, and plan the specific approach to use. The subordinate should be prepared to participate in the discussion in order to arrive at a fair appraisal. If a specific self-appraisal is required, the subordinate should be given plenty of notice so that adequate preparation can be made.

_____ Conducting the Appraisal Interview _____

The purpose of the appraisal interview is to discuss performance, not personality. It is future-oriented rather than past-oriented. Emphasis should be on what the subordinate will do in the future and not on what has been done in the past. However, a discussion of past performance is essential as the basis for the future.

Ten Guidelines to Remember

The following general principles apply to all performance interviews regardless of the form that is used or whether or not a self-appraisal has been completed.

1. *Establish and maintain rapport.* Rapport can be defined as the climate in which the interview takes place. First of all, as mentioned earlier, the location of the interview is important. It should be conducted in a place where both people can feel relaxed. The chairs should be comfortable. There should be a minimum of noise. No one else should be able to see the two people. If it will help to put the subordinate at ease, the boss and the subordinate should sit alongside each other rather than across the desk. The words as well as the non-verbal communications of the boss should make it clear that two-way communication will take place and that the subordinate should speak freely and frankly. A cup of coffee might help to create this comfortable climate.

It is debatable whether to begin the interview by talking about hobbies or some current event or whether to begin by saying, "As you know, the purpose of this interview is to. . . ." If the two people have a common hobby, that may be a good place to start. Or if there was an unusual political or sporting event that just happened, that may be a good opener.

Socializing for a few minutes is well worth the time if it creates rapport. The following list contrasts an interview climate of rapport to an interview climate without it.

Rapport	*Lack of Rapport*
At ease, relaxed	Nervous, fearful, anxious
Comfortable	Uncomfortable
Friendly, warm	Formal, cold
Not afraid to speak freely and frankly	Afraid to speak openly
Believing, trusting	Challenging, proving
Listening	Interrupting
Understanding	Misunderstanding
Open-minded	Closed-minded
Accepting criticism without resentment	Resenting criticism
Disagreeing without offending	Arguing, downgrading

2. *Clearly explain the purpose of the interview.* Make it clear to the subordinate what you want to accomplish. State it in positive terms, such as: "The purpose of the interview today is for us to discuss your performance and agree on your strengths and areas that can be improved. Then we are going to talk about your future and how we can work together."

3. *Encourage the subordinate to talk.* The interview must include two-way communication. Some subordinates are most anxious to talk, while others are reluctant because of shyness or fear. The establishment of rapport will help to overcome this reluctance. In some situations, the boss must ask specific questions to get the subordinate to talk. In others, the subordinate will talk freely with little encouragement.

4. *Listen and don't interrupt.* The word "listen" here means to *really listen*. It means more than merely keeping quiet or not talking. It is an active process of finding out the thoughts as well as the feelings of the other person. And if both parties start to talk at the same time, the boss should quit talking and encourage the subordinate to go ahead. This backing down is quite difficult for some bosses, but it pays off in maintaining two-way communication throughout the interview. It tells the subordinate, "What you have to say is more important to me than what I have to say to you!"

5. *Avoid confrontation and argument.* Even though differences of opinions are expressed, the boss should avoid confrontation and argument. It is obvious to both parties that the boss has more authority and power than the subordinate. Therefore, there is a chance of ending up in a win-lose situation where the boss wins and the subordinate loses. Unfortunately, winning by the boss might be

very costly, because it might destroy rapport and result in the subordinate deciding not to communicate freely and frankly. If this happens, the interview will not achieve its objectives and might even do more harm than good. By keeping the discussion free and open, a win-win situation can be created so that the needs of both people are met.

6. *Focus on performance, not personality*. This is a performance appraisal interview, and emphasis should be on performance, not personality. This does not mean that such items as attitude, integrity, dependability, appearance, or initiative are not mentioned. It means that these characteristics are mentioned only as they relate to performance.

7. *Focus on the future, not the past*. This does not mean that past performance will not be discussed. But the emphasis is on what can be learned from the past that will help in the future.

8. *Emphasize strengths as well as areas to improve*. Every employee has strengths as well as areas of performance that can be improved. Don't ignore the strengths. Recognize and build on these strengths, and also discuss job segments that must be corrected if performance is to improve.

9. *Terminate the interview when advisable*. Don't hesitate to terminate an interview at any point if you think it's a good idea. Any number of reasons could justify the termination, including loss of rapport, boss or subordinate being anxious to go somewhere, quitting time, lack of progress being made, fatigue, or an important interruption. If you end the interview before accomplishing all the objectives you set, agree on when the interview will continue.

10. *Conclude on a positive note*. Be sure that the subordinate leaves the interview in a positive frame of mind instead of resentful toward the negative aspects of the discussion. After the interview is over, the subordinate should say (or at least feel), "Thanks, boss. I'm glad we had a chance to get together and discuss my performance. Now I know where I stand and what I should do in the future. And I know that you are going to work with me."

A warm handshake at the conclusion of the interview is one way to end on a positive tone. Another is for the boss to say, "Thanks for coming in. I feel that this has been a very profitable discussion, and I know I can count on you in the future. I'll be glad to help you in any way I can."

Techniques for Successful Interviews

As explained earlier, there really shouldn't be any great surprises if the significant job segments and standards of performance have been clarified and agreed on as the basis for the appraisal. The subordinate's appraisal, whether mental or written, should be very close to the written appraisal by the manager.

The problem the manager faces is to be sure he or she gets honest agreement or disagreement from the subordinate on the appraisal. Obviously, the establishment of rapport is essential for this. Specific interviewing techniques are also important. Here are some specific suggestions:

1. Be open. Show the form to the subordinate. Don't hide it.
2. Explain your appraisal. Describe how you arrived at it. If you checked records or talked to other people, say so. If you did it by yourself, say so. Also, be sure to emphasize that you want frank comments from the subordinate because your appraisal may not be accurate. Admit, for example, that the subordinate may have done some things you've forgotten or don't even know about.
3. Be sure your appraisal is tentative. Be willing to change your appraisal if the subordinate's input convinces you that you were wrong. Don't be afraid to admit a mistake.
4. Summarize. When the entire appraisal has been discussed, go over it with the subordinate. Have a copy made for the subordinate so that he or she has the same information you have.

All four of these techniques demonstrate to the subordinate that there is nothing secret about what you are doing. A manager simply wants to come up with a fair and accurate appraisal that will make it possible to work with the subordinate and help him or her improve performance in the future. The manager may want to start with strengths or with the first item on the appraisal form and go straight down the form. Whatever way is most natural and comfortable is the best way. After completing the discussion, the entire appraisal should be summarized.

Interview Checklist

Walter Mahler suggests the following six items as a checklist to be used by managers when conducting appraisal interviews with subordinates:[3]

1. *Coach on results.* Were results or traits stressed? If traits were stressed, were they related to end results? Was criticism personal or job-centered?

2. *Get down to cases.* How specific were the reasons given for my opinions? Were specific incidents used well? How frank was I?

3. *Determine causes.* Was an attempt made to get at causes? Did we get at several causes? Did we get at the real causes?

4. *Make interview a two-way process.* Was I dominant? Who did the most talking? Was there good give-and-take discussion? Were questions used to stimulate thinking?

5. *Set or reset goals.* Were goals set against which the subordinate could measure progress? Were goals specific or general? Were goals imposed or developed jointly?

6. *Provide motivation.* Did I show concern about the subordinate? Did I use positive motivation? Was the subordinate motivated to act differently in the future?

Using the Self-Appraisal

If the subordinate has made a written self-appraisal, it is easier for a boss to conduct an effective performance appraisal interview. The best way to start is to put both forms side by side and compare them. The manager can say, "You've made out an appraisal just as I have. Let's see where we agree and where we disagree. I'll read off my appraisal and you mark it on your form. Then you read off your appraisal and I'll mark it on my form."

After this has been done, it's helpful to start with the items where there is agreement, then go to items of disagreement. Ask the subordinate to explain his or her rationale. Then the manager can do the same. Through discussion, differences can be resolved and agreement reached on a fair appraisal.

Evaluating the Interview

After the interview has been completed, the manager should evaluate it to determine its effectiveness as well as glean ideas for improving future interviews. Seymour Levy has suggested that interviewers can evaluate a completed interview by asking themselves the following questions:[4]

Did the interview achieve its purpose? Did I help the subordinate? How could I have made it more productive?

If I had it to do over again, what changes would I make in my approach? What things would I cover that were omitted this time? What things would I omit that were discussed, perhaps unnecessarily?

Did I learn something new from the interview? About counseling techniques? About the individual? About myself? About my organization?

Who did most of the talking? Did I really listen to what the subordinate had to say?

Was I satisfied with the interview? Do the subordinate and I understand each other better as a result?

Do I feel that I'll be able to conduct my next interview more effectively?

Summary

Conducting the interview is one of the most important and difficult parts of a performance review program. Good preparation, as described in this chapter, is essential. In addition, there are specific interviewing approaches and techniques that can be used for maximum effectiveness. Here are ten important principles to remember:

> Establish and maintain rapport.
> Clearly explain the purpose of the interview.
> Encourage the subordinate to talk.
> Listen and don't interrupt.
> Avoid confrontation and argument.
> Focus on performance, not personality.
> Focus on the future, not the past.
> Emphasize strengths as well as areas to improve.
> Terminate the interview when advisable.
> Conclude on a positive note.

In addition to these principles, this chapter gave other interviewing suggestions. For example, openness is important. Show the appraisal form to the subordinate and describe where you got the information and how you arrived at the ratings. Be willing to change the appraisal if the subordinate provides information to justify a change. Finally, summarize the appraisal discussion when it is over, and give a copy of the final completed form to the subordinate.

References

1. George Odiorne, *Management by Objectives*. New York: Pitman, 1965.
2. J. C. Flanagan and R. K. Burns, "The Employee Performance Record: A New Appraisal and Development Tool." *Harvard Business Review,* September–October 1955. Reprinted with permission.
3. Walter Mahler, *How Effective Executives Interview*. Homewood, Ill.: Dow Jones-Irwin, 1976.
4. Seymour Levy, *A Guide to Counseling*. New Rochelle, N.Y.: Martin M. Bruce Publishers, 1976.

4
The Performance Improvement Plan

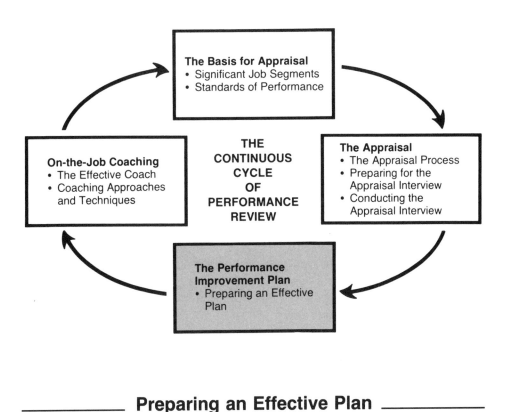

The Basis for Appraisal
- Significant Job Segments
- Standards of Performance

The Appraisal
- The Appraisal Process
- Preparing for the Appraisal Interview
- Conducting the Appraisal Interview

THE CONTINUOUS CYCLE OF PERFORMANCE REVIEW

The Performance Improvement Plan
- Preparing an Effective Plan

On-the-Job Coaching
- The Effective Coach
- Coaching Approaches and Techniques

——— Preparing an Effective Plan ———

A performance improvement plan is a specific course of action to be taken to improve the performance of the subordinate. It should describe what will be done, by whom, and when.

In the appraisal interview, segments of the job to be improved by the subordinate should be identified. The next step is to select the *one* segment of performance that should be worked on first. If too many are worked on, there is a good probability that the task will be overwhelming and nothing will be accom-

61

plished. The one job performance segment should be jointly determined by boss and subordinate. Four criteria should be used to select it:

1. What does the boss feel is most important? Perhaps the subordinate could improve a weakness that is causing serious problems, or maybe the boss wants improvement in an already strong area.
2. What area does the subordinate think should be worked on? This factor probably reveals the motivation of the subordinate to improve, because the subordinate usually won't pick an area that he or she does not want to improve.
3. What area of improvement would bring prompt results? This would provide a successful experience and could lead to improvement in other areas.
4. What area of improvement would have the greatest payoff in advantages versus time, energy, and money expended? This would be an objective decision based only on facts and logic.

Seymour Levy has suggested a strategy for making the selection,[1] which is illustrated in Figure 1. The very process of jointly picking the one job segment to improve can build rapport and understanding between boss and subordinate.

Ingredients of a Plan

The performance improvement plan should meet four criteria:

1. *It should be practical.* The specifics of the plan should be related to the job performance to be improved. Reading a theoretical book or taking a three-credit university course on industrial psychology might not be practical.

2. *It should be time-oriented.* Specific deadline dates should be set. These should be realistic and jointly determined.

Figure 1. Strategy for selecting areas to improve.

Areas of Performance	Difficult to Change	Easy to Change
Greater Need to Change	Put these on the long-range improvement schedule, or help the employee to compensate for them or work around them.	Work on these first!
Lesser Need to Change	Don't worry about these now!	Work on these second. They may help prepare for more difficult changes.

3. *It should be specific.* It should clearly describe what will be done. For example, if the area to be improved is poor communication with subordinates, the reading of a book by the subordinate would be one action to take. The name of a specific book should be listed instead of saying, "Read a book on communications."

4. *It should involve commitment.* Both boss and subordinate should be sold on the plan and committed to its implementation. They agree that it will be done.

Requirements for Behavior Change

The performance improvement plan is designed to bring about a change in the behavior of the subordinate. If this change is going to take place, five requirements must be met:

1. *Desire.* The employee must want to change.

2. *Knowledge and skill.* The employee must know what to do and also how to do it.

3. *Climate.* The employee must operate in a climate that provides an opportunity to behave in a different way. The most important factor in this climate is the boss. Bosses can provide the following types of climate:

(a) *Preventing.* This means that the boss does not allow the subordinate to do what he or she wants to do.

(b) *Discouraging.* The boss doesn't say, "You can't," but does say, "I wouldn't recommend it," or "I wouldn't do it if I were you," or "I'm not saying you can't do it, but if you do it and it doesn't work out, you are in trouble!" These statements discourage a subordinate from changing behavior.

(c) *Neutral.* The boss leaves it up to the subordinate. The typical attitude of the boss is: "I just want results. If you want to do it, it's up to you."

(d) *Encouraging.* The boss says, "It sounds like a good idea. Why don't you try it?"

(e) *Requiring.* The boss says, "Do it and I'll help you."

It's pretty obvious that the climate must be neutral or better if the subordinate is going to change his or her behavior. If the boss establishes a preventing or discouraging climate, it is almost certain that no change in behavior will take place. Therefore, the entire process leading up to the desired change in behavior must build the right climate between boss and subordinate.

4. *Help and support.* If an employee is going to improve, encouragement and help are needed. The person may be afraid to try something new because of fear of failure. Or an employee may intend to do it but won't get around to it

unless encouraged. Also, the person may not have the confidence or skill to do it without encouragement and assistance. The help can come from the boss, from a training or personnel professional, or from both.

5. *Rewards*. People who know they will be rewarded for changing are apt to change. Also, if the rewards really come, they will be motivated to change in the future. Rewards for changing behavior may be of a monetary or nonmonetary nature. Monetary rewards include salary increases, bonuses, or other financial incentives. Nonmonetary rewards include self-satisfaction, praise, increased responsibility, and more freedom and authority to act.

Who Develops the Plan?

Plans should be practical, time-oriented, and specific. The implementation of the plan requires the commitment of both boss and subordinate. These requirements suggest and almost necessitate that the plan be jointly developed by boss and subordinate. In addition, a training and development professional may be required to help. Line managers and subordinates are able to work out special job assignments, but they usually do not know what books to read or conferences to attend. Training professionals can recommend these from experience.

How Should the Plan Be Developed?

When the need for improvement has been determined, the first step is to determine the causes of the problem. Why isn't performance as good as it could and should be? According to George L. Morrissey, there are three different categories of reasons: the subordinate, the boss, and the situation.[2]

The subordinate may be doing something wrong or not doing what he or she should do. The reasons could be not understanding what's expected, lack of skill, or lack of motivation.

The boss could be doing counterproductive things that prevent the subordinate from performing to the maximum. Or the boss might not be doing something that would help the subordinate perform better. Some examples are:

Doing what shouldn't be done
Supervising too closely.
Criticizing every mistake.
Requiring the subordinate to come to the boss for all decisions and solutions to all problems.
Putting undue pressure on the subordinate.

Not doing what should be done
Not clarifying what's expected on the job.

Not seeing that the subordinate had necessary skills to do the job.

Not giving praise for a job well done.

Not being available to the subordinate.

Not listening and considering ideas of the subordinate.

Not keeping the subordinate informed.

Not taking a personal interest in the subordinate.

Not encouraging the subordinate to grow through delegation, special assignments, and education.

Not encouraging the subordinate to try out new ideas.

The third category, the situation, encompasses the conditions in which the subordinate performs. Obstacles could include:

Inadequate tools or equipment to work with.

Shortage of materials.

Poor working conditions, including noise, distractions, inadequate lighting, lack of space, and interruptions.

Unsatisfactory co-workers.

Changes in methods, procedures, or equipment that create problems for the subordinate.

Consider All Possible Solutions

A list should be made of all the possible things that can be done to improve performance. These should be listed under the categories of what the subordinate can do, what the boss can do, and what situations should be changed.

On the basis of extensive research concerning the growth and development of managers, Norman Allhiser of the Management Institute at University of Wisconsin—Extension identified some job-related growth activities. These were the results of his research listed in order from most effective to least effective.

Attendance at staff meetings

Job rotation

Discussions with staff specialists

Study of manuals and procedure guides

Attendance at technical department programs

Temporary assignments to other departments

Allhiser found that the example set by the boss was the single most important factor in the growth and development of subordinates.

These are possible approaches to consider when preparing the performance improvement plan. Off-the-job activities are also important ingredients of a performance improvement plan. The most common are programs to attend, books and articles to read, and active participation in professional and/or trade organizations.

Following are sample lists of possible actions for improving performance in orienting and training new employees, jointly developed in interviews between Tom Severson, the boss, and John Green, the subordinate. After the lists you will see the final performance improvement plan that was developed from them.

Possible Actions by John Green

1. Talk with another supervisor who does an effective job of orienting and training new employees.
2. Observe that supervisor when he or she orients and trains a new employee.
3. Attend the orientation meeting conducted by the personnel department with new employees.
4. Determine the best time for new employees to come into the department.
5. Set aside sufficient time to orient and train each new employee.
6. Have an ''expert'' observe the next time John orients and trains a new employee. Have the ''expert'' critique and offer suggestions.
7. Attend a seminar on orienting and training employees.
8. Read books on the subject.

Possible Actions by Tom Severson

1. Talk with each of John's new employees at the end of the first week of employment to find out how they are doing and how they feel about their jobs. Look for indications of good and bad things that happened in their orientation and training. Discuss this information with John.
2. Be sure that no special pressure or assignments are given John to prevent him from doing an effective job of orienting and training new employees.
3. Work with personnel department to be sure that new employees are sent to John's department when he wants them to come.
4. Suggest the name of an effective trainer for John to talk with and watch.
5. Correct any of the situations that hinder or prevent John from doing an effective job.
6. Find an ''expert'' (possibly from personnel or training department) to observe John the next time he orients and trains a new employee.
7. Find out what training courses are available that John might attend.
8. Find out the names of specific books that John can read to learn about effective ways to train new employees.

Possible Situations to Be Corrected

1. New employees will come to John's department when it is most convenient for John.
2. A quiet office will be provided for John so that he can spend time talking with and orienting each new employee.
3. A special place will be set aside for training new employees. No employee will be placed into a production situation until the training has been completed.

Finalize the Plan

This list of possible actions does not constitute a plan. It must be converted into specifics of what will be done, by whom, and when.

Figure 2 shows the specific plan that John and Tom worked out together. Larry Jackson, the training director, assisted. This performance improvement plan illustrates the requirements of being practical, specific, and time-oriented. It spells out what each person will do and by when. Most important, both John and Tom are committed to it.

The Dayton-Hudson Approach

Dayton-Hudson Corporation has developed a practical approach to individualized development, under the leadership of Paul Chaddock, vice president of organization planning and development. The feedback from the operating companies that have used this approach has been very positive.

A booklet called "Individual Development Plan" (IDP) was developed as an aid for managers.[6] It has two purposes: To help employees improve performance on present jobs, and to help employees with future potential to prepare for possible promotion through a preplanned series of learning activities. Emphasis is placed on improving present job performance.

The IDP grows directly out of performance reviews. Figure 3 shows the relationship between performance and the plan and is designed to improve performance on the present job. It is used to help a person overcome weaknesses and build on strengths. Figure 4 shows the form used when a person is preparing for promotion.

The specific plan for performance improvement at Dayton-Hudson consists of three different kinds of approaches, as illustrated in Figure 5: from outside sources, intraorganizational activities, and personal self-regulatory activities.

Figure 6 shows an example of a completed form to improve an employee's performance in the management of time. Emphasis is placed on intraorganiza-

Figure 2. Performance improvement plan.

Employee: John Green, Supervisor
Boss: Tom Severson, Department Head
Date: October 1
Performance to Be Improved: Orienting and Training New Employees

Action to Be Taken	By Whom	When
1. Talk with Phil Taylor about his approach.	John Green	October 15
2. Watch Phil Taylor when he orients and trains a new employee.	John Green	The next time he does it
3. Attend new employee orientation meeting conducted by personnel department.	John Green	The next time it is done
4. Decide on the best time for new employees to come to the department.	John Green working with personnel department	By October 20
5. Attend a seminar on "How to Train New Employees."	John Green	November 15 University of Wisconsin— Extension, Milwaukee
6. Read the following books: a. Self-Development for Supervisors and Managers, by Norman Allhiser[3] b. No-Nonsense Communication, by Donald Kirkpatrick[4] c. The Supervisor and On-the-Job Training, by Martin Broadwell[5]	John Green	by October 15 by November 10 by December 12
7. Observe John Green orienting and training a new employee.	Larry Jackson, Training Director	The next time John trains a new employee
8. Talk with John Green's next three new employees.	Tom Severson	One week after hire
9. Provide a check list to John for orienting new employees.	Larry Jackson	October 15
10. Arrange for a special office for John to use when orienting each new employee.	Tom Severson	October 15
11. Arrange for a permanent special training place for new employees.	Tom Severson	January 1

Figure 3. IDP form for improving performance on the present job.

Things to Change	Individual Development Plan	Done
Position responsibilities not achieved during the past 12 months, or areas of weakness: Individual strengths to build on:		

Figure 4. IDP form for preparing for promotion.

Positions to which you aspire:	Steps to take to get ready:	Done

Figure 5. IDP form for ideas for an individual development plan.

Performance Area to Improve: _____		
From Outside Sources	Interorganizational Activities	Personal Self-Regulatory Activities

Figure 6. Completed IDP form for improving time management.

Performance Area to Improve: Time Management		
From Outside Sources	Interorganizational Activities	Personal Self-Regulatory Activities
(To be done by subordinate)	(To be done by boss)	(To be done by subordinate)
Read Lakein's book, *How To Get Control of Your Time And Your Life.*[7]	Set up interview with or assign subordinate to a task force led by a skilled time manager.	Interview a manager who spends time wisely, and select two or three practices to adopt for yourself.
Attend a time management workshop.	Every day for one week show your subordinate how you schedule and manage your own time.	Make daily "To Do" lists, and set priorities for all items.
		Keep a written record of your completion score.
	Ask to see the "To Do" and "Deadlines Made or Missed" lists that you assign this employee. Reinforce every single indication of effective time management.	Supplement your "To Do" list with projected time allocations for each task.
		Keep written records of dead-lines made or missed.
		Refuse to allow yourself to stay overtime or come in early as a way to bail yourself out of your backlogs.
		Review your calender for the last three months. Identify activities that were unnecessary or that used an inappropriate amount of time. Then plan your next month to correct those situations.

tional activities and personal self-regulatory activities. A manager and subordinate working together can do more to produce growth than any other force inside or outside the organization.

The Secondary Performance Improvement Plan

It was emphasized that a plan should be developed to cover only *one* area to improve. This is important to be sure that improvement will take place in at least one part of the job. It was also suggested that three areas to improve be identified along with three areas of strengths. This means that when one performance improvement plan has been implemented wholly or at least partially, a new plan should be developed for a second area needing improvement. If the plans aren't too complicated, boss and subordinate can work on more than one performance improvement plan at a time.

The Boss and the Performance Improvement Plan

When any type of plan is developed between boss and subordinate, the boss automatically assumes the final responsibility for the implementation of the plan. This responsibility falls into five practical steps:

1. Be sure the subordinate understands the plan that was developed. The joint development of the plan almost ensures this. Both boss and subordinate get a copy of the plan.

2. Discuss a change in plan if any circumstances occur to warrant it. Make changes on the written plan.

3. Periodically, remind the subordinate of commitments before their due date. This helps the subordinate to meet the due dates and prevents failures because of forgetting.

4. Provide continuous help in the implementation of the plan. At the time of a reminder, the manager can ask, "Do you see any problems in meeting the deadline? Can I help you in any way?"

5. Correct the subordinate if certain parts of the plan are not met on schedule. It has been suggested above that prevention is much better than cure. But if a failure occurs, the manager must see that the situation is corrected and the subordinate gets back on schedule.

The problem is to accomplish these five steps without causing resentment. The solution depends on the rapport that is maintained between manager and subordinate. If the tone is kept positive and the manager controls his or her emotions, there is a very good chance that the plan will be implemented on schedule and everyone will be happy.

The Subordinate and the Performance Improvement Plan

The agreement on the performance improvement plan is the beginning of the on-the-job coaching. The boss immediately picks up an obligation to see that the plan is carried out. Likewise, the subordinate picks up an obligation to implement the plan or to let the boss know as soon as anything happens that makes the plan impractical. When a plan becomes unrealistic, a revision in the plan is just as necessary as a revision in a standard when the standard is no longer appropriate. If something comes up that makes it impossible or impractical to carry out any phase of the plan, the subordinate must realize that it is his or her responsibility to call it to the attention of the boss.

Summary

A specific written performance improvement plan is very helpful toward improving performance. This plan should include what will be done, by whom, and when.

To be effective the plan should be practical, time-oriented, and specific, with commitment on the part of both boss and subordinate. The best way to accomplish these four requirements is for boss and subordinate to develop it together. A training professional, if available, can provide valuable assistance.

A good approach is to identify three specific kinds of actions to be taken: what will be done by the subordinate, what will be done by the boss, and what situations or conditions will be changed. The implementation of the plan becomes the joint responsibility of boss and subordinate, with the boss playing the role of coach.

References

1. Seymour Levy, *A Guide to Counseling*. New Rochelle, N.Y.: Martin M. Bruce Publishers, 1976.
2. George L. Morrissey, *Appraisal and Development Through Objectives and Results*. Reading, Mass.: Addison-Wesley, 1972.
3. Norman Allhiser, *Self-Development for Supervisors and Managers*. Madison, Wis.: University of Wisconsin—Extension, 1977.
4. Donald Kirkpatrick, *No-Nonsense Communication*. Elm Grove, Wis.: K & M Publishers, 1979.
5. Martin Broadwell, *The Supervisor and On-the-Job Training*. Reading, Mass.: Addison-Wesley, 1978.
6. Dayton-Hudson Corporation, "Individual Development Plan." Minneapolis, 1979.
7. Alan Lakein, *How to Get Control of Your Time and Your Life*. New York: Peter H. Wyden, Inc., 1973.

5
On-the-Job Coaching

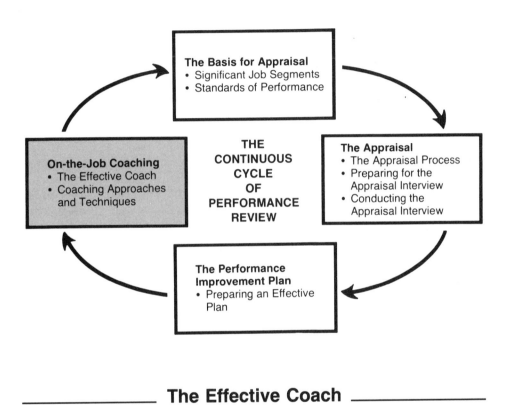

The Effective Coach

As soon as the word "coach" is mentioned, thoughts turn to athletics. And different coaches come to mind. People begin to identify effective coaches and analyze why they were successful, and the arguments begin as to who was the best and what characteristics and approaches are most effective.

What Makes a Good Coach?

What are the characteristics of an effective coach? Are these characteristics only of athletic coaches, or would they apply to managers as "coaches" in industry, business, and government? To answer these questions, I wrote letters to some well-known coaches and asked them this question: "What are the characteristics (qualities, approaches, and so on) of an effective coach?" Here are the replies I received.

J. Frank Broyles, director of athletics at the University of Arkansas:

> In my opinion, an effective coach should be a living example of the virtues he teaches.

Paul F. Dietzel, director of athletics at Louisiana State University:

> It is extremely important that the coach have a fine technical knowledge of the sport he or she is attempting to coach. That is third in line of importance. The second most important thing is how hard this coach works at the profession. How hard you work at your profession shows when no one is watching you. However, the single most important ingredient is the loyalty the coach displays to his fellow coaches, to his team, and to the organization that he represents. In other words, does the coach have a genuine "like" for the people he or she coaches and an abiding interest in them after they are no longer able to participate for that coach? Maybe that could be spelled out in another way: "Do you really want to be of service to young people?" Whatever it is, that ingredient—a genuine concern for the athlete—has to be of number one importance.

John Erickson, president of the Fellowship of Christian Athletes (former basketball coach of the University of Wisconsin, and general manager of the Milwaukee Bucks):

> I have always thought that to be effective, a coach must be an excellent teacher and a person with leadership qualities. These two general but important characteristics include more specific requirements such as:
>
> 1. Solid knowledge of what one is teaching.
> 2. Good motivation skills as well as effective communication.
> 3. A deep personal concern for each team member.
> 4. Ability to make decisions under pressure and live with these decisions without second-guessing oneself.
> 5. Willingness to confess mistakes and build on the experience.
> 6. Complete honesty in all situations.
> 7. Willingness to be an example for players in all areas of life.
> 8. Ability to keep all things in perspective, recognizing priorities of life—God, family, others, and my work.

Elroy Hirsch, director of athletics at the University of Wisconsin:

> I firmly believe that you cannot put a coach into a mold. In other words, I feel that successful coaches are different in their makeup and their tactics. For instance, John McKay, a loose, even-going coach with a great sense of humor, is far different from a Bo Schembechler or a Woody Hayes. Likewise, Dave Mc-

Clain is far different from a Bear Bryant. One thing all these people do have in common, however, is their dedication to the job—that is, they know no bounds on the hours they work, there are no days in the week—they are totally dedicated to the work at hand. Through their individual personalities they conquer the job before them.

If the coach has other qualities, so much the better. In other words, he should be very good on his feet, be able to meet the public well, be friendly and warm to one and all. Many times this is very, very difficult in the face of criticism from alumni, fans, and so on. He must have patience with young people, for it is his job to teach as well as to coach. He must be a very strong supervisor, for his assistant coaches must do his every bidding and do the job properly. Along this line, the selection of his staff is most important. He must not be afraid of having very sound, good people around him. He must not be afraid that someone underneath him is trying to take over his job. He must surround himself with strength, and of course this requires him to be an effective manager of personnel.

To a somewhat lesser degree, he must also understand the budgetary process. It is very easy to give a coach a free hand and let him spend all the money he wishes to accomplish the job; however, in our situation and in most situations in intercollegiate athletics, we are restricted by budget limitations, and the coach must understand the budget process and live within those limitations.

What we, in effect, are looking for is a "perfect man." It is very difficult to find one that possesses all the qualities for the ideal coach, but we try to come as close to it as possible. The structure of intercollegiate athletics is wrong in my estimation . . . in effect we are telling our income-sport coaches . . . who generate nearly all of the income which supports the entire 27-sports programs . . . , "If you are not successful, and if you don't draw large crowds and generate large amounts of income, we are going to fire you." I think that is totally unfair. However, this is part of the pressure that the head coach in the income-producing sports must work under.

Bob Knight, basketball coach at Indiana University:

The most important characteristic, I think, that an effective coach must have is the ability to make decisions. This applies not only to what transpires on the court or around basketball but on a day-to-day involvement he has with his program. I have long felt that the most important thing that a coach can teach is discipline. Discipline to me is doing something when it has to be done, as well as it can be done, and doing it that way all the time.

Tom Landry, football coach of the Dallas Cowboys:

An effective athletic coach must be a teacher, a psychologist, and a motivator. He must possess leadership qualities, and at the same time, he needs the confidence and concentration to operate at maximum efficiency under great stress.

Al McGuire, Al McGuire Enterprises, Inc. (former basketball coach at Marquette University):

A good coach is a person that stands the test of time. He uses team plays the same exact way the last five minutes of the game as the first five. He is also a person that has no other outside interest. They are usually guys that are not interested in having smoke rings blowing at them and are not continually trying to make supplemental income.

Ray Meyer, basketball coach at DePaul University:

I believe a coach has to put the sport in its proper perspective. It is a game, and one's life does not depend upon it. When he understands this, he coaches without putting extra pressure on the players. They will play freer and better. A coach must have patience. He can't expect too much too soon. He is a teacher. Probably the greatest quality a coach can have is understanding. He must understand that each player is an individual and must be treated as such. All players cannot be treated alike. Some you can improve by loud criticism, and others need encouragement. No coach can treat all players alike, for each one is an individual.

Tom Meyer, baseball coach at the University of Wisconsin:

The qualities of an effective coach include:
1. Honesty—season your speech with appropriate words.
2. Being yourself—also working to improve what "yourself" is all about.
3. Consistency.
   a. Attitude and lifestyle being . . . a springboard from which to communicate to others.
   b. Trying to treat each game the same and encouraging the team to do likewise, no matter what the competition.
4. Working hard, but not allowing priorities to be misplaced.
   a. God.
   b. Family.
   c. Job.
   d. Other ministries.
5. Anticipating various problems and possibilities in advance.
6. Thorough preparation.
7. Being open toward fresh ideas.
8. Creating a climate where criticism can be expressed and viewed as healthy.
9. Being part of a team effort, where no one thinks himself better than another, including coaches and players, even though responsibilities may differ.
10. Doing "your work heartily, as for the Lord rather than for men" (Colossians 3:23 NAS).

Ralph Miller, basketball coach at Oregon State University:

The qualities for effective coaching primarily embody three basic requirements for good teaching, because coaches merely teach physical skills and related material for competitive purposes. First, know your subject matter. Second, simplify the material for easy consumption and understanding by the pupil. Third, organize and simplify teaching methods to fully utilize the time allotment for the good of the group. The only difference between teaching and coaching involves preparation for testing. Classroom tests provide time for thought prior to requiring answers, but this luxury does not exist in athletic contests.

Tom Osborne, football coach at the University of Nebraska:

I believe that the qualities of an effective coach are good organizational skills, a capacity to work long hours, an ability to communicate effectively with his athletes, an ability to maintain composure and to think clearly in pressure situations, and an ability to communicate a genuine sense of concern for the general well-being of his players.

Ara Parseghian, Ara Parseghian Enterprises (former football coach at Notre Dame University):

Defining the characteristics of an effective coach is not easily done. In responding, a series of words came to mind . . . , and I won't attempt to weigh them. Here are some of the words that have crossed my mind.

Dedicated	Communicator
Confident	Enthusiastic
Consistent	Disciplinarian
Hard-working	Perseverance
Leader	Strategically abreast of trends
Loyal	Articulate
Honest	Flexible
Knowledgeable	Humble

I guess the last man that had these qualities, they put on the Cross.

Joseph Paterno, football coach and athletic director at The Pennsylvania State University:

An effective athletic coach must possess sound moral values and the ability to relate to all types of people. He must be dedicated, loyal, and sincere about his beliefs and philosophies and must be willing to accept success and failure as part of the game. Above and beyond all things he must have a true love for the sport and at all times realize the responsibility he has to his players.

Richard "Digger" Phelps, basketball coach at the University of Notre Dame:

My advice would be to know the game and be ready to make adjustments. But most importantly, a coach must always be himself.

Dean E. Smith, head basketball coach at the University of North Carolina:

1. The coach should care about the people under his guidance.

2. He should decide how best to use his personnel and then have the ability to teach.

3. It is important to motivate each individual to work to the best of his ability.

Bart Starr, football coach of the Green Bay Packers:

To begin, I believe he is goal-oriented and has a plan by which to accomplish those goals and a method by which to measure progress along the way. Additionally, he is extremely self-confident, very poised, has the ability to accept criticism, and receive coaching himself, has a strong faith in God, and a good sense of humor. Further, I think that all successful coaches tend to be so because they operate within their own personality and framework.

John Wooden, former basketball coach at UCLA:

These are the essential personal traits and abilities for a coach:

Primary Traits	*Secondary Traits*
Industriousness	Affability
Enthusiasm	Appearance
Sympathy	Voice
Judgment	Adaptability
Self-control	Cooperativeness
Earnestness	Forcefulness
Patience	Accuracy
Attentiveness to detail	Alertness
Impartiality	Reliability
Integrity	Optimism
Organization	Resourcefulness
Discipline	Vision

A coach must communicate with those under his supervision; listen and not be disagreeable when there is disagreement; keep in mind that criticism is to improve, prevent, correct, or help and not to punish; make those under his supervision feel that they are working with him rather than for him; be more interested in finding the best way rather than having his own way; be well organized and not waste time; and be genuinely concerned about his players.

In his book *They Call Me Coach,* this same coach adds:

No coach should be trusted with the tremendous responsibility of handling young men under the great mental, emotional, and physical strain to which they are subjected unless he is spiritually strong. If he does possess this inner strength, it is only because he has faith and truly loves his fellowman. This was the belief of Amos Alonzo Stagg, who also felt that the obligations, opportunities and responsibilities in coaching are manifold. The coach who is committed to the Christlike life will be helping youngsters under his supervision to develop wholesome disciplines of body, mind, and spirit that will build character worthy of his Master's calling. He must set the proper example by word and by deed.[1]

I also asked Jon McGlocklin, former basketball star with Indiana University and the Milwaukee Bucks, what he thought were the qualities of an effective coach. He replied:

I feel that a successful coach must possess the ability to communicate and relate to his players as people and athletes. He must be disciplined and command the respect of his players. He must be knowledgeable in his sport and yet capable of admitting a mistake. And, finally, it helps to have talented players if winning is everything! If not, he builds his players as athletes and men.

A Composite Image of the Ideal Coach

If we piece together the different comments of these well-known and successful coaches, a picture of the ideal coach begins to emerge. He or she has knowledge—of the players, the game, and finance and budgets. He or she has many skills and abilities, including these:

Recruiting players and staff of assistants.
Establishing goals and objectives.
Planning and organization.
Communication.
Motivating each person as an individual.
Teaching.
Correcting and criticizing without causing resentment.
Making decisions.
Listening.
Discipline.
Measuring performance and progress toward goals.
Finding the best way, which is not necessarily the coach's way.
Establishing and executing proper priorities.
Operating effectively under stress.
Relating to all types of people.

The ideal coach has the following personal qualities:

Enthusiasm and dedication	Self-confidence
Self-control	Humility
Patience	Perseverence
Impartiality	Genuine concern for players
Integrity and honesty	Warmth
Friendliness	Willingness to admit mistakes

Optimism	Willingness to accept criticism
Resourcefulness	Sense of humor
Vision	Flexibility
Forcefulness	Love of the sport
Consistency	Willingness to accept success and
Being part of the team	failure as part of the game
Open-mindedness	Strong sense of moral values

Finally, a good coach sets an example. Frank Broyles and John Erickson both emphasized that the coach must be a living example for the players. John Wooden quotes this poem to illustrate the importance of this:[2]

A careful man I ought to be, a little fellow follows me.
I do not dare to go astray for fear he'll go the self-same way.

Not once can I escape his eyes, what e'er he sees me do, he tries.
Like me he says he's going to be, the little chap who follows me.

I must remember as I go through summer sun and winter snow,
I'm building for the years to be, that little chap who follows me.

The Manager as "Coach"

The manager in industry, business, and government is a person who supervises a number of subordinates. His or her situation is almost identical to that of the athletic coach in many ways.

First of all, the manager must get the best effort and performance from each subordinate, and is constantly trying to help subordinates improve, both for their own benefit and for that of the organization.

In many situations, the manager is concerned with a team of workers as well as with the performance of each individual worker. This is similar to coaches of team sports like basketball, football, and hockey. In other situations, the manager is primarily concerned with individual workers because each person pretty much works alone. This is similar to sports like swimming, track, tennis, and golf.

If employees performing under a manager don't like the situation, they have available options such as letting up on performance, complaining, causing dissension among the other workers, and quitting. Athletes can do all these things too.

Managers have some employees who are better than others and who therefore receive higher rewards than others. Sometimes the subordinates make more money than the manager does.

Managers are under constant pressure to produce with the people and resources available. Sometimes accidents, sickness, and other problems reduce these resources. Like coaches, managers are concerned about competition. In order to stay in business, they must meet or beat the competition—with whatever resources they *do* have.

Finally, managers have the same opportunities to give rewards that coaches have, and the same limitations on them. Most managers are limited in how much money they can give, but they have ample opportunities to give nonfinancial rewards such as praise, more responsibility, more freedom, special job assignments, and asking for ideas.

Summary

Because the job of a manager is very similar to the job of an athletic coach, many of the characteristics of an effective athletic coach also apply to a good manager. Just as athletic coaches have different types of players to work with, managers have employees with differences in attitudes, knowledge, and skills. In both situations, the challenge is to mold people into an effective team to accomplish the goals of the organization and to help subordinates accomplish their own goals at the same time.

_____ Coaching Approaches and Techniques _____

The terms "coaching" and "counseling" are frequently used to describe the on-the-job conversations that take place between boss and subordinate. Some organizations use the words interchangeably to mean the same thing. Others differentiate between the two words. In this book, the word "coaching" will be used with a different meaning than "counseling." Here are the characteristics of each:

Counseling
1. The subordinate usually initiates discussion.
2. Counseling takes place when a problem arises or when the subordinate feels a problem needs solving.
3. The problem can be personal or job-oriented.
4. Emphasis is on listening on the part of the manager.
5. The manager avoids giving specific advice and helps the subordinate solve his or her own problem.
6. The objectives are to solve a specific problem and/or to relieve tension on the part of the subordinate.

Coaching
1. The manager usually initiates discussion.
2. It is done on a regular basis.
3. It is job-oriented.
4. It is positive or corrective, with emphasis on telling, training, and teaching by the manager.
5. The manager frequently gives specific advice on what to do and how to do it.
6. The objective is to improve the job performance of the subordinate as an individual and a team member.

What Coaching Is Not

According to George Odiorne,[3] managerial coaching is *not* a specific set of instructions that a boss has developed about activities or behavior of the subordinate. It is *not* a set of tasks to be performed with demands for vaguely determined outcomes such as ''hitting the ball.'' And it is *not* some action or policy that inhibits movement, requires sitting overly long in one position, or extols the virtues of patience and humility.

The following three examples represent what is often the bulk of the activities of the manager who imagines that he or she is coaching subordinates.

1. The plant manager who daily calls his or her staff together and pours forth wisdom about the mistakes of the day before, with somber warnings of ''Let's watch that one,'' is seriously attempting to coach but is lamentably ineffective at it.

2. The sales manager who uses staff meetings to divulge deep insights about top-management goals and thinking, in the form of ten-minute speeches, is often doing nothing more than using communication as a club to beat down any incipient rise of new ideas or change from subordinates.

3. The staff manager who counterpunches with subordinates, insisting that they produce new ideas but shooting these full of holes when they appear, may be utterly sincere but is also utterly incompetent in coaching.

What Coaching Is

The effective coaching function is more apt to take the form of working on forward-looking plans and objectives for subordinates in a way that keeps them moving constantly toward new areas of experience, new demands for personal skill development, and application of ingenuity and problem solving. On-the-job coaching improves job performance in two ways, and the principles and approaches involved are the same for both. First, day-to-day coaching takes place whenever the need arises, and it bolsters the relationship between the manager and the subordinate. If an employee makes a mistake, the boss helps the employee correct it, and this coaching should prevent the same mistake from happening again. If, on the other hand, the employee does an especially good job, the boss compliments the employee. This is also part of the coaching process.

The other reason for coaching is to help the subordinate implement the performance improvement plan that was developed as part of the performance review program. The manager should periodically see how the subordinate is progressing and provide help in implementing the plan.

Day-to-Day Coaching

The manager must play a day-to-day coaching role, which is based on observing the performance of the subordinates. If the subordinate performs well, the manager provides positive reinforcement. If the subordinate fails to so something that should be done, the manager calls it to the attention of the subordinate to find out why it wasn't done and to see that it is done. Or the subordinate may do something that should not be done. This requires the manager to find out the reason for the mistake and take whatever action is appropriate.

The key to effective coaching is to handle problem situations without causing resentment on the part of the subordinate. Resentment can easily be created by an eager coach who is overly anxious to correct an error. For example, a direct approach to pointing out the mistake and ordering the subordinate to do it right could well end up in resentment. To avoid resentment, a tactful approach is usually required.

If the manager sees an employee make a mistake, there are four possible courses of action to take:

1. Ignore the situation and hope that the subordinate will see the mistake and correct it.

2. Call immediate attention to the mistake and ask the subordinate to do the right thing.

3. Use an indirect approach such as, "How are things going?" If the subordinate knows about the mistake, he or she may frankly admit the mistake and tell the manager, "Don't worry, boss, I'll take care of it." If the subordinate doesn't realize that a mistake has been made, the answer might be, "Fine, boss, no problems!" In this case the manager will have to call attention to the mistake and ask, "What can we do to correct it?"

4. Use the "sandwich" approach. This means to praise the subordinate for good work, call attention to the mistake, and end up with a positive statement such as, "I'm sure that this won't happen again." Some people ridicule this

approach by saying that the subordinate will recognize the technique and after the first words of praise will immediately react, "O.K., what have I done wrong?" Obviously, the success or failure of the "sandwich" technique depends on the frequency of its use. If the only time a manager praises a subordinate is to provide the first part of the "sandwich," the approach will backfire. But if praise is regularly used by the manager to recognize good work, the technique can be successful. In any case, it must be remembered that praise is recognizing good work that has actually been done, not just using complimentary words when they aren't true. Wooden[4] said, "I try to follow any criticism with a pat on the back, realizing that I cannot antagonize and influence at the same time."

Among these four choices for correcting poor work, there is no guarantee that any will be successful or unsuccessful. For example, if the manager uses the first approach (doesn't say anything), the worker may or may not recognize the mistake and correct it. Likewise, the "sandwich" method may be successful with one employee and unsuccessful with another.

The important point is that the coaching must be done to correct the situation—now and in the future—and not to cause resentment. It's like a prisoner who goes to jail. After paying for the crime, the prisoner may come out with an attitude that says, "I've learned a lesson. Next time I won't get caught!" Or the prisoner may come out with an attitude that says, "I've learned my lesson. I won't do it again." Obviously, the second result is the one to seek from subordinates as well as prisoners. Here are some specific suggestions that will help you achieve this.

If the employee has done a good job, the manager has a very pleasant situation. Positive reinforcement should be done immediately. If there are other people within hearing distance, so much the better. They realize that the employee has done something well, and they are pleased to see a boss recognize it. Obviously, they hope to be treated the same way when they do something worthy of praise. Even if the performance wasn't perfect, a compliment can be sincerely given to show improvement. And complimenting improvement generally leads to continued effort by the employee and better results in the future.

Some managers compliment warmly when a job is well done. Others ignore it and act as if they thought, "That's what we are paying you for; why should I have to tell you besides?"

In sporting events, some coaches do not give praise when a player does an exceptionally good job. Other coaches openly show signs of enthusiasm and give praise for good work. Ara Parseghian is an example of the latter type of coach. When he was head football coach at Notre Dame and a player made an exceptionally good play, Ara would jump up and down, give his player a hug or pat on the back, and pay him a nice compliment like "Good play!" That spirit and outward expression brought out the best in his players.

If the employee has done a poor job, the coach should usually correct a situation as soon as it occurs. Sometimes, however, this isn't a good idea because it might not be the right time and place. For example, there may be other people around when the employee has made a mistake. Also, the coach may be emotionally upset. In these situations, it is important to correct the employee as soon as practical, but in private. One good approach might be to say, "Can I see you in my office in five minutes?" This gives the manager time to cool down and also to do a little preparation for the coaching interview. The preparation might include:

Thinking of some good things the worker has recently done that can be mentioned.

Trying to determine the reason why the employee made the mistake.

Thinking how the interview should end. The employee should say or feel, "Thanks for calling this to my attention," rather than, "I'll get even with you."

Dr. Earl Planty, former executive, consultant, and teacher, has some good tips for handling emotional conversations. These are listed in Table 2. Typical

Table 2. Handling problems filled with emotions.

Do	*Don't*
Set a supportive, quiet situation for the discussion.	Be interrupted by phone, secretary, and so on.
Draw off emotions, encourage release of pressure.	Interrupt.
Listen, listen, listen.	Talk too much (or the problem employee won't).
Listen to emotions as well as facts.	Disagree.
Expect and prepare to hear negative, critical comments and confused, distorted ones.	Correct, deny.
Restrain your own emotions in response to the other person's.	Play FBI.
Understand, empathize.	Blame.
Echo back, reflect to the person the feelings expressed.	Judge.

emotional situations managers must deal with involve fear, anxiety, bias, distortion, confusion, or selfish or neurotic behavior.

Coaching on the Performance Improvement Plan

While day-to-day coaching takes place as needed to discuss the ongoing performance of an employee, coaching regarding the performance improvement plan is a planned activity.

In Chapter 4, an example was given of a performance improvement plan that was jointly developed between John Green, subordinate, and Tom Severson, his supervisor. In this plan, John agreed to do a number of things. And Tom, his boss, became his coach to be sure they would be done. It will be noted that the plan was developed on October 1. The first commitment was October 15, by which time John agreed to talk with Phil Taylor about his approach. Therefore, sometime before October 15, Tom should talk with John to see if he has made arrangements to talk with Phil. The same approach should be used regarding the other commitments.

Figure 7 is the same performance improvement plan that was described in Chapter 4, with the coaching contacts added. This is the working tool that the manager, Tom Severson, needs to be sure that effective coaching takes place. Otherwise he and John may forget the details of the plan until the deadlines have gone by. By following through on the plan, Tom will emphasize to John that the planning process was an important one and that it will be implemented. The coaching should be done in a very positive manner. In most cases, Tom will check with John before the agreed-on date to serve as a reminder. This continues to maintain the rapport that has been built up throughout the entire performance review program. And the coaching will probably result in improved performance.

Coaching Practices of Managers

Walter Mahler has conducted surveys regularly to measure the coaching practices of managers.[5] He divides his survey into ten major categories. For each category, he asks five questions about the activities that are occurring on the job, and each question has four possible answers. Typical questions are:

1. How well do you understand what is expected of you in your current position?
   _____ a. I have some idea of what is expected of me.
   _____ b. I have a fairly good idea.

Figure 7. Coaching on the performance improvement plan.

Name: John Green, Supervisor

Boss: Tom Severson, Department Head

Date: October 1

Performance to Be Improved: Orienting and Training New Employees

	The Performance Improvement Plan			Coaching Contact by Tom Severson	
Action to Be Taken	By Whom	When		When	Results
1. Talk with Phil Taylor about his approach.	John Green	October 15		October 14	Has made arrangements to talk to Phil tomorrow.
				October 15	Did talk with Phil. Got some good ideas.
2. Watch Phil Taylor when he orients and trains a new employee.	John Green	The next time he does it		October 15	Phil plans to train a new employee on Nov. 13. John will observe.
				November 15	Phil trained a new employee and John watched. John felt it worth-while.
3. Attend new employee orientation meeting conducted by personnel department.	John Green	The next time it is done		October 15	Checked with personnel department and learned that it will be done Nov. 18. Asked John to be there.
				November 18	Asked John for his report of the orientation meeting. He had suggestions that were passed on to personnel department.
4. Decide on the best time for new employees to come to the department.	John Green working with personnel department	By October 20		October 19	Worked out the starting time for all new employees; 9 A.M. on Monday instead of 7 A.M.
5. Attend a seminar on "How to Train New Employees."	John Green	November 15 University of Wisconsin—Extension, Milwaukee		November 10	Discussed program schedule and details.
				November 18	Discussed program and benefits John got from it.

The Performance Improvement Plan   Coaching Contact By Tom Severson

Action to Be Taken	By Whom	When	When	Results
6. Read the following books: a. Self-Development for Supervisors and Managers, by Norman Allhiser	John Green	by October 15	October 3	Arranged to order the three books John has agreed to read.
			October 14	Learned that John has read half of Allhiser's books.
			October 31	Learned that John has read half of Kirkpatrick's book and all of Allhiser's.
b. No-Nonsense Communication, by Donald Kirkpatrick		by November 10	November 5	Learned that John had finished Kirkpatrick and Broadwell books.
c. The Supervisor and On-the-Job Training, by Martin Broadwell		by December 12		
7. Observe John Green orienting and training a new employee.	Larry Jackson, Training Director	The next time John trains a new employee	October 20	Learned that John is scheduled to hire a new employee on November 15.
			November 20	Got good feedback from Larry Jackson on John's training of new employee.
8. Talk with John Green's next three employees.	Tom Severson	One week after hire	November 25	Talked with Ralph Cador, John's new employee, about his start with company. Generally felt good about orientation and training. Still confused about benefits. Doesn't feel secure in his job yet.
9. Provide a checklist to John for orienting new employees.	Larry Jackson	October 15	October 13	Checked with Larry Jackson on checklist. List not yet ready. Promised by October 21.
			October 21	Checked with Larry on new checklist. Not quite done.
			October 25	Checklist completed and given to John.

	The Performance Improvement Plan			Coaching Contact By Tom Severson	
Action to Be Taken	By Whom	When	When	Results
10. Arrange for a special office for John to use when orienting each new employee.	Tom Severson	October 15	October 10	Tried to find a special office to let John use in orienting new employees. Arranged for conference room in training department when not in use. Told John he could use his office if needed. Asked for 24-hour notice. Will try to find another permanent place.
11. Arrange for a permanent special place for training new employees.	Tom Severson	January 1	December 1	Tried to locate a place for training new employees. Nothing available.
			December 20	Tried to locate a place for training new employees. There is a possible place in the shipping room.
			December 28	Arranged for a temporary place in a corner of shipping with temporary partitions. Will continue to try to get a permanent place.

_____ c. I have a good understanding.

_____ d. I have a very good understanding.

2. How well do you know what your supervisor thinks of your performance (results, accomplishments)?

_____ a. I don't know what he or she thinks of my performance.

_____ b. I have some idea.

_____ c. I have a good idea.

_____ d. I have a very definite idea.

3. On the basis of the results you have secured over the last few years, do you think you have been accorded the recognition by your supervisor that you deserve?

_____ a. I haven't been accorded deserved recognition.

_____ b. Yes, I have, but with quite a few exceptions.

_____ c. Yes, I have, with almost no exceptions.

_____ d. I've always received the recognition I deserved.

4. How helpful has your supervisor been in your development and growth over the past few years?

_____ a. He or she has helped very little.

_____ b. He or she has helped somewhat.

_____ c. He or she has helped considerably.

_____ d. He or she has helped a great deal.

The results of Mahler's survey are shown in Table 3. For each question, the first two answers are considered unfavorable and the last two favorable.

These results point out some serious problems related to performance appraisal and review. For example, 30 percent of the subordinates gave negative answers to an understanding of their responsibilities and goals. This kind of confusion is bound to have negative repercussions when appraisals are made and discussed. Even more serious is the response to the questions dealing with knowledge of performance. Nearly 50 percent of the subordinates who replied indicated that they didn't have a clear idea of what the boss thought of their performance. The other results point to problems that exist because of inadequate communication, appraisal, and on-the-job coaching.

Summary

This chapter has emphasized the two different situations for on-the-job coaching. The first is day-to-day coaching to compliment good work and correct and improve performance that does not meet expectations and standards. The second reason for coaching is to be sure that the performance improvement plan

Table 3. Coaching practices survey.

| | Favorable Responses | |
| | Top and Middle | Lower-Level |
Factors having to do with:	Management*	Management†
Responsibilities and goals	75%	68%
Delegation	68%	62%
Knowledge of performance	58%	45%
Assistance as needed	72%	61%
Motivation	61%	46%
Working relationship	80%	82%
Benefiting from experience	50%	40%
Group activities	60%	48%
Future responsibilities	38%	32%
Coaching results	70%	65%

*From survey of 1,000 subordinates of 200 top and middle managers.
†From survey of 2,037 subordinates of 779 lower-level managers.

is properly implemented. The principles and approaches for both kinds of coaching are essentially the same, and the desired results—best possible performance—are identical.

According to Mahler, managers generally do not do an effective job of coaching. Approximately 30 percent of employees surveyed do not understand their responsibilities and goals. And almost 50 percent do not know what their manager thinks of their performance. In summarizing his research, Mahler stated that less than 70 percent of managers were achieving favorable coaching results.

References

1. John Wooden, *They Call Me Coach*. New York: Bantam, 1973.
2. Ibid.
3. George Odiorne, *Training by Objectives*. New York: Macmillan, 1970.
4. John Wooden, op. cit.
5. Walter Mahler, "Coaching Practices Survey." Unpublished paper, Midland Park, N.J., 1980.

6
Five Program Requirements

Up to this point, the specifics of a performance review program have been discussed. Significant job segments and standards of performance were emphasized and described in order to clarify what is expected of a subordinate. The appraisal of performance was then discussed with a suggestion that a self-appraisal be included. Specific suggestions were then given on how to prepare and how to conduct an appraisal interview. The preparation of a performance improvement plan was described in detail. The next chapter dealt with the characteristics and techniques of an effective coach. Throughout the book, emphasis has been placed on boss and subordinate working together to accomplish improved performance on the part of the subordinate.

This chapter will take a broader view and describe the five requirements for an effective performance review program.

The Program Fits the Organization

Some programs are quite complicated and require considerable paperwork. Other programs use simple forms and procedures, and paperwork is kept to a minimum. Some programs require appraisals and interviews on a quarterly or semiannual basis, while others require it only annually. In choosing a program, every organization must be sure that its program can be properly implemented.

For example, a program that requires frequent appraisals and much paperwork will fail if there is a minimum of time available for those who must do the appraisals and complete the forms. It would probably also fail unless the person responsible for administering the overall program has enough time to do an effective job. Another important consideration is support from top management. Therefore, care should be taken to select a program that fits the needs, personnel, and priorities of the organization.

The Program Is Communicated

The word "communicate" means to create understanding. This means that everyone involved in the program must understand the what, why, when, where, and how. In most cases, it will require meetings to explain and discuss the program as well as a manual that describes the forms and procedures.

I attended a recent meeting in which a supervisor said that his organization was using the Hay System of performance appraisal. He went on to say that those involved in the program called it the haze system because everyone was confused.

When introducing a new performance review program I had developed for a large corporation, the general manager of the Carlsbad plant scheduled a dinner meeting of all employees who were included in the program. Secretaries, engineers, and foremen were included, for example, even though they were not going to conduct appraisals and interviews with subordinates. We wanted to be sure they understood the program because they were going to be appraised and interviewed. In order to accomplish this communication, we prepared slides and a small booklet that supplemented the oral presentation I made. A question-and-answer session followed the presentation. By using this approach, we were confident that there would be much better understanding of the program than if we left it up to the reviewers to communicate the program to their subordinates.

The Program Is Sold

Understanding isn't enough. Those who implement the plan must be convinced that their time and effort are going to be rewarded. Initially, this can probably be done through persuasion. As time goes on, though, the benefits must be real.

When I introduced the performance review program at Carlsbad, the process of selling included the following steps:

1. Explanation of the program to the general manager, industrial relations manager, and management development supervisor. We discussed it and made some minor changes.

2. Explanation of the program to the eight department heads. We discussed it and made some changes, on the basis of their recommendations.
3. Communication of the program at the dinner meeting. Benefits to the individuals employees as well as to the company were stressed.
4. Individual discussion with those who weren't sold on the program.
5. The general manager stressed that it was *their* program and not a program that had been imposed by the corporate office. He emphasized that I had been invited to help them implement the program.

The program must be sold not just initially, but continuously. Managers constantly battle with priorities. The more they are sold on the program, the more likely they are to give time and energy to it and do it effectively.

The Reviewers Are Trained

It's not enough to create understanding and sell the managers on the program. They must have the necessary skills to implement the program. To get them to understand the forms and procedures is relatively easy, but to get them to develop the required skills is difficult. And a well-written manual isn't going to do it.

With our program, the necessary skills were:

How to identify significant job segments
How to develop standards of performance
How to appraise performance
How to conduct the appraisal interview
How to develop a performance improvement plan
How to coach

All these skills required practice. So we established a training program as follows:

FIRST MEETING (2 hours)

Objectives	1. Understand the performance review program. 2. Learn how to identify significant job segments.
Agenda	1. Overview of the program. 2. Description of significant job segments. 3. Examples of significant job segments. 4. Each person lists significant job segments for his or her own job.
Assignment	Get together with one of your subordinates and jointly develop significant job segments for his or her job.

SECOND MEETING (3 hours)

Objectives	1. Review significant job segments.
	2. Learn how to write standards of performance.
Agenda	1. Discussion of significant job segments that were developed as an assignment.
	2. Meaning of standards of performance.
	3. Characteristics of standards of performance.
	4. Examples of standards of performance.
	5. Each person writes one standard of performance.
Assignment	Jointly develop with the subordinate standards of performance for *one* of the significant job segments from the previous assignment.

THIRD MEETING (2 hours)

Objectives	1. Review standards of performance.
	2. Understand appraisal by the boss.
	3. Understand self-appraisal.
	4. Learn how to complete appraisal form.
Agenda	1. Discussion of standards of performance that had been developed as an assignment.
	2. Explanation of the appraisal process.
	3. Explanation of the appraisal form.
	4. Samples of completed appraisal forms.
	5. Each person completes a sample appraisal form.
Assignment	1. Complete an appraisal form on the subordinate.
	2. Get the subordinate to complete the self-appraisal form.

FOURTH MEETING (3 hours)

Objectives	1. Review the appraisal process and forms.
	2. Understand guidelines for an effective appraisal interview.
	3. Learn how to conduct an appraisal interview.
Agenda	1. Discussion of completed appraisal forms from the assignment.
	2. Explanation of guidelines for an effective appraisal interview.
	3. Demonstration of a poor appraisal interview.
	4. Demonstration of a good appraisal interview.
	5. In groups of three, each person in turn takes the role of

interviewer, interviewee, and observer. The observer leads the critique after each practice interview.

Assignment   Conduct an appraisal interview with the subordinate.

FIFTH MEETING (2 hours)

Objectives
1. Review the appraisal interview.
2. Understand a performance improvement plan.
3. Learn to prepare a performance improvement plan.

Agenda
1. Discussion of the appraisal interview completed as an assignment.
2. Explanation of a performance improvement plan.
3. Examples of a performance improvement plan.
4. Each person writes a performance improvement plan.

Assignment   Jointly develop with subordinate a performance improvement plan for one aspect of the job.

SIXTH MEETING (2 hours)

Objectives
1. Review the performance improvement plan.
2. Understand on-the-job coaching.
3. Review the entire performance review program.

Agenda
1. Discussion of the performance improvement plan that was developed as an assignment.
2. Explanation of characteristics of an effective coach.
3. Explanation of coaching techniques.
4. Review of the entire program.

The length of the six training meetings (two or three hours each) was established to accomplish the objective. The amount of time between sessions was determined by the group at the end of each session by discussing how long it would take to do the assignment. When agreement was reached, the next session was scheduled accordingly.

Each assignment was done by the managers with the same subordinate. When the training program was completed, each manager had completed the following steps of the performance review program with one subordinate:

Jointly developing significant job segments.

Jointly developing standards of performance for one significant job segment.

Completing an appraisal form.

Having subordinate complete a self-appraisal form.

Conducting an appraisal interview.
Jointly developing a performance improvement plan.

After the training program was completed, the managers were scheduled to conduct performance reviews with all subordinates. The management development supervisor at Carlsbad was available as a resource for anyone who needed help.

According to William Simpson, management training manager at Kemper Insurance, that company's performance review training was done on a more concentrated basis. For example, a two-day workshop was conducted with Kemper managers on how to write performance standards. Here is a brief outline of the approach, adapted with permission from *Education Exchange*, a publication of the Insurance Company Education Directors Society.

FIRST DAY

Morning	1. Welcome
	2. Objectives of workshop
	3. Introductions
	4. Background of performance standards within Kemper Insurance
	5. Principal (explains *what, who, how,* and *when*)
	Film (29 minutes)
	Quiz
	Discussion
	6. Need for performance standards (explains *why*)
	Filmed case study (4 minutes)
	Discussion questions
	Other
	7. Procedures and techniques (explains *how*)
	Booklet, "Guidelines"
	Handout material
	Other
Lunch	
Afternoon	1. Workshop: practice in writing performance standards
	Consultation with discussion leader as needed
	2. Periodic summaries by participants

SECOND DAY

Morning	1. Continuing workshops in writing performance standards
	Periodic evaluation of progress by participants
	Continued consultation with discussion leader as needed

2. Assignment changes as necessary or desirable
3. Periodic summaries by participants of progress, problems, and so on
4. Informal session with guest speaker
      Presentation
      Questions and answers

Lunch

Afternoon   1. Continuing workshops
      Include periodic evaluation, periodic summaries, assignment changes, and so on
2. Summary
3. Close

This concentrated workshop was designed to develop and sharpen skills through extensive practice and critique.

Appropriate Controls Are Established

There are two philosophies of management. One says that people will do what the boss *expects*. The other says that people will do what the boss *inspects*. The first philosophy applies in many situations, but in performance appraisals, the second seems to predominate.

Even if managers are sold on the performance review program and their boss expects them to do it, there is a good chance it will be considered a should-do instead of a must-do. In most cases, the managers have so many must-do's that many of the should-do's don't get done. And if the manager discovers that nothing serious happens if the performance reviews aren't completed on schedule, the program becomes "voluntary" even though it began as a compulsory part of the job.

At one plant of a large company, the general manager was most enthusiastic when the new performance review program started. He conducted reviews with his subordinates as scheduled, and he expected them to do the same. The industrial relations department sent him a monthly report of schedules and completions. If any reviews were not completed on time, he talked with the manager about it. So all reviews were completed, and most of them on time.

During the second year of the program, the general manager didn't complete his reviews as scheduled. In spite of reminders from the industrial relations department, he fell further and further behind. Because he hadn't completed his, he didn't say anything to his subordinates who hadn't completed theirs. Managers soon discovered that the program was now "voluntary." Some did it and some didn't.

During the second year, this general manager transferred to the corporate office and was replaced by a general manager from a different plant. When the new general manager learned of the performance review situation, he called the department heads together and said, "I understand you have the same performance review program here that we have at the other plant. I believe in the program. I will do it on schedule with each of my subordinates. I expect you to do it on schedule with your subordinates. I've asked the industrial relations manager to send me a monthly report of performance reviews scheduled and those completed. If the reviews are not completed as scheduled, I will not approve any salary increases for you or anyone else in your department until they are completed. In other words, I'm going to *require* that you do it, because I believe that it is beneficial to every employee as well as to the company. Any questions?"

Naturally, there weren't any questions. The managers knew that the program had just returned from "voluntary" to compulsory. Controls like this are usually needed to put performance review in the must-do category.

Summary

Performance of subordinates can be improved through performance appraisal and coaching. It won't happen, however, unless a program is carefully planned and effectively implemented. It won't be perfect at the beginning. Therefore, it is probably wise to start slowly, perhaps by means of a pilot program in a department where the manager is eager to try it. If the program is effective, other managers will hear about it and request that it be implemented in their departments. Eventually it may become company policy for all departments.

The five requirements described in this chapter are essential to the success of a performance review program. If any one of them is missing, there is a good chance that the program will fail. Every organization, therefore, should be sure that:

> The program fits the organization
> The program is communicated
> The program is sold
> The reviewers are trained
> Appropriate controls are established

An effective performance review program can be highly beneficial, not only in terms of financial savings, but also in terms of the morale of boss and subordinate alike.

─────────────── Posttest ───────────────

Write "yes" in front of each statement if you agree and "no" if you disagree.

_____ 1. Every employee has responsibility for his or her own development.

_____ 2. Every manager has responsibility for the growth and development of all subordinates.

_____ 3. Every organization has responsibility for the growth and development of all employees.

_____ 4. Most people want to know how they are doing their job as the boss sees it.

_____ 5. Most employees would like to improve their performance.

_____ 6. Less than maximum performance of an employee is often due to factors over which the employee has no control.

_____ 7. The same performance review program (forms, procedures, interview) should be used both for improved performance and for salary administration.

_____ 8. Performance appraisals and reviews should be voluntary on the part of managers.

_____ 9. The more writing required of the boss on the appraisal form, the more effective the program.

_____ 10. The less paperwork required in a performance appraisal program, the more effective the program.

_____ 11. Appraisal forms should include about a 50-50 balance between items dealing with performance and those dealing with personality.

_____ 12. Agreement on significant job segments and standards of performance is an important prerequisite to the appraisal of job performance.

_____ 13. The word "appraisal" connotes both judgment and communication.

_____ 14. A group appraisal of a person's performance is better than having an appraisal just by the boss.

_____ 15. A self-appraisal by the subordinate is a good idea.

_____ 16. The main objective of the appraisal interview is for the boss to explain and sell his or her prepared appraisal to the subordinate.

_____ 17. In the interview discussing the performance of the subordinate, there should be no surprises.

_____ 18. In an appraisal interview, it's a good idea to have at least three people present (for example, the boss, the subordinate, and a neutral party such as a representative of the personnel department).

_____ 19. Appraisal interviews should be a pleasant experience for both boss and subordinate.

_____ 20. In the appraisal interview, the boss should not show his or her completed form to the subordinate.

_____ 21. An organization can be assured that an effective appraisal interview has been conducted if the employee is required to sign the form.

_____ 22. In an appraisal interview, the boss should always give his or her appraisal of the subordinate and then ask the subordinate for reactions and comments.

_____ 23. It's a good idea to divide the appraisal interview into two or three separate interviews.

_____ 24. An appraisal interview should always end on a positive note.

_____ 25. A specific written performance improvement plan is an important part of a performance review program.

_____ 26. A performance improvement plan should include what should be done, by whom, and when.

_____ 27. It's a good idea for employees to work toward performance improvement in several areas at once.

_____ 28. Coaching means the same as counseling.

_____ 29. Coaching a group of employees is similar to coaching a team of athletes.

_____ 30. On-the-job coaching is necessary to be sure that the performance improvement plan is implemented.

_____ 31. Coaching on the job should include praise for good work as well as constructive criticism and help to improve poor work.

_____ 32. Improvement in performance should be immediately rewarded by the boss.

_____ 33. Rewards should be based on performance rather than seniority.

_____ 34. Both the boss and subordinate should have a copy of all completed forms.

_____ 35. A copy of the completed appraisal forms should be put in the personnel file of the subordinate.

_____ 36. A standard of performance should be:

_____ a. Established for a job.

_____ b. Established for an individual.

_____ c. An "acceptable" level of performance.

_____ d. A "well done" level of performance.

_____ e. Challenging (requires stretch but can be reached).

_____ f. Unattainable (requires stretch and can't be reached).

_____ g. Agreed on between boss and subordinate.

_____ h. Determined solely by the boss.

_____ i. Determined solely by the subordinate.

_____   j. Jointly determined by boss and subordinate.

_____   k. Clear to boss and subordinate.

_____   l. Written.

_____   m. Time-oriented.

_____   n. Specific (numbers, percentages, dollars, wherever possible).

_____   o. The basis for performance appraisal.

_____   p. Subject to change.

_____   37. The same appraisal forms and procedures can be effectively used by any kind of organization.

_____   38. The people supervising a performance appraisal program must do more than simply oversee paperwork. They must communicate the program and sell it to those involved.

_____   39. It takes no real training to conduct performance reviews effectively.

_____   40. Administrative controls must be established for performance review programs.

Test Answers and Reasons for Them

1. Yes, but it must be supplemented by items 2 and 3.
2. Yes, but it must be supplemented by items 1 and 3.
3. Yes, but it must be supplemented by items 1 and 2 to show a complete picture of the responsibilities.
4. Yes, because it relieves feelings of insecurity.
5. Yes, because it can bring rewards such as self-satisfaction, promotion, and merit salary increases.
6. Yes. Other reasons for less than maximum performance include the boss, poor working conditions, defective equipment or materials, and personal problems the employee cannot directly control.
7. No. There is much emotion involved in discussing salary, and usually the objective of improved performance is hard to accomplish simultaneously.
8. No. Appraisals and reviews should be compulsory to be sure they are done.
9. No, not necessarily.
10. No, not necessarily. Effectiveness may have nothing to do with the amount of paperwork.
11. No. All or nearly all of the items on an appraisal form should deal directly with performance.
12. Yes, because these two factors clarify what's expected and provide a sound basis for the appraisal.
13. No, ''appraisal'' connotes judgment but not communication.
14. No. Although group appraisals can help avoid bias and increase objectivity, they are very time-consuming and dilute the role of the boss in the performance review process.
15. Yes, because it gets subordinate involvement and also helps show the boss how the subordinate feels about his or her own performance.
16. No. The main purpose is to get understanding and agreement. The best approach is to discuss the appraisal that each of them has completed.
17. Yes, because the joint development of significant job standards and standards of performance will clarify what is expected of the subordinate. If expectations are clear to both boss and subordinate, the boss's opinion will not be a surprise. Also, the day-to-day communication and coaching should keep the subordinate informed of how he or she is doing.
18. No, only the boss and the subordinate should be at the appraisal interview. A third party should be added only for a specific purpose, such as to help prepare a performance improvement plan.

19. Yes, both should feel good about the interview when it is over.
20. No. The boss should not hide anything from the subordinate, including the appraisal form.
21. No. The only thing that a signature assures is that the person signed the form.
22. No, this is only one possible approach. Another is to have the subordinate give his or her self-appraisal first.
23. Yes. This is advisable because the interview must accomplish several objectives: to agree on the appraisal, to develop a performance improvement plan, and to clarify significant job segments and standards of performance for the next appraisal period.
24. Yes. This gives both boss and subordinate a constructive attitude toward improving the subordinate's performance.
25. Yes, because it helps clarify future action for both boss and subordinate.
26. Yes. It is important for the plan to be specific.
27. No. In most cases, it is best to concentrate on only one area at a time to be sure that improvement occurs. Sometimes a second area can also be worked on.
28. No. Coaching is always job-oriented and is initiated by the boss. Emphasis is placed on telling. Counseling is usually initiated by the subordinate and may deal with personal rather than job-related problems. Emphasis is on listening by the boss.
29. Yes. In both situations, the "coach" is trying to get maximum individual as well as team performance.
30. Yes. After the performance improvement plan is jointly developed by boss and subordinate, on-the-job coaching both reminds and helps the subordinate to implement the plan.
31. Yes, coaches should praise good work as well as correct poor work.
32. Yes. Immediate positive reinforcement by praise or other means is the best way to encourage and stimulate continued improvement in performance.
33. Yes, in order to encourage maximum effort and the best possible performance.
34. Yes. Each should have a copy for regular referral to ensure understanding and good working relationships.
35. Yes, these forms should be used in considerations for salary increases, promotions, and other personnel decisions.
36. Items a, c, g, j, k, l, m, n, o, and p should be marked "yes."
37. No, forms and procedures must fit the requirements of the specific organization. Some organizations are better equipped to handle detailed paperwork than others, for example.

38. Yes. No matter how good a program looks on paper, the people who use it must understand it and believe in it before it can really work.
39. No, training is very important. Conducting performance reviews requires skills that must be learned.
40. Yes. Unless higher management establishes requirements and controls, managers will tend to regard it as a should-do rather than a must-do.

Part II
Applications: Examples from Various Organizations

7
Sample Forms

In this chapter I have gathered a number of performance appraisal forms that are in actual use. They come from many types and sizes of organizations. (The names of the specific organizations have been taken off the forms.) They also reflect many different approaches to appraising employee performance, and you may find it helpful to compare them.

Each form or set of forms is preceded by my observations on its strong and weak features. As you study the forms, look for ideas that you can use or adapt. Keep in mind the following criteria:

1. The forms must accomplish your objectives.
2. They must be successfully communicated and sold to those who will use them.
3. Your organization must be able to handle the paperwork.
4. The forms should be useful both for clarifying what's expected and for appraising performance.
5. They should result in improved performance on the part of the subordinate.
6. They should help to maintain rapport between boss and subordinate.

Example 1

Instead of establishing standards ahead of time, appraisers are asked to describe the employee's status regarding each factor. This invites a great deal of subjective evaluation even though the form suggests that judgment should be based on facts and figures whenever possible.

Too much writing is required. It would be better to have ratings with possible comments to explain them. Also, the last question is too subjective to be of any value. ("Is there understanding and acceptance of standards to measure future performance?")

The overall performance rating symbols stand for:

$$
\begin{array}{ll}
\text{I} = \text{Incompetent} & \text{S} = \text{Satisfactory} \\
\text{Cd} = \text{Conditional} & \text{C} = \text{Commendable} \\
\text{M} = \text{Marginal} & \text{O} = \text{Outstanding}
\end{array}
$$

PERFORMANCE APPRAISAL
Salaried Non Exempt Employees

This Review Date

Last Review Date

Next Review Date

Name_____ Dept _____ Serial _____

Position_____ Code _____

Employment Date_____Birth Date _____ Date Assigned Position_____

Is this position correct? Yes____No____   If no, explain _____

_____

Give a clear concise statement identifying employee's status regarding each of the factors below. Judgment should be based on facts and figures whenever possible.

Production: Volume of work performed.

_____
_____
_____
_____

Quality: Quality of work performed, including cost.

_____
_____
_____
_____

Initiative and Ingenuity: Ability to decide and take proper action outside the area of specific instructions.

_____
_____
_____
_____
_____

Dependability: Acceptance of responsibility; reliability; a realistic approach to assignments and problems.

_____
_____
_____
_____

Attendance/Promptness: Absenteeism, tardiness.

_____
_____
_____

Relationships: Cooperation with and attitude towards others.

_____
_____
_____

Knowledge: Possesion of knowledge valauable to performance of the job.

_____
_____
_____

Significant Area(s) of Improvement Since Last Apprasial

_____
_____
_____

Significant Area(s) for Improvement

_____
_____
_____

Is there understanding and acceptance of standards to measure future performance?   Yes   No

PERFORMANCE RATING   ☐ I   ☐ Cd   ☐ M   ☐ S   ☐ C   ☐ O

RATING PRIMARILY BASED ON: ☐ Performance   ☐ Progress

SIGNATURES:

Supervisor:_____ Position _____ Date_____

Supervisor's
Supervisor:_____ Position _____ Date_____

Employee:_____ Date_____

This signature confirms that an interview took place.
It does not necessarily imply agreement.

Example 2

For a simple form, this has some good features. It has been designed for a specific job (sales) and excludes sales volume, which is evaluated in objective terms.

Five major segments have been identified. After each one, each rating is explained instead of using general rating words such as *outstanding* or *satisfactory*. It also encourages examples and comments.

Another positive feature is the requirement to identify strengths and areas to improve. It also asks for suggestions regarding training or experience to make the individual a more valuable employee. This is far short of a performance improvement plan but goes further than most forms do to consider improved performance.

This form would lend itself nicely to self-appraisal.

SALES PERFORMANCE EVALUATION

(OTHER THAN SALES VOLUME)

SALESPERSON'S NAME _____ TIME ON THIS JOB _____ _____

(years)   (months)

DATE THIS

EVALUATOR'S NAME _____ REPORT COMPLETED _____

ITEM TO BE EVALUATED	FOR EACH ITEM ON LEFT, PLEASE CHECK STATEMENT BELOW THAT MOST ACCURATELY DESCRIBES WORK, AND GIVE ACTUAL EXAMPLES OR COMMENTS AS TO WORK PERFORMANCE.			
1 CUSTOMER SERVICE	GIVE CUSTOMER PROMPT AND EFFECTIVE SERVICE. BUILDS VOLUME THROUGH GOOD SERVICE. ☐	SERVICE TO CUSTOMER IS GENERALLY SATISFACTORY ☐	SOME IMPROVEMENT NEEDED IN HANDLING SERVICE ☐	SERVICE TO CUSTOMER IS UNSATISFACTORY ☐
	Examples/Comments:			
2 TERRITORIAL COVERAGE	OUTSTANDING COVERAGE, TRIPS PLANNED WITH EXCELLENT REGARD FOR COST OF TRAVEL RELATIVE TO POTENTIAL OF CUSTOMER. ☐	GOOD COVERAGE, TRIPS USUALLY WELL PLANNED AS TO FREQUENCY IN RELATION TO CUSTOMER POTENTIAL AND COST. ☐	SOME IMPROVEMENT NEEDED COVERAGE FAIR AND NOT AS WELL PLANNED AS IT SHOULD BE. ☐	MUCH IMPROVEMENT NEEDED. COVERAGE IS INADEQUATE ☐
	Examples/Comments:			
3 EXPENSE CONTROL	USES EXPENSE ACCOUNT WISELY AND WITH INTEGRITY. EXCEPTIONALLY CAREFUL AND EFFECTIVE USE OF EXPENSE ACCT. ☐	USUALLY USES GOOD JUDGEMENT IN HANDLING EXPENSES. ☐	SOMETIMES MAKES UNWISE USE OF EXPENSE ACCOUNT IN THE MATTER OF TELEPHONE CALLS, ENTERTAINMENT OR OTHER CHARGES. ☐	ABUSES EXPENSE ACCOUNT, REQUIRES FREQUENT CRITICISM. ☐
	Examples/Comments:			
4 REPORTS AND RECORDS	ALL RECORDS AND REPORTS UP-TO-DATE AND ON TIME. RECORDS AND REPORTS ARE COMPLETE AND ACCURATE. ☐	REPORTS AND RECORDS ARE GENERALLY ON TIME, UP-TO-DATE, AND COMPLETE ☐	SOME INPROVEMENT NEEDED ☐	LATE, INADEQUATE OR INCOMPLETE REPORTS AND RECORDS ☐
	Examples/Comments:			
5 KNOWLEDGE OF PRODUCTS, PRICES AND POLICIES	UNUSUALLY WELL INFORMED. KEEPS ABREAST OF NEW PRODUCTS, POLICIES AND REQUIREMENTS. ☐	GOOD GENERAL UNDERSTANDING OF PRODUCTS, PRICES, AND POLICIES ☐	NEED FOR SOME IMPROVEMENT INDICATED. SOME BUSINESS MAY BE LOST BECAUSE OF LACK OF KNOWLEDGE ☐	INADEQUATE KNOWLEDGE. NOT SUFFICIENT EFFORT TO LEARN. ☐
	Examples/Comments:			

ANSWER THE FOLLOWING QUESTIONS FULLY:

What various things does this individual do especially well? _____

_____

_____

_____

In what respects does this individual need to improve? _____

_____

_____

_____

What added training or experience would make this individual a more valuable employee? _____

_____

_____

_____

What is this individual's all-around job performance? *(Please check the statement that best describes your appraisal)*

DESCRIPTION OF ALL-AROUND JOB PERFORMANCE	CHECK
1. One of the best performers	☐
2. A good performer	☐
3. A satisfactory performer.	☐
4. Some improvement needed to become satisfactory	☐
5. Much improvement needed to become satisfactory	☐

REMARKS _____

_____

_____

_____

_____

_____

_____

_____

REPORT PREPARED BY_____   DATE_____

REPORT REVIEWED BY_____   DATE_____

RECORD OF INTERVIEW: This report was discussed with the incumbent

BY _____   _____
          (SIGNATURE)   (DATE)

Example 3

Again, for a simple form, this has some good features. Eight major factors have been selected. Although standards have not been developed, each rating is explained. In order to encourage objectivity on the part of the appraiser, major weak points as well as strong points of the subordinate are required.

The form's major weakness is the lack of specifics regarding improved performance. One question asks what further training would be helpful, but this is inadequate to accomplish the objective of improved performance.

This type of form would also work well for a self-appraisal.

																				DATE DUE				

EMPLOYEE PERFORMANCE RATING

EMPLOYEE NO.	NAME		SERVICE DATE	LABOR GRADE	JOB CLASS/DESCRIPTION

PROBATION MONTH	PROBATION END	ANNUAL	SEMI-ANNUAL	SPECIAL	PERIOD COVERED	RATING

FACTORS	UNSATISFACTORY					MARGINAL					GOOD					VERY GOOD					EXCELLENT				
	1	2	3	4	5	6	7	8	9	10	11	12	13	14	15	16	17	18	19	20	21	22	23	24	25

1. QUALITY OF WORK

Disregard volume. Consider only whether his work is accurate, neat, thorough.

No Opportunity To Observe ☐

Work is very slip-shod with frequent and avoidable errors.	Makes frequent errors; work is often careless.	Work is generally satisfactory. Occasionally uncorrected errors slip through.	Work is almost always accurate and neat; corrects errors himself.	Work is always of superior quality.

Remarks:

2. COOPERATIVENESS

Consider his attitude toward his work, associates, and company; his willingness to work for and with others; his readiness to give new ideas and methods a fair trial.

No Opportunity To Observe ☐

Seems unable to cooperate with others; is argumentative over every innovation.	Often fails to cooperate and is frequently disagreeable; difficult to get along with.	Gets along well with others much of the time; is occasionally obstructive.	Usually cooperates very well; willing to try new methods.	Works effectively with co-workers and supervisors; falls in readily with new ideas; gets along very well with others.

Remarks:

3. JOB KNOWLEDGE

Does he know the requirements of his job; the methods, systems and equipment pertaining to his job?

No Opportunity To Observe ☐

Does not know enough about most phases of his job.	More knowledge of some phases of the job would be desirable.	Knows his job well enough to get along.	Thorough knowledge of practically all phases of his work.	Has excellent mastery of all phases of his work.

Remarks:

4. INITIATIVE

Consider his ability to proceed with his job without being told every detail; to be generally resourceful; to get along without constant supervision.

No Opportunity To Observe ☐

Routine worker; usually waits to be told what to do; needs constant supervision.	Often at a loss in other than routine situations; frequent check-up	Does regular work without waiting for directions; requires some supervision on anything new.	Resourceful; needs minimum supervision; alert to opportunities for improvement of work.	Always gets on with the job on his own, seeks and sets for himself additional tasks; highly ingenious.

Remarks:

5. INDUSTRY

Consider the extent to which he applies himself to the duties of the job.

No Opportunity To Observe ☐

Soldiers on the job whenever possible. Frequent socializing.	Frequently neglects his work.	Usually sticks to the job but with occasional wandering.	Conscientious most of the time but sometimes needs reminder to get on with his work.	Can always be relied upon to get things done.

6. QUANTITY OF WORK

Disregard quality; consider only volume produced.

No Opportunity To Observe ☐

Very slow; never turns out job on time.	Below average in output.	Turns out required volume, seldom more.	Above average producer.	Unusual output; exceptionally fast; does more than is expected.

Remarks:

7. ABILITY TO LEARN

Consider the ease and speed with which he grasps instructions and new methods; follows directions; remembers and applies new knowledge.

No Opportunity To Observe ☐

Unable to grasp without constant re-instruction.	Learns slowly but usually remembers well or seems to grasp quickly but can not retain what he has learned.	Learns moderately fast and remembers with occasional check with supervisors.	Learns fast; remembers well.	Unusually quick and complete grasp.

Remarks:

8. ATTENDANCE

Consider the regularity and punctuality with which he reports to work.

No Opportunity To Observe ☐

Excessively absent or tardy.	Frequently absent or tardy.	Occasionally absent or tardy.	Rarely absent or tardy — then only for good cause.	Never absent or tardy.

Attendance Record for Rating Period _____ Times Tardy _____ Excused Absences _____ Unexcused Absences _____

SUPERVISOR'S COMMENTS

Overall Evaluation = Score/2

Unsatisfactory (1-20)	Marginal (21-40)	Good (41-60)	Very Good (61-80)	Excellent (81-100)

Major Weak Points: _____ Major Strong Points: _____

What further training would be helpful to this employee? _____

Does employee seem to be suited for this job?   ☐ Yes   ☐ No

If not, what would be better? _____

Has employee taken any schooling after work in order to better himself or herself? _____

What company-sponsored training or activities has employee participated in? _____

Additional Comments: _____

EMPLOYEE'S COMMENTS

What can I as your supervisor do to help you to do a better job and improve yourself in the future? _____

Can you offer any constructive criticism, regarding your job, your supervisors, or working conditions in general? _____

What other jobs or training do you feel you would be interested in that would afford you opportunity for advancement? _____

Additional Comments: _____

Rated By _____   Date _____   Date Discussed with Employee _____

Reviewed By _____   Date _____

IMPORTANT: *This is your opinion of this employee's performance over the past review period. He or she will gain a better understanding only if you have communicated with and listened to him or her frequently during this period.*

Remember: *Strive for a better understanding between the employee and yourself—Clarify your mutual objectives— Be sure review is job-oriented rather than personality-oriented—Listen—Indicate your satisfaction in areas in which he or she has been effective—Reach an understanding of how the performance can be improved and establish a determination to improve it.*

Example 4

This form has some strong features and some weak ones. On the good side, three simple rating categories are described for Part II of the form: below requirements, meets requirements, and exceeds requirements. (I'd like to see another category here called *outstanding*.) Supporting statements are requested of the supervisor, and strengths and improvement needs must be identified.

On the negative side, major end results must be described by the supervisor in order of importance. This probably requires much time, effort, and frustration on the part of the person developing them. Much training would be required to implement this form. Also, there is no reference to what can be done to improve performance.

PERFORMANCE APPRAISAL

NAME _____

POSITION _____

DEPARTMENT _____

DATE OF EMPLOYMENT _____

DATE ENTERED PRESENT POSITION _____

— INSTRUCTIONS —

1. ACCOUNTABILITIES

List in Section I each of the accountabilities—or major end results—expected of the individual being evaluated. Depending upon the specific position, there are typically 3 to 8 major position accountabilities. List them in order of importance, from the most important to the least important.

2. EVALUATION OF ACCOUNTABILITIES

In Section II, perform an annual evaluation of the employee's progress toward fulfilling the requirements of each accountability by checking the appropriate box. Note that there are three boxes provided which are labeled "Exceeds Requirements", "Meets Requirements" and "Below Requirements."

3. SUPERVISOR'S SUPPORTING STATEMENTS

In Section III, briefly discuss the employee's performance on each accountability and explain how each evaluation was determined. Give examples where possible.

4. ADDITIONAL COMMENTS

The three items presented in Section IV should be answered as completely as possible.

5. OVERALL EVALUATION

In Section V make an overall evaluation of the employee's performance by considering the evaluation of each separate accountability and the data presented in Section IV. Assign a rating from one to five. In general, those rated 1 and 2 combined would represent the upper 20%, those rated 3 would represent the middle 60% and those rated 4 and 5 combined would represent the lower 20%. The definitions which are provided on the rear cover are designed to assist you in making your evaluation.

6. CAREER PLANNING

The two items related to Career Planning which are presented in Section VI should be answered as completely as possible.

7. COMPLETED EVALUATION

Both the employee and the Supervisor should sign the completed evaluation form.

I. MAJOR END RESULTS
(Rank in order of importance.)

1.

2.

3.

4.

5.

6.

7.

8.

II. SUPERVISOR'S RATING			III. SUPERVISOR'S SUPPORTING STATEMENTS
EXCEEDS REQUIREMENTS	MEETS REQUIREMENTS	BELOW REQUIREMENTS	(Give examples where possible.)

IV. ADDITIONAL COMMENTS

Summarize the employee's major strengths. _____

_____

Sumarize areas for improvement. _____

_____

Discribe additional factors which favorably or adversely influence the evaluation of this
individual. _____

_____

V. OVERALL EVALUATION
(Place check on scale).

| 1 | 2 | 3 | 4 | 5 |

DEFINITIONS: PERFORMANCE LEVELS

1 = OUTSTANDING — Outstanding performance is that which is consistently characterized by work of exceptionally high quality.

2 = VERY GOOD — Very good performance is that which is noticeably better than that usually expected in the position.

3 = GOOD — Good performance is that which meets the requirements of the position in a consistently satisfactory manner.

4 = ADEQUATE — Adequate performance is that which usually meets the minimum requirements of the position but where performance may leave something to be desired.

5 = NEEDS IMPROVEMENT — Performance is inadequate and performance requirements are not being met.

VI. CAREER PLANNING

1. Does this person have an interest in other positions or types of work? If so, what
are they? _____

_____

2. What further training and development is appropriate for this individual? _____

_____

This appraisal has been reviewed and discussed with the employee.

_____	_____
Date	Employee's Signature
_____	_____
Date	Supervisor's Signature
_____	_____
Date	Manager's Signature

Example 5

This simple form breaks the subordinate's job down into 16 different segments, which helps to pinpoint the specific factors to be judged. The descriptions help to clarify the factors but fall far short of standards. The three categories of appraisal are simple and quite descriptive.

This type of form may be useful in an organization that is not paperwork-oriented. It might also be helpful where managers are not going to spend much time on performance appraisal because they are too busy meeting production schedules. Though it won't achieve the results that could be accomplished by the approach recommended in this book, it sure beats nothing. The form would help to communicate how a subordinate is doing and at least suggest job segments to be improved. Finally, it would lend itself very well to a self-appraisal.

APPRAISAL OF SUPERVISORY PERFORMANCE

Name of Subordinate_____ Title _____

POSITION PERFORMANCE

Job Segment	Description	Strong	O.K.	Weak
1. Job Knowledge	Knows jobs of people supervised.			
2. Planning and organizing	Develops and organizes plans and schedules.			
3. Delegation	Delegates work to qualified subordinates.			
4. Induction	Orients and inducts new employees.			
5. Training	Trains, coaches, and develops subordinates.			
6. Responsibility	Cares for equipment, tools, materials, and so on.			
7. Record keeping	Maintains adequate records and reports.			
8. Empathy	Knows people personally, puts self in their shoes.			
9. Sociability	Gets along with people, is well liked.			
10. Discipline	Enforces rules and regulations, handles grievances.			
11. Judgment	Makes proper decisions, solves own problems.			
12. Follow-through	Follows through on plans and assignments.			
13. Cooperation	Cooperates with other departments and with management.			
14. Production	Gets out work on time.			
15. Quality	Maintains high-quality standards.			
16. Costs	Holds costs down.			

Form Completed by _____ Date_____

Example 6

This form has many positive features. First, it has identified the major segments of the job. Although standards have not been established, the descriptions of each rating convey quite clearly the performance to be evaluated. And the instructions suggest that the appraiser should compare each employee to the same standard. The form offers some practical help for appraising and interviewing. It also suggests that an employee development plan should be prepared with the employee.

The problem with this form is that the form itself requires little time and effort to complete. To implement the many suggestions on the instructions would require much initiative, time, and paperwork on the part of the appraiser, and most of the time it won't be done.

PERFORMANCE EVALUATION

INSTRUCTIONS TO THE RATER

PURPOSE OF PERFORMANCE EVALUATION

To review individual's performance of presently assigned duties and responsibilities, to communicate performance expectations, and to discuss individual's future career plans.

SET THE DATE FOR PERFORMANCE EVALUATION CONFERENCE

Set the date, time and place for the performance evaluation conference with the employee, perferably at least a week in advance.

Ask employee to review the "Employee Guide, Performance Characteristics Evaluation" to prepare for the conference. The employee may be given a copy of the evaluation form.

EVALUATE EMPLOYEE PERFORMANCE

Review employee's responsibilities as noted on your copy of the Position Description. If appropriate, revise the Position Description.

Reflect on employee's performance since the last evaluation.

COMPLETE PERFORMANCE EVALUATION FORM

Study each characteristic carefully before rating the employee. Evaluate each of the characteristics separately.

Compare each employee rated to the same standard. At no time should prejudice, partiality, or other factors influence the rating. Each employee's progress, or lack of progress, between each period of evaluation should be measured.

Modify the qualifiers for each performance characteristics, if necessary, by striking or adding words, as long as the general intent remains the same.

Write any comments in the space provided. If more space is needed, attach additional sheets which are adequately identified.

Give the employee an overall performance evaluation.

With the employee, prepare an employee development plan to correct areas in need of improvement, to improve skills needed for the current job, and to develop the skills needed for the employee's career advancement.

CONDUCT PERFORMANCE EVALUATION CONFERENCE

Meet alone with employee.

Solicit employee comments and questions.

Review employee's duties and responsibilities, resolving any misunderstandings.

Comment on employee's strengths, areas in need of improvement and ways to improve job performance.

Review Performance Evaluation form.

Answer any questions.

INSTRUCTIONS

Send the WHITE copy to the Personnel Office, the YELLOW copy is kept by the supervisor and the PINK copy will be kept by the employee. NO CARBON REQUIRED.

EMPLOYE PERFORMANCE AND DEVELOPMENT REPORT
BASED ON PERFORMANCE DURING PERIOD
FROM _____ TO _____

_____   _____
Name of Employe (First, Middle, Last)   *Civil Service Title*

_____   _____
Division   *Department*

PERFORMANCE CHARACTERISTICS: Check the statement for each characteristic which most appropriately describes the employe. *YOU MAY CROSS OUT OR ADD WORDS TO MODIFY THE PERFORMANCE CHARACTERISTIC AS LONG AS THE BASIC INTENT REMAINS THE SAME.*

PRODUCTIVITY: Measure the volume of work accomplished and rate of progress on assignments.
☐ Fast worker. Rate of progress on assignments and volume of output is above average. Well organized.
☐ Work output satisfactory. Works at a steady pace. Work done timely.
☐ Works slowly. Only occasionally is output considered average.
☐ Very slow worker. Quantity of output is well below average of others in the same class. Does not utilize time effectively.

JOB KNOWLEDGE: Evaluate the employe's ability to grasp the procedures, techniques, instructions of the job and the degree to which requires skills have been mastered.
☐ Has thorough knowledge of all aspects of work assignments and performs with high degree of skill.
☐ Has sufficient knowledge of duties and responsibilities of the work to satisfy requirements of the job. Degree of skill is met in most respects.
☐ Learns work assignments slowly. Requires much instruction and guidance. Attainment of required skills is marginal. Needs further training.
☐ Demonstrates little or no understanding of work assignments and seems unable or uninterested in mastering the skills required.

QUALITY OF OUTPUT: Evaluate the accuracy, thoroughness and appearance of work assignments.
☐ Work frequently incomplete or needs to be done over. Often repeats same kind of mistakes. Work is sloppy in appearance and poorly arranged.
☐ Work not completely unsatisfactory, but generally substantial improvement is necessary.
☐ Work is usually neat and presentable. Seldom needs major redoing. Seldom repeats mistakes. Generally adheres to applicable instructions.
☐ Work is complete, attractively presented and accurate.

ATTITUDE: Consider interest and enthusiasm in work, reactions to constructive criticisms, support of management policies, reaction to supervisor's instructions.
☐ Demonstrates sustained motivation to do the best possible job.
☐ Reasonably conscientious and generally enthusiastic in performing assigned tasks. Makes an effort toward overcoming difficulties and volunteers when assistance is sought.
☐ No real interest in job. Satisfied if he/she can do the minimum.

HUMAN RELATIONS: Consider employe's ability to maintain harmonious working relations with others, both within and external to work unit.
☐ Has trouble getting along with others. Makes little or no attempt to improve person-to-person working relationships.
☐ Usually gets along with others.
☐ Very effective in meeting and dealing with others.
☐ An asset to the image of the work unit or office. Considerate of others' views and interests. Elicits cooperation from among others in the unit.

ATTENDANCE AND DEPENDABILITY: Consider whether the employe can be relied upon to appear for work on time and to meet work schedules.
☐ Extremely conscientious in meeting work schedules and in fulfilling responsibilities and commitments. Attendance is excellent and can always be depended upon for appearing and getting job done, regardless of circumstances.
☐ Can usually be depended upon to meet schedules and commitments. Makes effort to be punctual and to complete assignments on schedule. Seldom absent or tardy and reports absences and tardiness in advance.
☐ Occasionally is late in reporting to work or in keeping appointments. Requires more supervision than should be necessary.
☐ Can seldom be relied upon to meet work schedules without constant supervision. Frequent tardiness and apparent abuse or misuse of leave privileges. Does not usually report leave in advance.

RESOURCEFULNESS: Consider the employe's determination and energy displayed in overcoming obstacles within scope of the job, in finding solutions to problems and in keeping productively occupied.
☐ Generally initiates action and finds solutions to problems. Makes creative and innovative contributions to work.
☐ Displays considerable energy and moves ahead on own initiative to complete assignments. Demonstrates resourcefulness and originality.
☐ Occasionally takes initiative in the performance of assigned duties.
☐ Usually relies on others to find solutions to problems.
☐ Almost never initiates action on the job without specific instructions. Work effort stops when an obstacle is encountered. Doesn't seek assistance.

Evaluate Employe's Overall Performance

☐ Outstanding   ☐ Very Good   ☐ Competent   ☐ Improvement Desired   ☐ Unacceptable

SUPERVISOR'S COMMENTS* _____

_____

_____

EMPLOYE'S COMMENTS _____

_____

_____

_____
Supervisor Making Report

_____
This report was discussed with me

Example 7

This form combines the writing of goals and achievements with the checking of boxes regarding specific aspects of performance. It requires the appraiser to use the position description to clarify the prime responsibility results. General statements instead of standards of performance are used to explain the factors being rated.

The degrees of performance range from *poor* to *superior*, with *average* in the middle. The word *average* should not be used because it suggests a comparison with other people instead of evaluating the performance against a standard.

This type of form requires much thought, time, and effort to fill out. Appraisers would need careful training in how to use it effectively.

PERFORMANCE APPRAISAL

ADMINISTRATION/MID-MANAGEMENT/PROFESSIONALS

NAME _____ JOB TITLE _____

DEPARTMENT _____ EVALUATION PERIOD FROM_____
_____ TO_____

JOB DESCRIPTION ☐ ATTACHED ☐ UNDER REVISION, WILL BE FORWARDED

I. RESULTS ACHIEVED LAST YEAR

Summarize the results achieved for each major goal established last year. Attach a copy.

GOAL #1 ☐ Met ☐ Failed to Meet

GOAL #2 ☐ Met ☐ Failed to Meet

GOAL #3 ☐ Met ☐ Failed to Meet

GOAL #4 ☐ Met ☐ Failed to Meet

GOAL #5 ☐ Met ☐ Failed to Meet

II. EMPLOYEE APPRAISAL

PRIME RESPONSIBILITY RESULTS — To what degree the responsibilities listed on position description were fulfilled.

☐ Superior   ☐ Outstanding   ☐ Average   ☐ Acceptable   ☐ Poor

EVALUATION COMMENT:_____

_____

MANAGEMENT SKILLS — Effectiveness in planning, organizing, leading, and controlling.

☐ Superior   ☐ Outstanding   ☐ Average   ☐ Acceptable   ☐ Poor

EVALUATION COMMENT:_____

_____

COMMUNICATIONS — Degree of effectiveness of both oral and written communications.

☐ Superior   ☐ Outstanding   ☐ Average   ☐ Acceptable   ☐ Poor

EVALUATION COMMENT:_____

_____

INTERPERSONAL RELATIONS — Success in dealing with supervisors, subordinates, peers and other business contacts.

☐ Superior   ☐ Outstanding   ☐ Average   ☐ Acceptable   ☐ Poor

EVALUATION COMMENT:_____

_____

DECISION MAKING AND JUDGMENT — Effectiveness in analyzing problems and determining appropriate actions.

☐ Superior   ☐ Outstanding   ☐ Average   ☐ Acceptable   ☐ Poor

EVALUATION COMMENT:_____

_____

INITIATIVE & CREATIVITY — Ability to initiate action and develop new ideas and handle unusual work situations.

☐ Superior   ☐ Outstanding   ☐ Average   ☐ Acceptable   ☐ Poor

EVALUATION COMMENT:_____

_____

(II. CONTINUED)

ADAPTABILITY — Consider ability to cope with change.

☐ Superior ☐ Outstanding   ☐ Average   ☐ Acceptable   ☐ Poor

EVALUATION COMMENT:_____

_____

_____

_____

_____

III. SUMMARY

Change in overall performance level since last appraisal dated _____

☐ Improved   ☐ Same   ☐ Less Effective

Considering all the items discussed in this appraisal and any others you feel are important, summarize your assessment of this staff member's total effectiveness on the job. Specifically comment on the conditions influencing the environment in which the job was performed, i.e., degree of challenge presented. Also comment on the manner in which results were achieved, noting how the staff member's methods impact others in the organization, i.e., the degree of support given others.

_____

_____

_____

_____

_____

_____

_____

_____

_____

_____

_____

_____

_____

_____

_____

_____

_____

_____

IV. NEGOTIATED GOALS FOR NEW YEAR

GOAL #1

    DETAIL _____

_____

_____

    EXPECTED RESULTS _____

_____

_____

    ANTICIPATED OBSTACLES IN ACHIEVING _____

_____

_____

    HOW WILL THEY BE RESOLVED? _____

_____

_____

GOAL #2

    DETAIL _____

_____

_____

    EXPECTED RESULTS _____

_____

_____

    ANTICIPATED OBSTACLES IN ACHIEVING _____

_____

_____

    HOW WILL THEY BE RESOLVED?_____

_____

_____

GOAL #3

    DETAIL_____

_____

_____

    EXPECTED RESULTS _____

_____

_____

(GOAL #3 CONTINUED)

ANTICIPATED OBSTACLES IN ACHIEVING _____

_____

_____

HOW WILL THEY BE RESOLVED? _____

_____

_____

GOAL #4

DETAIL _____

_____

_____

EXPECTED RESULTS _____

_____

_____

ANTICIPATED OBSTACLES IN ACHIEVING _____

_____

_____

HOW WILL THEY BE RESOLVED? _____

_____

_____

GOAL #5

DETAIL _____

_____

_____

EXPECTED RESULTS _____

_____

_____

ANTICIPATED OBSTACLES IN ACHIEVING _____

_____

_____

HOW WILL THEY BE RESOLVED? _____

_____

_____

V. PERFORMANCE IMPROVEMENT

List those areas in which you feel the staff member should work in order to improve effectiveness on the job, and recommendations for specific actions you would like to encourage the staff member to take to improve performance.

AREA	ACTION FOR IMPROVEMENT

ONE-OVER-ONE

_____   _____
Appraiser's Signature   Reviewed by Appraiser's Manager

_____   _____
Date   Date

COMMENTS OF ONE-OVER-ONE REVIEWER (OPTIONAL)

STAFF MEMBER'S COMMENTS

Each staff member is encouraged to express views on the fairness and accuracy of this Performance Appraisal.

_____   _____
Staff Member's Signature   Date

Example 8

This is a complicated approach that requires much time and writing. It would also require extensive training so that reviewers have the necessary understanding and skills to implement it effectively.

A number of positive features are included, such as the identification of strengths, job segments needing improvement, and specific action plans.

EMPLOYEE PERFORMANCE PLANNING
AND EVALUATION

CONFIDENTIAL

EMPLOYEE NAME (LAST, FIRST AND INITIAL)				DATE OF PERFORMANCE PLAN	
POSITION PLAN				DATES OF PROGRESS REVIEWS	
DATE EMPLOYED	DATE ASSIGNED PRESENT POSITION	DATE ASSIGNED TO THIS SUPERVISOR			
COMPANY	DIVISION	LOCATION	DEPARTMENT		
				DATE OF PERFORMANCE EVALUATION	

PERFORMANCE PLANNING

RESPONSIBILITIES* (Major headings of job responsibilities.)	PERFORMANCE FACTORS AND OR RESULTS TO BE ACHIEVED A specific statement of the goals employee can reasonably be expected to achieve in the coming period for each responsibility. Indicate how results will be measured. When specific quantitative indicators are not possible, state the conditions which exist when a job is well performed.	PRIORITY ** AND/OR TARGET
CHANGES IN PERFORMANCE PLAN - Use this section for any changes in plans before the end of the PPE period.		

PERFORMANCE EVALUATION

LEVEL OF ACTUAL ACHIEVEMENT

ADDITIONAL SIGNIFICANT ACCOMPLISHMENTS

_____
_____
_____
_____
_____
_____
_____

CONTINUING RESPONSIBILITIES - Indicates additional responsibilities whenever they have had a significant positive or negative effect on the overall results achieved.

_____
_____
_____
_____
_____
_____

RELATIONSHIP WITH OTHERS - (JOB RELATED) Give significant positive or negative influence this employee has had on the results achieved by other employees.

_____
_____
_____
_____
_____

OVERALL RATING

Review actual level of achievement against overall performance plans. Consider performance in key results areas, that is actual performance against important priorities, dates, amounts and other factors listed above. Check the definition which best describes the employee's overall performance.

☐ Results achieved were unsatisfactory - performance did not meet expectations and must improve.

☐ Results achieved were acceptable - performance met expectations in most key results areas

☐ Results achieved were satisfactory - performance exceeded expectations in a few key results areas

☐ Results achieved were above average - performance exceeded expectations in many key results areas

☐ Results achieved were outstanding - performance exceeded expectations in most key results areas

* ALL MANAGERS ARE EXPECTED TO INCLUDE EEO. OSHA, AND EMPLOYEE DEVELOPMENT RESPONSIBILITIES AS AN INTEGRAL PART OF THE PERFORMANCE PLAN.

** USE THE FOLLOWING CODES TO CLASSIFY PRIORITIES:

A - MOST IMPORTANT   C - IMPORTANT
B - VERY IMPORTANT   D - OPTIONAL

NOTE: ● TARGET REFERS TO COMPLETION DATES, AMOUNT, ETC.

● TRANSFER RATING TO EDR FORM TEN 4788.

COUNSELING SUMMARY

EMPLOYEE STRENGTHS: _____

_____

_____

DEVELOPMENT NEEDS: _____

_____

_____

SIGNIFICANT INTERVIEW COMMENTS

Record additional significant items discussed by you or the employee during the Development/Evaluation interview.

_____

_____

_____

_____

_____

_____

| _____ | _____ | _____ |
| (Manager's Signature) | (Print Name) | (Date of Interview) |

EMPLOYEE REVIEW

The employee should use the space below to express any agreement or disagreement concerning the Performance Plan and/or Evaluation if he/she wishes to do so.

_____

_____

_____

_____

I have reviewed this Performance Plan and/or Evaluation with my manager. My signature means that I have been advised of my performance status and does not imply that I agree with this evaluation.

| _____ | _____ | _____ |
| (Employee's Signature) | (Print Name) | (Date) |

MANAGEMENT REVIEW

Optional Comments _____

_____

_____

_____

| _____ | _____ | _____ |
| (Reviewer's Signature) | (Print Name) | (Date) |

EMPLOYEE DEVELOPMENT REPORT

A. PERFORMANCE PLANNING AND EVALUATION

1. HOW DID YOU RATE THIS EMPLOYEE'S OVERALL PERFORMANCE DURING THE LAST PERIOD (TRANSFER RATING FROM TEN 4789):

   ☐ Results achieved were unsatisfactory - performance did not meet expectations and must improve.

   ☐ Results achieved were acceptable - performance met expectations in most key results areas

   ☐ Results achieved were satisfactory - performance exceeded expectations in a few key results areas

   ☐ Results achieved were above average - performance exceeded expectations in many key results areas

   ☐ Results achieved were outstanding - performance exceeded expectations in most key results areas

2. DATE OF RATING:

3. WHAT IS THE BASIS FOR YOUR OVERALL RATING? (INCLUDE SPECIFIC RESULTS THAT THE EMPLOYEE ACHIEVED AND USE ADDITIONAL SPACE ON BACK IF NEEDED.)

   _____

   _____

   _____

   _____

B. DEVELOPMENT PLANNING

1. DEVELOPMENT NEEDS
   WHAT EDUCATION, PERSONAL IMPROVEMENT, SPECIAL IMPROVEMENTS, OR OTHER FUNCTIONAL/DIVISIONAL EXPERIENCES WOULD INCREASE EMPLOYEE'S POTENTIAL FOR ADVANCEMENT AND/OR IMPROVE PERFORMANCE IN CURRENT POSITION.

   _____

   _____

2. ACTION PLANS
   WHAT SPECIFIC ACTIONS ARE PLANNED TO MEET THESE DEVELOPMENT NEEDS? WHEN? WHOSE RESPONSIBILITY TO IMPLEMENT?

   _____

   _____

3. PREVIOUS ACTION PLANS
   WHAT SPECIFIC RESULTS WERE ACHIEVED UNDER THIS EMPLOYEE'S DEVELOPMENT PLAN FOR THE PRIOR PERIOD?

   _____

   _____

C. POTENTIAL FOR PROMOTION

1. EMPLOYEE'S INTEREST AND ASPIRATIONS (BASED ON EMPLOYEE'S VIEW AND COMMENTS TO YOU IN YOUR ONGOING RELATIONSHIP.)

2. WHAT INDICATIONS DO YOU HAVE THAT THE EMPLOYEE IS CAPABLE OF ACCEPTING MORE RESPONSIBILITY?

3. IN WHAT AREAS DOES THE EMPLOYEE HAVE POTENTIAL FOR ADVANCEMENT?

4. PROMOTABILITY (HOW DO YOU RATE THE EMPLOYEE'S PROMOTABILITY?)

   ☐ Employee is not promotable at this time for one of the following reasons:
   * ☐ Was promoted/transferred to present job _____ months ago.
       (i.e., has potential, but needs further experience on present job).
   ☐ Must achieve specific developmental goals before being considered for promotion.
   ☐ Personal (i.e., health, interest, family/relocation problems, etc.). Please indicate: _____

   * ☐ Employee has potential for one or more positions.
   * ☐ Employee has outstanding potential for one or more positions.

If the employee has potential for promotion (*ratings) please specify the positions for which employee should be considered: (consider other locations, Divisions, and/or Tenneco companies): _____

● HOW DOES EMPLOYEE FEEL ABOUT RELOCATION? _____
(CONSIDER FAMILY AND OTHER COMMITMENTS.)

REVIEWER'S COMMENTS

(X) _____
(REVIEWER'S SIGNATURE)

D. REPLACEMENT PLANNING

PLEASE REVIEW EACH ITEM BELOW AND CHECK AND COMPLETE THE REPLACEMENT STATUS FOR THE EMPLOYEE BEING RATED.

☐ QUALIFIED REPLACEMENT - EMPLOYEES IN MY AREA OF RESPONSIBILITY AND QUALIFIED TO REPLACE THE EMPLOYEE BEING RATED ARE:

☐ 18-MONTH REPLACEMENT - EMPLOYEES IN MY AREA OF RESPONSIBILITY WHO CAN BE DEVELOPED INTO A "QUALIFIED REPLACEMENT" THROUGH A PLANNED PROGRAM IN 18 MONTHS OR LESS ARE:

☐ NONE - NO EMPLOYEE IN MY AREA OF RESPONSIBILITY IS "QUALIFIED" OR AN "18-MONTH REPLACEMENT."

☐ POSSIBLE REPLACEMENT - EMPLOYEES OUTSIDE MY AREA OF RESPONSIBILITY WHO MIGHT BE "QUALIFIED" OR 18-MONTH REPLACEMENTS ARE:
(CONSIDER OTHER LOCATIONS, DIVISIONS, AND/OR TENNECO COMPANIES.)

COMMENTS _____

REPORTER
SIGNATURE: (X) _____ (DATE)

PRINT NAME: _____

_____ _____
(PRINT NAME) (DATE)

Example 9

This form requires the reviewers to establish their own standards and appraise performance against these standards. It leaves too much to the individual appraiser and requires much writing.

It isn't clear whether each factor should be rated from *poor* to *superior* or whether the reviewer should simply describe the performance. The only specific rating required is for overall performance. This may be sufficient for salary administration purposes, but it is unsatisfactory if improved performance is the objective. The word *average* should not be used.

A great deal of communication and training is required for this approach, and the results may not warrant the time and effort.

PERFORMANCE APPRAISAL

Employee's Name	Job Title
Department	Evaluation Period From To
Job Description ☐ Attached	☐ Under Revision, will be forwarded

REVIEW THE STANDARD JOB DESCRIPTION WITH THE EMPLOYEE.
Summarize the specific duties of the job and establish expected standards.

_____

_____

_____

_____

_____

_____

_____

_____

_____

Does the employee understand the responsibilities and results? ☐ Yes   ☐ No

CONSIDER THE FOLLOWING AREAS CAREFULLY AND DISCUSS EACH WITH THE EMPLOYEE. Be specific in your descriptions. Keep in mind the job to be performed and the standards of performance desired.

How does the employee's work measure up to your standards in terms of the following?

1. THOROUGHNESS, ACCURACY, AND NEATNESS. Consider work organization and appearance.

_____

_____

_____

2. AMOUNT OF SATISFACTORY WORK ACCOMPLISHED. Consider quantity, quality, and ability to complete tasks.

_____

_____

_____

3. EMPLOYER AND STAFF RELATIONSHIP.   Consider salesmanship, service, enthusiasm, courtesy and co-operation.

_____

_____

_____

4. KNOWLEDGE OF THE JOB. Consider comprehension and acceptance of counseling, guidance, procedures, rules and regulations.

_____

_____

_____

5. OTHER ATTRIBUTES OR SKILLS NECESSARY IN THIS JOB. (If additional room is required, please attach a sheet to this appraisal.)

_____

_____

_____

OVER-ALL PERFORMANCE. Carefully review each of the five areas discussed and give an over-all rating on the employee on the following scale.

Poor	Acceptable	Average	Outstanding	Superior

Comments on over-all rating.

_____

_____

_____

PROGRAM OF DEVELOPMENT
1. WHAT HAS BEEN DONE SINCE THE LAST APPRAISAL INTERVIEW?

_____

_____

_____

_____

_____

_____

_____

2. DESCRIBE THE NEW PROGRAM OF DEVELOPMENT AND WHAT PLANS HAVE BEEN DISCUSSSED. BE SPECIFIC.

_____

_____

_____

_____

_____

_____

_____

_____

3. INDICATE THE EMPLOYEE'S REACTION TO THIS APPRAISAL. Indicate reaction to counseling session and employee's goals or aspirations.

_____

_____

_____

_____

EMPLOYEE'S COMMENTS, IF ANY

_____

_____

_____

_____

_____

This appraisal was
reviewed with me on: _____

Employee's Signature: _____

Appraiser's Signature: _____

Reviewed by Appraiser's
Manager: _____

Example 10

This complicated approach requires much writing. It combines responsibilities with objectives in one column and asks for comments in the next column. This is more confusing and less beneficial than identifying job segments and standards and then using specific ratings.

Although the general content of the form is satisfactory, and although there is a section on plans for improvement, too much writing and initiative are required of the appraiser. This makes the form impractical. This approach could not be used for self-appraisal.

STEP I. POSITION RESPONSIBILITIES & OBJECTIVES — PERFORMANCE RATING

NAME_____   LOCATION_____

JOB TITLE_____   DEPARTMENT_____

List the principal responsibilities for which the individual is accountable and the specific objectives which were established for the appraisal period.	Comment on the individual's discharge of responsibilities and attainment of objectives. Explain special difficulties, changes, etc. affecting accomplisment.

OVER-ALL EVALUATION OF ACCOMPLISHMENTS

Evaluate over-all performance of position responsibilities and objectives by checking one of the following:

OUTSTANDING ☐   GOOD ☐   ADEQUATE ☐   UNSATISFACTORY ☐

STEP II. EVALUATION OF MANAGERIAL ABILITY

Comment briefly on use of managerial skills and demonstrated leadership ability.

Consider such factors as: Knowledge of job . . . Control of expenditures . . . Communications . . . Teamwork . . . Delegating responsibility . . . Assuming responsibility . . . Planning and organizing . . . Contributing workable ideas . . . Making decisions . . . Relations with others . . . Training and development of subordinates. (Use specific examples, when possible.)

STEP III. SELF-DEVELOPMENT ACTIVITIES

1. What is the person's attitude toward self-development? Does he or she have a real desire to improve and broaden capabilities?

2. List the special training and development activities, inside and outside the Company, which the individual has engaged in during the past year.

3. List the individual's participation in professional, civic, and community activities. Indicate where the individual provided leadership in these areas.

STEP IV. PLANS FOR IMPROVEMENT

As the last phase of planning future job performance, supervisor and subordinate will develop specific plans to help the individual improve his or her performance and encourage personal development. Consider actions by the individual and actions by you as the supervisor.   Indicate any training programs and related activities in which he or she should participate.

If the appraisal is limited because the individual is new on the position, check here: ☐

Appraisal Period: FROM_____ TO_____

APPRAISED BY:

_____   _____
              (Immediate Supervisor)   (Date)

APPROVED BY:

_____   _____
              (Next Higher Supervisor)   (Date)

Performance discussion held with individual on _____
                                                                          (Date)

SUMMARY — PERFORMANCE & POTENTIAL

NOTE: This summary is confidential and should not be discussed with the individual appraised. It is to be completed by the supervisor after the discussion with the individual concerning plans for improvement of future job performance.

SUMMARY EVALUATION — PRESENT PERFORMANCE

1	2	3	4
OUTSTANDING (Overall perform- ance is clearly exceptional)	EXCEEDS REQUIREMENTS (Very good)	MEETS REQUIREMENTS (Satisfactory performance)	UNSATISFACTORY

FUTURE POTENTIAL

☐ 1. No indication of growth potential beyond present job.

☐ 2. Is ready for more responsibility and/or promotion.
       If so, to what specific positions — what greater responsibilities?

_____

_____

☐ 3. Will be ready for more responsibility and/or promotion with further development and experience.
       If so, what specific experience and development is needed?   Could then fill what positions?

_____

_____

SPECIAL SKILLS AND AMBITIONS

1. What special skills and talents does the individual possess?

_____

_____

2. Indicate the individual's ambitions within the Company. Does he or she have interest in other types or areas of work within the Company?

_____

_____

_____

_____

_____

HEALTH

1. Does health affect present performance? If so, explain.

   _____

   _____

2. Would health be a factor in a position of increased responsibility?

   _____

   _____

GENERAL

1. Particular individuals, for good reasons, may be giving only mediocre performance today. This may be due to age, health, inability to adjust to change, etc. Does this individual fall into this categroy? If yes, explain and recommend action to be taken.

   _____

   _____

   _____

   _____

2. Add additional pertinent comments, including significant events occuring during the discussion of planning future job performance.

   _____

   _____

   _____

   _____

   _____

   _____

   _____

   _____

Example 11

This form has many positive features. Although specific standards are not used, the descriptions of each job segment help to clarify what is expected as the basis for appraisal. Additional comments are encouraged. The five ratings are described in detail so that objectivity is encouraged. (See the performance category definitions following the form itself.) This form would lend itself to a self-appraisal.

Its weakness is its lack of emphasis on and specific guidelines for improved performance.

EMPLOYEE PERFORMANCE REVIEW
(Non-Exempt Salaried Employees Only)

_____	Dept. No. _____ Hired Date _____
Name	
_____	Salary Grade _____
Job Classification Title	

Rate the employee on each of the factors below by placing an X in front of each factor which most closely describes the employee being rated. Should a particular description fail to adequately describe the employee's performance, feel free to delete or add words as appropriate.

QUANTITY OF WORK

_____ High volume producer; frequently does more than is expected or required.
_____ Turns out satisfactory volume of work; occasionally does more than is required.
_____ Output is generally satisfactory but requires occasional prodding; does only what is required.
_____ Very slow worker; output consistently low.

QUALITY OF WORK

_____ Consistently produces error-free work; work is always neat and orderly.
_____ Usually produces error-free work; work is usually neat and orderly.
_____ Generally produces satisfactory work both as to accuracy and neatness.
_____ Room for improvement; errors frequent; work requires checking and re-doing.

RELIABILITY

_____ Always gets the job done on time; excellent attendance and tardiness record; dependable under pressure.
_____ Usually gets the job done on time; seldom absent or tardy; works fairly well under pressure.
_____ Performs satisfactorily; requires occasional prompting and checks on performance; generally satisfactory attendance record.
_____ Reluctant to accept responsibility; frequently careless or forgetful; frequently absent or tardy; fails to complete work on time.

INITIATIVE

_____ Displays unusual drive and perseverance; anticipates needed actions; frequently suggests better ways of doing things.
_____ A self starter; proceeds on own with little or no direction; makes some suggestions for improvements.
_____ Does not proceed on own but waits to have procedures outlined; seldom makes suggestions for improvements.
_____ Continually needs prompting to complete assignments; never makes suggestions for improvements.

UTILIZATION OF TIME

_____ Always on the job; looks for additional work; does not distract others.
_____ Usually on the job; generally does not distract others.
_____ Easily distracted; room for improvement.
_____ Spends too much time off the job; disturbs others.

JUDGMENT

_____ Uses exceptionally good judgment and makes sound decisions.
_____ Handles most situations well and makes sound decisions under normal conditions.
_____ Uses questionable judgment at times; room for improvement
_____ Uses poor judgment in dealing with people and situations.

JOB KNOWLEDGE

_____   Expert in job; has thorough grasp of all phases of job; seldom requires assistance or instruction.
_____   Understands and performs most phases of job well; occasionally requires assistance and instruction.
_____   Limited knowledge of job, further training required; frequently requires assistance and instruction.
_____   Inadequate; lacks basic understanding of job; constantly requires assistance and instruction.

ADDITIONAL FACTORS

Please comment on factors such as clerical skills, technical proficiency, attendance or personnel relationships which have an **important** effect on employee's performance. If appropriate make recommendations or suggestions for future personnel action.

Considering the specific ratings given above, indicate an overall performance rating of either:

(1) Marginal   (2) Fair   (3) Competent   (4) Commendable   (5) Exceptional

OVERALL PERFORMANCE RATING _____

Date	Reviewing Supervisor	Date	Approved By

PERFORMANCE REVIEW DISCUSSION WITH THE EMPLOYEE

Performance Review discussed on _____ by _____
                                        (Date)   Supervisor's Signature

                                                                                 Employee's Signature

Employee's Reaction to the Performance Review Discussion:

Expanded Definitions of Performance Categories

Marginal—1

Use of this performance category implies:

- Has been on the job long enough to have shown better performance. Probably should be told time is running out.
- Is creating a bit of a morale problem with those who have to help carry his or her load (including yourself).
- Just doesn't seem to have the drive or the know-how to do the job. Would be better off on some other job for which qualified.
- The employee's work is holding up that of the other positions with which it interrelates.
- It is more than likely that the employee probably recognizes that the job is not getting done.
- If performance continues at this level, the employee should be replaced.
- Just doesn't seem to get things accomplished.
- The work keeps falling behind. If you keep the employee much longer, you will be in real trouble.
- Seems to make one mistake after another; some of them are repeats.
- Apparently does not have the background to grasp the work.
- You have had adverse comments from outsiders concerning the employee's performance.

Fair—2

Use of this performance category implies:

- This employee is doing the job reasonably well. Performance meets the minimum requirements for the position and many of the normal performance requirements.
- The employee's performance is not really poor, but if *all* your people were at this performance level, you would be in trouble.
- You would like to see the employee improve, but in the meantime you really don't have too much to complain about.
- May be the kind of employee who needs some pushing and follow-through, but does the job under close guidance.
- You may have to keep a close watch, otherwise you would consider the employee competent.
- The employee shows drive but needs to acquire more know-how.
- You may have to plan the employee's programs or assignments step by step. After that, the job usually gets done.
- Some of your people have to "carry" the employee on occasion.
- Can't always depend on the employee to complete the assignments or the daily work unless you keep checking.

Competent—3

Use of this performance category implies:

- This employee is doing a full, complete, and satisfactory job. Performance is what is expected of a fully qualified and experienced person in the assigned position.
- You would not require significant improvement. If improvement *does* occur, it's a plus factor for your group's effectiveness. If it *does not,* you have no reason to complain.
- If all your employees were as good, your total group's performance would be completely satisfactory (in your judgment and your manager's too).
- You get few complaints from others with whom the employee's work interfaces.
- Errors are few and seldom repeated.
- Demonstrates a sound balance between quality and quantity.
- Does not spend undue time on unimportant items, neglecting problems or projects that should have priority.
- You feel reasonably secure in quoting the employee's input or recommendations.
- Requires only normal supervision and follow-up and usually completes regular work and projects on schedule.
- Has encountered almost all the activity fields of the position and has proved quite capable in each.
- You consider the employee a good, solid member of your team and feel reasonably secure in making any kind of an assignment within the scope of the job and level.

Commendable—4

Use of this performance category implies:

- This employee exceeds position requirements even on some of the most difficult and complex parts of the job. Takes the initiative in development and in implementation of challenging work goals. Normally, this individual would be considered for promotion.
- You are getting *more* than you bargained for.
- You find the employee accomplishing *more* than you expect.
- Is able to take on extra projects and tasks without defaulting in other assigned activity fields.
- Each project or job tackled is done thoroughly and completely.
- The employee's decisions and actions have paid off to a higher degree than would be expected.
- Often provides "extras."
- Requires only occasional supervision and follow-up.
- Frequently exceeds objectives.
- Does own advance planning, anticipates problems and takes appropriate action.

- Shows a good grasp of the "big picture." Thinks beyond the details of the job, and works toward the overall objectives of the department.
- "If you had four like this employee, you would only need three."

Exceptional—5
Use of this performance category implies:
- Employee demonstrates a knowledge that normally can be gained only through long periods of experience in this particular type of work.
- Recognized by all as a real expert in this job area.
- This employee can usually be a prime candidate for promotion when a higher level position in this or a related field becomes open.
- The employee's actions show an understanding of work well beyond the assigned area. Outsiders seek the employee out because of knowledge of *many* facets of the department's work.
- Requires little or no supervision or follow-up.
- Shows unusual initiative and is a self-starter.
- Almost invariably takes the best approach to getting the job done.

Note: This level of performance must be looked at in terms of both *quantity* and *quality.* Use of this category shows that you are recognizing really outstanding worth to the company within the level of this position.

Example 12

On the positive side, this form is simple to understand and easy to complete. It is very much oriented toward behavior and lends itself well to a self-appraisal.

Nothing is included about the identification of strengths or weaknesses. Also, there is no form or procedure for planning and implementing improved performance.

EMPLOYEE JOB PERFORMANCE EVALUATION

Department: Production

Employee's Name: _____

Job Title: Shop Foreman　　　　Date: _____

Instructions: Immediately to the left of each job behavior is a line on which you are to indicate the level of performance. Enter a numerical value on each line, indicating one of the following:

+2　Superior
+1　Commendable
　0　Good
−1　Marginal
−2　Unsatisfactory

Job Behaviors

_____ Carries out work as directed by Production Manager.
_____ Plans and supervises shop work.
_____ Assists with monthly inventory.
_____ Spot-checks craftsmanship on finished products.
_____ Supervises truck loading and unloading.
_____ Makes out bills of lading.
_____ Maintains storage areas in good condition.
_____ Enforces safety rules and regulations.
_____ Monitors for efficient use of materials.
_____ Trains new employees.
_____ Works well with employees.
_____ Meets production standards.
_____ Repairs salvageable materials when practical.
_____ Organizes work efficiently.
_____ Interviews and screens job applicants.
_____ Maintains high morale among employees.
_____ Motivates employees to higher productivity.
_____ Employs and terminates shop employees with discretion.
_____ Is flexible.
_____ Maintains shop in cleanliness and in order.

Comments: _____
_____
_____
_____

From Robert W. Carsell, "Evaluation Dynamics." Columbia, S.C.: The Interaction Press, 1979.

Example 13

This form is simple to understand and administer. It would be appropriate for a self-appraisal, and it is job-oriented.

The word *average* is used, which would confuse the appraiser because of the dual standard of the job and other people. No forms or procedures are included for improving performance.

PLANNING   RATING

1. Does employee set both short-term and long-term goals for the department unit in verifiable terms (either qualitative or quantitative) that are related in a positive way to those of his or her superior and company?   _____

2. To what extent does he or she make sure that the goals of the department are understood by subordinates?   _____

3. How well does he or she assist subordinates in establishing verifiable and consistent goals for their operations?   _____

4. To what extent does he or she utilize consistent and approved planning premises and see that subordinates do likewise?   _____

5. Does he or she understand the role of company policies in decision making and ensure that subordinates do likewise?   _____

6. Does he or she attempt to solve problems of subordinates by policy guidance, coaching, and encouragement of innovation, rather than by rules and procedures?   _____

7. Does he or she help subordinates get the information they need to assist them in their planning?   _____

8. To what extent does employee seek out applicable alternatives before making a decision?   _____

9. In choosing from among alternatives, does he or she recognize and give primary attention to factors that are limiting, or critical, to the solution of a problem?   _____

10. In making decisions, how well does he or she bear in mind the size and length of commitment involved in each decision?   _____

11. Does he or she check plans periodically to see if they are still consistent with currect expectations?   _____

12. To what extent does he or she consider the need for, as well as the cost of, flexibility in arriving at a planning decision?   _____

13. In developing and implementing plans, does he or she regularly consider longer-range implications of decisions along with the shorter-range results expected?   _____

14. When submitting problems to a superior, or when a superior seeks help in solving problems, does this employee submit considered analyses of alternatives (with advantages and disadvantages) and recommend suggestions for solution?   _____

RATINGS

5.0   = *Superior:* a standard of performance that could not be improved upon under any circumstances or conditions known to the rater.

4.0 or 4.5 = *Excellent:* a standard of performance that leaves little of any consequence to be desired.

3.0 or 3.5 = *Good:* a standard of performance above the average and meeting all normal requirements of the position.

2.0 or 2.5 = *Average:* a standard of performance regarded as average for the position involved and the people available.

1.0 or 1.5 = *Fair:* a standard of performance that is below the normal requirements of the position, but one that may be regarded as marginally or temporarily acceptable.

0.0   = *Inadequate:* a standard of performance regarded as unacceptable for the position involved.

From Harold Koontz, *Appraising Managers as Managers*. New York: McGraw-Hill, 1971.

Example 14

This form has good features. First of all, ten significant job segments are listed. Although no standards were established, the various appraisal terms (unsatisfactory, marginal, and so on) are defined. Space is allowed for remarks, and the form would lend itself nicely to a self-appraisal.

The main weakness of the form is its lack of emphasis and specifics in terms of development of the subordinate.

PERFORMANCE | **Engineering Personnel Annual Appraisal**

1 QUALITY OF WORK

UNSATISFACTORY	MARGINAL	ACCEPTABLE	COMMENDABLE	OUTSTANDING
Poor quality of work, continually makes errors, requires excessive checking and rework.	Careless, inclined to make mistakes, work barely acceptable.	Meets minimum requirements of accuracy and neatness, average quality of work, needs normal supervision.	Exceeds minimum requirements of accuracy and neatness, very few errors, carries out instructions well, needs little supervision.	Consistent high degree of accuracy and neatness, work can be relied upon, very little rework, seldom needs supervision.

REMARKS: _____

2 ATTENDANCE

UNSATISFACTORY	MARGINAL	ACCEPTABLE	COMMENDABLE	OUTSTANDING
Often absent or tardy. Does not report absence or tardiness in advance. Very Undependable.	Erratic in attendance and punctuality. Seldom reports absence or tardiness in advance. Not dependable.	Occasionally absent or tardy. Reports absence or tardiness in advance.	Seldom absent or tardy. Always reports absence or tardiness in advance. Dependable.	Excellent attendance record. Always at work and on time. Very dependable.

REMARKS: _____

3 JOB KNOWLEDGE

UNSATISFACTORY	MARGINAL	ACCEPTABLE	COMMENDABLE	OUTSTANDING
Definite lack of knowledge. Very little understanding of job duties. Needs considerable instructions.	Inadequate knowledge of duties. Understanding of job duties not sufficient.	Has adequate knowledge of duties. Needs a little additional instruction.	Good knowledge of duties. Well informed. Occasionally needs direction.	Excellent understanding of job assignments. Requires very little direction. Extremely capable.

REMARKS: _____

4 ATTITUDE

UNSATISFACTORY	MARGINAL	ACCEPTABLE	COMMENDABLE	OUTSTANDING
Difficult to work with. Chip-on shoulder attitude. Uncooperative. Rude.	Occasionally unwilling to follow orders without argument. Inclined to be stubborn.	Tries to cooperate. Usually agreeable and obliging.	Cooperative most of the time. Interested in work. Quick to offer assistance.	Always cooperative. Shows a high interest in work. Goes out of way to help. Pleasant.

REMARKS: _____

5 QUANTITY OF WORK

UNSATISFACTORY	MARGINAL	ACCEPTABLE	COMMENDABLE	OUTSTANDING
Slow worker. Does very little work, wastes time.	Works at a slow pace. Needs encouraging and urging.	Works at a steady pace. Meets minimum requirements.	Works fast. Often exceeds requirements.	Very fast and prompt worker. Consistently exceeds requirements.

REMARKS: _____

6 VERSATILITY

UNSATISFACTORY	MARGINAL	ACCEPTABLE	COMMENDABLE	OUTSTANDING
Seems unable to learn new tasks. Cannot adjust from one job to another. Resists change.	Learns new tasks slowly. Has difficulty in understanding and going from one assignment to another.	Neither slow or fast. Able to perform several related tasks. Handles new assignments with some difficulty.	Catches on fast. Learns new tasks easily. Handles new assignments with minimum amount of difficulty.	Very adaptable and flexible. Masters new tasks easily. Handles various assignments without difficulty.

REMARKS: _____

7 PLANNING

UNSATISFACTORY	MARGINAL	ACCEPTABLE	COMMENDABLE	OUTSTANDING
Is very poorly organized.	Poorly organized. Just gets job duties completed.	Makes some mistakes, but generally is organized in completing tasks.	Very seldom makes mistakes. Most of the time is well organized in completing tasks.	Hardly ever makes a mistake. Always well organized in completing duties.

REMARKS: _____

8 INITIATIVE

UNSATISFACTORY	MARGINAL	ACCEPTABLE	COMMENDABLE	OUTSTANDING
Never volunteers to undertake work. Requires constant prodding to do work. Has no drive or ambition.	Needs some prodding to do work. Dislikes responsibilities. Has very little drive. Believes in just getting by.	Seldom seeks new tasks. Will accept responsibilities when necessary but does not go out of way. Routine worker.	Occasionally seeks new tasks. Works well when given responsibility. Makes occasional suggestion.	Definitely a self-starter. Goes out of way to accept responsibility. Very alert and often constructive.

REMARKS: _____

9 CREATIVITY: Consider whether subject has evidenced imagination and ingenuity in solving problems that accompany job responsibilities.

UNSATISFACTORY	MARGINAL	ACCEPTABLE	COMMENDABLE	OUTSTANDING
Rarely contributes any new ideas or suggestions.	Occasionally contributes some new adaptation of established principles or procedures.	Has been alert to find better ways to carry out responsibilities.	Readily produces new solutions to problems and evidences ingenuity in solving them.	Has produced unique solutions to problems that have application in or beyond the area of job responsibility.

REMARKS: _____

_____

_____

10 PERSONAL APPEARANCE: ☐ Needs Improvement   ☐ Satisfactory

This quality refers to the employee's personal grooming, attire, and overall appearance. Does the employee's personal appearance meet the standards for the job? An employee's attire is usually dictated by the nature of his/her work, which should be considered in evaluating this quality.

_____
Signature of Supervisor

The above rating has been reviewed with me.

_____
Interview date

_____
Signature of employee

11 DISCUSSION

A What does employee feel is necessary to improve his/her efficiency?

_____

_____

_____

B Is employee satisfied with his/her job?

_____

_____

_____

C What can/should be done to improve employee's value as a ▄▄▄▄ employee?

_____

_____

_____

D Goals:

_____

_____

_____

E Additional comments:

_____

_____

_____

_____

Example 15

This set of forms illustrates the principles described in this book. It begins with a blank form that can be used in any department. The specifics in the first two columns (significant job segments and standards of performance) must be developed by boss and subordinate. The appraisal headings are the ones suggested in this book: *does not meet standards, meets standards, exceeds standards*, and *outstanding*. A space for comments is also included.

The second form requires agreement on outstanding performance and performance needing improvement. The development of a specific performance improvement plan is then required for one or possibly two performance areas needing improvement.

The final form is to be completed by the boss. It may or may not be communicated to the subordinate.

NAME _____

SUPERVISOR _____

DATE _____

APPRAISAL OF JOB

SIGNIFICANT JOB SEGMENTS

STANDARDS OF PERFORMANCE
(What conditions will exist when the job
is done in an acceptable manner?)

Significant job segments are discussed between subordinate and immediate supervisor
to reach understanding and agreement.
Standards of performance are developed to correspond with the significant job seg-
ments of Column 1.
Appraisal is made on the basis of standards of performances.
Comments should explain ratings given.

PERFORMANCE   APPRAISAL

Does not meet standards

Meets standards

Exceeds standards

Outstanding

COMMENTS

Appraisal Summary and
Performance Improvement Plan

I. **SUMMARY OF PERFORMANCE APPRAISAL**

A. Outstanding Performance (Order of Priority)

1.

2.

3.

B. Performance Needing Improvement (Order of Priority)

1.

2.

3.

II. **PERFORMANCE IMPROVEMENT PLAN**

Training Need*_____

Action To Be Taken	By Whom	By What Date

*It is strongly suggested that you concentrate on only one need at a time. If you are working on two needs that may be closely related, attach another sheet of paper to this form.

JUDGMENT OF PROMOTABILITY

I. **OVERALL PERFORMANCE ON PRESENT JOB**
(See copy of "Appraisal" form for a complete appraisal.)

☐ Outstanding ☐ Good ☐ Adequate ☐ Unsatisfactory

II. **PROMOTABILITY**

A. Estimate of level

☐ 1. Has potential for promotion to two or more levels above present job.

☐ 2. Has potential for pomotion to next higher level only.

☐ 3. Currently limited to present job.

☐ 4. Present level is too challenging.

B. Readiness for promotion (check only if A "1" or "2" was checked above).

☐ 1. Is ready for promotion now.
To what kind of job(s)?

☐ 2. Will be ready in two years or less.
What kind of training and experience is needed?

☐ 3. Will require more than two years.
What kind of training and experience is needed?

(Use back of page for additional comments.)

8
Case Study:
A Large Midwestern
Heavy Manufacturing
Organization

This organization developed a comprehensive performance review program in 1979. Details are provided so that the reader can get a picture of the total program including objectives, approaches, forms, and procedures. Practical tips are offered regarding the conducting of interviews as well as coaching and counseling. Not all forms and procedures are included.

In the foreword to the company publication describing its program, the authors quote the following passage from Douglas McGregor:

> In the last analysis the individual must develop himself, and he will do so optimally only in terms of what he sees as meaningful and valuable. If he becomes an active party to the decisions that are made about his development, he is likely to make the most of the opportunities that are presented. If, on the other hand, he is simply a passive agent being rotated or sent to school, or promoted, or otherwise manipulated, he is less likely to be motivated to develop himself.*

They go on to say:

> A business concern succeeds or fails according to the effectiveness or otherwise of the people who comprise its personnel, including its management. There is, therefore, nothing more important in industrial enterprise than the building of an effective workforce. . . . The major test of industrial worth must, of course, always be individual performance. . . . We want to build people—to help them help us and to help themselves. To that end, we will do our best to select, place, and continue employing them: to train, guide, and direct them; to inform, advise, encourage, reward, and caution them.

*Douglas McGregor, *The Human Side of Enterprise*. New York: McGraw-Hill, 1960.

174

Performance reviews in this organization serve four functions: (1) they directly relate compensation recommendations to the individual's contributions to the enterprise; (2) they should help the individual improve performance; (3) they should answer the employee's question, "How am I doing?" and (4) they should give managers data with which they may judge future job assignments.

The process is summarized by the following flow chart. It is important that the first 17 steps be performed to ensure fair treatment of all employees participating in the performance evaluation process. The last three steps are optional.

PERFORMANCE EVALUATION AND PERFORMANCE IMPROVEMENT PLANNING PROCESS

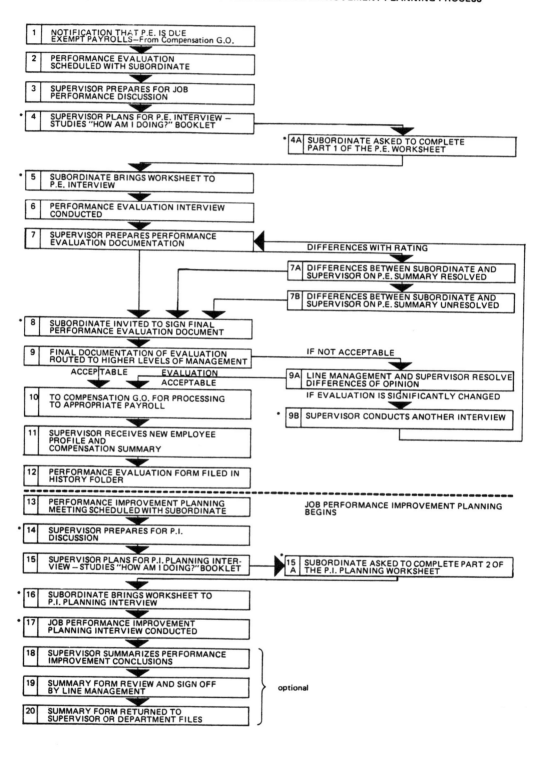

The performance of every employee on the exempt payroll must be evaluated at least annually. Annual Performance Review/Annual Salary Review forms are used for semimonthly and monthly roll employees.

The following elements are essential to an effective evaluation process:

- Performance evaluations must be objective, relevant, timely, results-oriented, and they must contain examples, illustrations and measurements to substantiate the evaluation.
- The appraisal interview should be well planned — with notes, facts and background data on observed and measured performance to permit a discussion which should summarize a continuing dialogue between supervisor and employee.
- The job-centered evaluation interview should be private, participatory, and conducted in a manner that will achieve a mutual understanding of the job requirements and how well the employee has satisfied these job requirements.
- A documented performance evaluation summary should be made of the job-centered evaluation interview between the employee and his or her supervisor for future reference and benefit to the employee, supervisor and other managers of the company.

Let's look at the sequential steps in the performance evaluation and performance improvement planning process and at the supervisor's responsibilities in carrying them out.

1	NOTIFICATION THAT P.E. IS DUE EXEMPT PAYROLLS — From Compensation G.O.

The process begins when you are notified that an employee is due for an evaluation.

Exempt payrolls — You'll receive copies of the Annual Salary review forms from Compensation G.O. in September of each year, with instructions outlining:

1. Computation of recommended salary action,
2. Preparation of the performance review, and

3.   Due dates for the return of completed Annual Salary and Performance Review forms to Compensation.

These forms (01-846-81799 for Semimonthly and 01-846-80662 for Monthly Payroll) are preprinted to include employee identification, position title, salary ranges and the current performance increase percentages that will assist you in preparing the Annual Salary and Performance Reviews.

Steps 2 through 4A outline the procedures to be followed by supervisor and subordinate to prepare for the performance evaluation interview.

As part of the evaluation process, supervisors will find it helpful to give the employee an opportunity to complete the Employee's Performance Evaluation Worksheet, Part 1. It permits the employee to prepare for the performance evaluation interview, and thus become a participant in the evaluation discussion by providing valuable input. As part of the supervisor's preparation, supervisors are encouraged to review any pertinent data, including reports, progress reports on objectives, notes, incident reports, or the judgment of others familiar with the performance of the employee, in preparation for conducting a job-related performance discussion with the employee. Objectivity is the key to fair, effective performance evaluation.

2	PERFORMANCE EVALUATION SCHEDULED WITH SUBORDINATE

A mutually convenient time is scheduled by the supervisor to meet with the subordinate. It is also appropriate at this step to introduce the subordinate to Part 1 of the Performance Evaluation Worksheet, encouraging him or her to complete it before the interview. Allow sufficient time between the introduction of the worksheet and the interview for adequate subordinate preparation to take place.

3	SUPERVISOR PREPARES FOR JOB PERFORMANCE DISCUSSION

The supervisor prepares for a job performance discussion with the employee by gathering together and organizing information about the employee's performance, utilizing performance measurements, observations, notes, facts, reports, consultations with others, critical incident notes, progress reports on objectives — whatever background material is most appropriate — for a factual, job-centered discussion. (The performance evaluation summary is not completed until *after* the performance discussion with the employee.)

*	4	SUPERVISOR PLANS FOR P.E. INTERVIEW — STUDIES "HOW AM I DOING?" BOOKLET

The supervisor plans the evaluation interview. If necessary, the supervisor reviews the "How Am I Doing?" booklet (included as Appendix A) on how to conduct an effective performance evaluation interview. A time and place for an unhurried, uninterrupted discussion has been selected. The supervisor develops a plan for the interview with major points to be made, views to be explored, and the sequence of discussion and tentative conclusions identified. Part 1 of the Worksheet may be used to lead the format of the discussion.

*	4A	SUBORDINATE ASKED TO COMPLETE PART 1 OF THE P.E. WORKSHEET

The subordinate's involvement in the process begins when the supervisor requests that the subordinate complete Part 1 of the Performance Evaluation Worksheet. The worksheet gives the subordinate an opportunity to prepare for the interview. The performance evaluation will be more complete, job-related, factual and valid if the subordinate is invited to provide input to the process. This input can best be developed if approached in an organized way. Part 1 of the Performance Evaluation and Performance Improvement Worksheet has been provided for this purpose. Part 2 of the Worksheet is for use by the subordinate during the subsequent Performance Improvement Planning Interview and is discussed in Step 15A.

*	5	SUBORDINATE BRINGS WORKSHEET TO P.E. INTERVIEW

At the time of the interview, both employee and supervisor may refer to a copy of Part 1 of the Performance Evaluation Worksheet and any notes providing meaningful input to the discussion.

6	PERFORMANCE EVALUATION INTERVIEW CONDUCTED

The purpose of the interview is to allow an exchange of communication so that the supervisor can provide full and accurate documentation of the employee's progress during the past year.

The performance evaluation interview is conducted by the employee's immediate supervisor. Supervisors should plan to provide suitable private arrangements for the interview. Employees should be encouraged during the interview to raise questions and to comment on results and events, circumstances or working conditions affecting those results. The supervisor should be prepared to answer questions about the employee's readiness for future positions and any other such questions that may be raised. The purpose of having a discussion with the subordinate prior to preparing final documentation is that it will permit you as a supervisor to develop a more valid, complete, accurate results-oriented performance evaluation.

7	SUPERVISOR PREPARES PERFORMANCE EVALUATION DOCUMENTATION

Documentation of the evaluation is prepared by the supervisor, who must exercise great care in objectively weighing his or her summary. The summary is prepared on a blue form for semimonthly roll employees and on a buff colored form for monthly roll. The "Overall Performance Summary and Comments on Above Rating" (Outstanding, Merit or Special Action) provides space to state the facts of the past year's performance and to substantiate the reasons for the rating you provided. In documenting the performance review, consider the subordinate's input and include all pertinent reasons for the results of the review. Additional sheets may be attached to complete the summary.

7A	DIFFERENCES BETWEEN SUBORDINATE AND SUPERVISOR ON P.E. SUMMARY RESOLVED	7B	DIFFERENCES BETWEEN SUBORDINATE AND SUPERVISOR ON P.E. SUMMARY UNRESOLVED

Differences of opinion regarding the subordinate's performance may arise during the interview or during the follow-up interview (Step 8) when you review the final performance evaluation summary with the subordinate. These differences should be discussed, and if possible, resolved. You may or may not wish to revise your summary as a result of a discussion of these differences. If no revision takes place, and the subordinate still disagrees with the summary, his or her opinion should be noted in the summary.

*	8	SUBORDINATE INVITED TO SIGN FINAL PERFORMANCE EVALUATION DOCUMENT

The summary of the performance evaluation should be communicated to the subordinate, making sure that the subordinate understands the reasons why his or her performance was evaluated as it was. At the conclusion of the discussion about the summary, the employee should be asked to acknowledge that the evaluation was shown and fully communicated, and he/she should be requested to sign the evaluation summary. The employee should be told that the signature does not necessarily represent agreement with the evaluation. It simply indicates that the evaluation was communicated and an interview took place. If the subordinate believes the appraisal does not accurately reflect performance, and such disagreement has not been resolved by the supervisor, the subordinate may add such comments to the Performance Evaluation form, or a comment sheet may be attached before routing the final document up the line for approval. This process will give higher levels of management an opportunity to follow up on the appraisal as the evaluation is now routed to them. The supervisor may also note that the subordinate has not signed the summary but has been advised of its contents. Whether the employee reads, reads and signs, or receives a copy is not critical. What is critical is full communication of the contents of the evaluation. The objective is to achieve a mutual understanding — if not agreement — on the supervisor's evaluation of performance results. A discussion of salary adjustment is inappropriate at this time.

9	FINAL DOCUMENTATION OF EVALUATION ROUTED TO HIGHER LEVELS OF MANAGEMENT

Routinely, the final documentation presented on the Annual Performance Review form is routed up the line to management for review and approval. While no formal appeal process is provided in the current performance evaluation process, if exceptions are noted by higher management, either because of the contents of the summary as prepared by the supervisor or comments of the subordinate noted in the summary, follow up is initiated at this level.

9A	LINE MANAGEMENT AND SUPERVISOR RESOLVE DIFFERENCES OF OPINION	* 9B	SUPERVISOR CONDUCTS ANOTHER INTERVIEW

Higher management and the supervisor get together at this time to resolve differences of opinion. When the disagreement by higher management levels results in a request to the immediate supervisor to make a significant adjustment to the ratings, the supervisor must have another interview with the subordinate to fully communicate this revised evaluation and the basis for the change. The purpose of complete and candid communications at each step in the appraisal process is to assure that the final evaluation and resultant salary action will be no surprise to the employee.

10	TO COMPENSATION G.O. FOR PROCESSING TO APPROPRIATE PAYROLL

The performance evaluation review process is almost complete now. Final documentation on the performance evaluation and recommended salary action (if a salary adjustment is involved) acceptable to higher levels of line management, is forwarded to Compensation Department, G.O. for processing by the appropriate payroll. It is still too early, however, to indicate any salary action to the subordinate, since many factors can influence the final salary adjustment. You will be notified by payroll of the amount and effective date of the salary adjustment.

| 11 | SUPERVISOR RECEIVES NEW EMPLOYEE PROFILE AND A COMPENSATION SUMMARY |

The new profile contains all the new data elements for historical purposes, including new salary, effective date and the relevant action codes for the particular salary action. A Compensation Summary is sent to supervisors of exempt payroll personnel, and this document notifies the supervisor that new salary information may now be communicated to the subordinate.

| 12 | PERFORMANCE EVALUATION FORM FILED IN HISTORY FOLDER |

The performance evaluation forms are then filed in the individual employee's history folder. Worksheets used by the employee and supervisor need not be retained; their function has been fulfilled. They may be destroyed following the final completion of the Overall Performance Summary.

Written performance evaluations should be periodic, factual, objective records of job-centered discussions between employee and supervisor. After approval by management in the line organization and required processing, if salary adjustments or changes in job status are involved, the performance evaluation is placed in the employee's history folder. Although the evaluations are not removed from the folder until the end of the relevant retention period — five years for weekly salary roll employees and ten years for exempt salary roll employees — the entire folder is available for review by management on the basis of "need to know."

Since the annual performance review primarily serves salary administration purposes, separate discussions between supervisor and subordinate should be conducted to plan for improved performance. Experience has shown that it is simply not effective to attempt to accomplish both functions — Performance Evaluation and Performance Improvement Planning — at the same time or during a single discussion.

| 13 | PERFORMANCE IMPROVEMENT PLANNING MEETING SCHEDULED WITH SUBORDINATE |

The performance improvement planning interview may be scheduled by the supervisor at the conclusion of the interview, when final documentation is reviewed about the subordinate's past performance. Or, the supervisor can set up the interview independent of this activity. It is probably wise to schedule the meeting as soon after the final interview as possible, however, so that both supervisor and subordinate have in mind the priorities established by their meetings during the review.

Steps 14, 15 and 15A outline the steps the supervisor and subordinate take to prepare for the planning interview. Again, preparation by both parties is the key to a successful interview.

| * | 14 | SUPERVISOR PREPARES FOR P.I. DISCUSSION |

The supervisor begins preparation for the planning interview by reviewing the summary of the employee's past performance and any other data about the employee's past and present status. The supervisor may also find it useful to complete Part 2 of the Planning Worksheet, keeping the growth and development plans of the subordinate in mind. As part of his or her preparation for the interview, the supervisor's answers should be based on how he or she perceives the subordinate's improvement needs, growth, and development potential. Answers should also be based on *how* the subordinate may achieve those goals and performance improvements. The purpose of this joint worksheet effort is to prepare for a discussion, at which time supervisor and subordinate will develop a mutual understanding of the subordinate's job responsibilities, improvement plans for the next review period, growth and development plans for the subordinate, if they exist, and ways in which the employee may achieve them. The supervisor and subordinate should also determine how the subordinate's performance results will be measured at the next performance evaluation. Reference to notes made on Part 1 used during the earlier performance evaluation discussion may be useful here.

15	SUPERVISOR PLANS FOR P.I. PLANNING INTERVIEW — STUDIES "HOW AM I DOING?" BOOKLET	*	15A	SUBORDINATE ASKED TO COMPLETE PART 2 OF THE P.I. PLANNING WORKSHEET

The supervisor can review the "How Am I Doing?" booklet or other coaching and counseling material before conducting the performance improvement planning interview. Preparation for the performance improvement planning part of the process for the subordinate begins when the subordinate completes Part 2 of the Performance Improvement Planning Worksheet. The sections of this worksheet focus on the short- and long-term future — improvement plans and growth and development goals. These are distinct from the items covered in the performance evaluation process which was a summary of accomplishments during the past review period. Part 2 of the Worksheet may be introduced to the subordinate at the time the performance improvement planning interview is scheduled. Sufficient time should be allowed to elapse for preparation by both supervisor and subordinate.

While Caterpillar believes employee development *opportunities* must be available to all, in practical terms this must mean *all who seek development*. Therefore, this process must be voluntary; if the individual does not wish to complete this part of the worksheet, particularly those elements dealing with improvement planning for the future, little purpose will be served by forcing him or her to go through the motions. Nevertheless, it is important to conduct the interview regardless of the subordinate's attitude toward the worksheet.

*	16	SUBORDINATE BRINGS WORKSHEET TO P.I. PLANNING INTERVIEW

The subordinate brings the worksheet and other notes to the performance improvement planning interview with the supervisor. If the subordinate does not choose to complete the worksheet, this does not eliminate either the need for a supervisor-subordinate discussion or the need for the employee's supervisor to explore the general subject of improving present job performance and assuring mutual understanding of current job responsibilities.

*	17	JOB PERFORMANCE IMPROVEMENT PLANNING INTERVIEW CONDUCTED

Both the supervisor and subordinate have completed their preparation based on independent analysis and evaluation. They are ready to share this information and discuss what is needed to improve results, and to plan any effort aimed at job performance improvement, future growth and individual development. Since the first questions seek agreement on current work objectives, key job elements, and measurement of results, the process automatically requires annual update and may be done either during the objective-setting process or immediately following approval of the annual performance review.

The remaining steps in the cycle are optional and may be used at the supervisor's discretion. However, it is recommended that these last three steps be included in the Performance Evaluation and Performance Improvement Planning Process whever possible. They round out the cycle in an organized manner and aid the supervisor in the beginning of the next measurement period.

18	SUPERVISOR SUMMARIZES PERFORMANCE IMPROVEMENT CONCLUSIONS

Following the discussion between supervisor and subordinate, the supervisor may use the Supervisor's Summary to summarize conclusions reached. This will become a working document and should be retained by the supervisor for future reference. It should serve to follow progress on objectives achieved and improvement plans accomplished.

The supervisor may also comment on the employee's readiness for other assignments, and promotability to the next level in the same function. Or the supervisor may define personal goals and objectives as indicated by the employee during the discussion.

19	SUMMARY FORM REVIEW AND SIGN OFF BY LINE MANAGEMENT

Completed Supervisor's Summary forms used in the performance improvement planning process are to be signed by both the employee and supervisor and may be routed for review to higher levels of supervision. The extent to which they are routed for review is at the discretion of the administrative head.

20	SUMMARY FORM RETURNED TO SUPERVISOR OR DEPARTMENT FILES

If reviewed by higher levels of management, the summary will be returned to the employee's supervisor to serve as a working tool for follow up on improvement commitments and to assist in monitoring progress toward work objectives.

Worksheets used by both the employee and the supervisor in developing their plans need not be retained; their function is to develop a meaningful performance improvement interview. They may be destroyed following the completion of the supervisor's summary or the conclusion of Step 17, the performance improvement planning interview.

Conclude this step by answering any questions the participants may have concerning the steps in the Performance Evaluation and Performance Improvement Planning Process.

Step 3 — Preparing for the Performance Evaluation Interview

Participants read Step 3 narrative.

HOW TO CONDUCT AN EFFECTIVE PERFORMANCE
EVALUATION INTERVIEW

There are three main steps: *Preparation, The Interview,* and *Follow-up.*

To obtain maximum benefits from the discussion — and to avoid an embarrassing and fruitless interview — carefully prepare a plan for discussion. As the first step in getting ready for an evaluation interview, both you and your subordinate should understand clearly what is expected in terms of results. There should be an awareness, *in advance,* of what the conditions, facts, results, and figures will be which indicate when a job is well done.

PREPARATION

Plan the meeting. Identify the key functions of the incumbent's job. Treat each key function as factually and impersonally as you would any business problem or objective.

- Have your performance expectations well in mind. Determine your subordinate's performance relative to your expectations. Have your background material well organized: agreed-upon objectives, standards of performance, results, facts, figures, data, reports, feedback from others, etc.

- Avoid speculating about the individual's personality or lifestyle. Avoid thinking about the kind of person he/she is. Avoid butting into things that are none of your business. Think and talk only about the individual's performance and accomplishments. This is your business as a manager.

Plan the content

- How you will tell the individual "how well he/she is doing."

- How you will *measure* each performance objective.

- How you will present and explain each performance *measurement.*

- In what sequence you will take up the various points.

- Be prepared with facts, results, measurements, examples, incidents to support any statements made during the interview.

Think about the employee's performance

- Think through, in objective terms, what you expect of the employee in this position. What *results* do you expect in each of the work areas for which he/she is responsible? What measurements do you and the employee have at hand to determine how well he/she is doing? Review the position description, job objectives, performance standards, and related operating records, such as budgets, long and short range plans. Review again such documents as personnel data sheet, employee record, employee's profile or Skills Inventory, as necessary, to refresh your memory on education, training and experience, both inside and outside the company.

- What results are being attained? *How* is he or she doing in each area of responsibility? Are there functions in which he or she is doing too well to the neglect of other important functions? Make notes of specific examples for your discussion of accomplishments and areas of less than satisfactory accomplishment.

- Determine what needs to be said during the discussion: The opening, the most effective approaches, the possible reactions (yours and the employee's). Tailor your approach to the employee and the situation. Get ready to listen with interest and understanding to what he or she has to say.

Make the necessary arrangements

- Select a time and place that will be convenient, completely private and comfortable.

- Be prepared to allow plenty of time for uninterrupted discussion. Avoid scheduling the meeting during a period of unusual stress, or too soon after any upsetting experience.

THE INTERVIEW

The main purpose of the interview is to come to an understanding, if not agreement, on the general level of performance during the period under review. Before getting into the specific things you talk over, here is a general pattern you might like to follow:

The general pattern

—   *Tell effectively* so that the subordinate understands you. Among the keys to effective telling are getting your own thoughts clear and knowing the individual.

—   *Be a good listener* so that you understand. Get the employee to talk! Listening is your opportunity to observe areas of agreement and to spot important differences. It enables you to check whether you are really understood. It gives the employee a chance to think things through. Summarize what he or she has said, before you go on, to be sure you've got it right.

—   *Discuss to agreement.* When you understand each other, you are ready for this final step. Bring important differences into the open, one by one.

  •   Be sure each difference really exists and that you know exactly what it is. If there is any doubt, encourage the individual to say more about the issue. Listen! You may learn something!

  •   Decide where you can concede and where a firm stand is necessary.

  •   Reconcile as many differences as possible.

  •   If your initial efforts to resolve a difference fail:

    1.   Summarize the status of the difference. Then table the issue temporarily so you can move on to other matters. Agree to resume it, either later in the meeting or on a specified date.

2.   Remember that *complete* agreement is not necessary for sound, give-and-take working relationships, provided we respect differences which cannot be resolved.

This pattern — *Tell, Listen, Discuss to Agreement* — is worth remembering. It is what we mean by "talking person-to-person." It is a way of exploring differences sincerely and honestly, to arrive at a conclusion which satisfies both of you to the fullest possible extent. Use it every time you have something important to tell the individual.

— *Get off to a good start.*

- Warm up.

- Begin in a natural way. Be sincere and objective. Your knowledge of the employee and of his/her functions in the organization will dictate a common ground on which you may meet in a natural way.

- Relax. Show your respect and general approval.

- Express confidence in his/her ability to develop. Be careful not to overstate and, consequently, mislead.

— *Tell the employee where he/she stands.*

- Convey the general impression of the performance evaluation. Begin by stating the extent to which you and your supervisor are satisfied with his/her performance. Then briefly comment on progress, future prospects and value to the organization, if it contributes to the overall evaluation you want to get across.

- Mention a few significant strengths which you honestly feel this individual has. Others will ordinarily come up when you discuss specific areas of performance.

— *Discuss one major area of performance at a time.*

- Discuss results and accomplishments against objectives, or

- Discuss results and accomplishments against principal accountabilities of the job description, or

- Discuss results and accomplishments against agreed-upon standards of performance.

- Be specific on areas of performance and accomplishments expected and measurements used.

- Clarify each objective of performance and be sure it is understood. There are several ways to do this:

  - Cite specific instances where he or she performed more nearly as you expect.

  - Discuss situations coming up where the individual will have a chance to show what he or she can do.

  - Arrange follow-up meetings to further clarify more complex objectives. Remind the employee that a future discussion will concentrate on improvement plans and development ideas.

  - Get the subordinate to talk.

— *Agree on action.*

Ordinarily, if you are using the Tell, Listen, Discuss pattern, you will end up with agreement on the plan you propose, or on a new and better one. But there are other possibilities:

- He or she may agree to give your proposals a try, despite reservations.

- The individual may think he or she is already performing the way you described. If so, agree to watch performance more closely to determine the facts.

- You may find it is desirable for the employee to develop the plan, despite your reservations. Set a date for consideration of the proposed plan.

- Whatever the outcome, depend upon follow-up to insure achievement of each performance objective.

— *Conclude the meeting.*

- Sum up. Some of the things that were said in the early part of the meeting may now be vague.

- Reassure. Some tension will inevitably build up during the meeting. Therefore, express honestly your satisfaction with the meeting and your confidence in the individual.

- End the meeting on a positive note. Let the employee know your emphasis is on the future. This will help channel his or her thoughts and energies in positive and constructive directions.

FOLLOW-UP

Time may easily erase the good effects of even the best of meetings. Therefore, follow-up is an essential of performance counseling. Here is what you do:

— Observe performance and progress with respect to objectives. The mere fact that you notice will make a big difference to him or her.

— Commend instances of good performance and progress as they occur. This is your most powerful device for performance improvement. It lets the employee know he or she is on the right track and stimulates effort to do better.

— Correct failures to measure up as they occur. Discuss these instances thoroughly and constructively so that the individual will learn how to handle them better the next time.

— Correcting is less effective than commending, since it may lead to fear and discouragement. It has its place nonetheless.

  • The extent to which you can correct mistakes without ill effects depends largely on the recognition given for jobs well done.

— Encourage. Changing habits and improving upon established ways of doing things are not easy. A word of encouragement from you will often keep an employee trying.

  • Encouragement will soon lose its effectiveness, however, if no real progress is made.

  • Therefore, prevent the individual from becoming discouraged by actually stimulating progress. Commend better performances even if they are not up to your standards when they represent an effort to improve. Discuss these performances to help him or her understand how they could be handled better.

— Teach *by example* in your own daily performance. This helps clarify the kind of performance you expect. It shows that you consider what you preach important enough to practice it.

— Follow-up counsel. Occasionally, review the whole picture, modifying plans as required.

— Keep your commitments, and see that the individual's commitments are kept also.

HOW TO CONDUCT AN EFFECTIVE PERFORMANCE IMPROVEMENT PLANNING INTERVIEW

As in the Performance Evaluation interview, there are three main steps: *Preparation, The Interview,* and *Follow-up.*

The previous discussion on Performance Evaluation was confined to developing an understanding on the general level of past job performance and accomplishments. We are now going to look ahead.

PREPARATION

To plan for this interview, both the employee and the supervisor may use worksheets containing identical questions (See Appendix B for samples). These are questions dealing with current job performance and questions dealing with future improvement. Best results will be achieved if both the employee and supervisor bring completed worksheets to the performance improvement planning interview. If the employee does not choose to complete the worksheet, this does *not* eliminate either the need for a supervisor-employee discussion or the need for the supervisor to explore the general subject of improving present job performance and/or assuring mutual understanding of current job responsibilities and performance objectives for the next review period.

Plan the meeting

Treat each development objective as factually and as impersonally as you would any business problem or objective.

- Have a summary of the previous performance evaluation well in mind.

- Think about what performance improvements are important to your function and the company.

- Consider how you and the subordinate can bring about the desired improvements. Plan how the improvement objectives can be reached. Such plans should include the initial meeting and follow-up, whether or not additional actions, such as courses of study or special assignments, are required.

- Avoid speculating about the individual's personality. Think only about performance improvement and growth plans.

Plan the content

- How will you summarize the most recent performance evaluation? (as lead-in to job improvement discussion.)

- How will you set performance improvements for the next evaluation?

- How will you establish work objectives for the next period?

- What are your thoughts on development objectives for this individual?

- In what sequence will you take up the various points on your worksheet?

- How will you present and explain each development objective?

- Be prepared with facts, results, measurements, examples, incidents to support any statements made during the interview.

- Complete PART II, Employee's Performance Improvement Planning Worksheet, as you believe it applies to the employee, and ask the employee to do the same, as preparation for your discussion.

Think about the employee's development needs in terms of job performance

- Think through in objective terms what you expect of the employee in this position. What results do you expect in each of the work areas for which he/she is responsible? What measurements do you and the employee have available to determine how well he/she is doing? Does an analysis of these suggest development needs? Review position description, job objectives, performance standards and related operating records. Do these help identify development needs? Review again such documents as employee profile, skills inventory, and personnel data forms, as necessary, to refresh your memory on education, training and experience, both inside and outside the company.

- What results are being achieved? How is he/she doing in each area of responsibility? Make notes of examples of specific accomplishments and areas where greater accomplishment would be desirable.

- Think through what *you* are doing to help improve performance. What more can *you* do in delegation, communications, coaching, counseling, facilities, tools, stimulation and recognition? What are you doing, or not doing, that might limit his/her performance?

COACHING AND COUNSELING

WHAT IS IT?

Coaching and counseling is (1) the use of managerial skill (2) to develop self analysis by the subordinate which (3) when combined with the manager's insights and knowledge (4) produces self-understanding on the part of the subordinate, commitment to mutually accepted objectives, and a plan of action for achieving them.

Coaching is distinguished from counseling in that coaching focuses on improving job skills and job knowledge, whereas counseling focuses on resolving problems of attitude and interpersonal deficiencies. In short, to coach is to *train,* to counsel, is to *advise.*

Coaching and counseling is probably the most common form of training in organizational use today. Formal training programs, seminars, conferences, meetings of one kind or another are all done intermittently from time to time in most organizations. But coaching and counseling is done every day, probably even several times each day. And it's done not only by professional trainers, but by managers, supervisors and executives of every kind, function, and level. It's important that it be done right.

In the broadest sense, any contact between a supervisor and a subordinate for purposes of developing the subordinate can be called coaching and counseling. But, generally, the term is used in a somewhat narrower sense, to refer to a specific kind of development — improving skills and knowledge. The table below shows how coaching and counseling is normally distinguished from the *less* formal daily contacts between boss and subordinate and the *more* formal annual performance evaluation.

Three Kinds of Subordinate Development Methods			
Type	Daily or Periodic Contacts	Coaching and Counseling	Annual Performance Evaluation
Nature	Informal	Semiformal	Formal
Subjects	Immediate problems and decisions, organization information	Skills, knowledge, progress toward objectives	Performance on objectives, new objectives, growth and development plans
Time Orientation	Immediate resolution	Measure immediate past performance. Improve immediate future performance	Measure past year's performance against objectives and other job requirements
Duration of Contact	Few minutes	Minutes to hour	Matter of hours

HOW DOES A MANAGER DO IT?

After all, it's a fairly simple matter to chew out and bully a subordinate, or to hem and haw and refuse to come to grips with issues, or to sweet-talk a subordinate and pretend there are only silver clouds, no linings. *But,* how does a manager go about communicating with a subordinate so as to produce optimal improvement in the subordinate's performance or attitude and, thereby, improvement in *results?*

To answer that, it should be observed that coaching and counseling is a four-phase process that follows a very deliberate and systematic process — *when it is done right.* The phases are:

1.   Preparation
2a.. Coaching: Identifying improvement areas
2b.   Coaching: Action planning
3.   Follow through

PREPARATION

Effective coaching stays in close touch with the real world. The manager doesn't waste time talking to subordinates about their performance as he/she *assumes* it to be; they are counseled about their performance as he/she *observes* and *measures* it. The manager approaches a coaching session armed with facts, data, records, evidence and gets this evidence by doing good, hard planning and preparation.

Then the manager *evaluates* his/her information and puts it in perspective. Before the manager can plan to "tell it like it is" he/she must first *learn it like it is.* That's what preparation for coaching is all about.

IDENTIFYING IMPROVEMENT AREAS

The next phase is the actual coaching session — the face-to-face meeting in which manager and subordinate grapple with this question: How is the subordinate doing, and how can he/she do even better? The coaching session is a two-part session because it tries to answer a two-part question. The first part (how is the subordinate doing?) underlies the first stage of the coaching session (identifying improvement areas); the second part (how can the person do better?) underlies the second stage (action planning).

If you don't know where you're going, any route will get you there; and in order to develop a route, you first have to know where you're at *now.* So the manager devotes the first stage of the coaching session to determining — with the subordinate's help — where they're at — how they're doing, where they most need to improve, what the priorities are.

Some suggestions at this point:

a.   The manager should explain the purpose of the sessions with the subordinate in terms that *mean something* to the subordinate.

b.   The manager should find out how the subordinate thinks he/she is doing — by asking. The manager digs and probes for evidence and words to know *why* the subordinate sees him/herself in a certain way. (It would be well, then, if the subordinate also *prepared* for the session.) The manager listens carefully — at a thinking level.

c.   The manager then responds to the subordinate's views as objectively as possible, setting forth pluses and minuses, explaining how the pluses can be maintained or strengthened and assigning priorities to the minuses.

d.   Now the subordinate and manager are ready to compare their views — drawing whatever conclusions appear justified. The whole idea is to get at the truth of the matter. It requires openness, candor, objectivity.

e.   It's unrealistic to expect anyone to change many aspects of behavior at one time — it's more realistic to concentrate on a few changes that really count. The two should set priorities on those improvements most significant to better *results.*

f.   Improvement priorities should be written — commitment to paper lends permanence to them. At this point, manager and subordinate have agreed on *what* needs to be done — they haven't discussed *how* to do it.

ACTION PLANNING

The manager now asks the subordinate for *specific* ideas on how to effect the improvements they've agreed on. Next, the manager presents his/her own ideas about what needs to be done, being as specific as the subordinate is expected to be. When possible, the manager *quantifies* how much of what, when, at what cost, and under what conditions. There is a difference between lecturing and action planning. Lecturing relies on vague complaining to "do better." The question is *how.* Detailed action planning can answer that.

At this point two action plans have been put forward: the subordinate's and the manager's. Now the manager asks the subordinate to compare them. Out of this comparison comes a specific action plan — a plan of improvement for the priority areas. The subordinate commits it to writing and, finally, the two agree on a review date.

REVIEW AND FOLLOW THROUGH

Before the follow-up session, the manager collects data about how the subordinate is doing — getting as much from direct observation as possible and reviewing whatever performance records are available.

The review session itself begins with the manager explaining its two-fold purpose: (1) to find out what problems the subordinate may be having in implementing the plan of action and (2) to find out if the plan is proving workable, and to change or revise it if necessary. The review/follow-up session focuses on *both* the subordinate and the plan of action. If the plan isn't working, the fault may be with the subordinate, with the plan, or with both.

The subordinate is then asked to summarize the priorities and the action plan — and what should have been done to achieve them. Now is the time to clear up any misunderstanding . . . if such should exist.

Next, the manager asks the subordinate's opinion of how he/she is doing, probing *specifics.*

Having heard the subordinate's thinking, the manager offers his/her thinking, backing it up with examples.

Now the manager asks the subordinate to compare the two analyses. Then the two try to agree on what (if anything) needs to be done differently . . . and they may hammer out changes in the action plan, they may modify objectives, they may realign priorities. The purpose is to emerge from the review with an updated action plan that fits *today's* realities . . . and tomorrow's *anticipated* realities.

Finally, the two agree on a *new* review date. Like the predecessor, today's action plan is not cast in concrete. It is considered a working tool and if it doesn't work as well as it should, then it, too, will be reviewed.

Ideally, what kind of results would a manager like to get out of effective coaching and counseling?

Ideally, managers would hope to achieve the following results:

1.   Improved performance

2.   An improved working relationship with the subordinate.

3.   Subordinate self-discovery — how he/she is *really* doing on the job and how it can be done better.

4.   Subordinate growth and development.

SUMMARY

Coaching and counseling, or training and advising, only *sounds* easy. It is not. Similar to performance evaluations, it is, in fact, one of the toughest jobs confronting any manager. But it is a job that must be done and done well if maximum benefits are going to accrue to the organization.

PERFORMANCE EVALUATION AND PERFORMANCE IMPROVEMENT WORKSHEET

NAME _____   JOB TITLE: _____   DATE _____

The performance evaluation process helps both you and the organization. Completing this worksheet and referring to it when your supervisor discusses your performance review will contribute to your appraisal in three ways:

- It will assure your viewpoints are considered as your performance is appraised.
- It will help make your appraisal interview more productive.
- It will help in your growth and development planning.

If you need more space, use separate sheet of paper. Be brief — use words and phrases sufficient for discussion reminders.

Section I — Key Job Functions and Responsibilities:

Describe your job as you see it in terms of key functions — In other words, major responsibilities, primary duties, important functions. Some questions to help identify key functions: What results are expected? What does your supervisor emphasize? On what things do you spend time and effort? What important things wouldn't get done if your job didn't exist. What were your objectives for this year? What were your major supervisory responsibilities (if you supervise others)?

_____
_____
_____
_____
_____
_____
_____
_____
_____
_____
_____

Section II — Major Contributions:

Review each job function, note your contributions. These may include important problems solved, an idea implemented, a job improvement, accomplishment of objectives or successful completion of a difficult assignment; significant results. Be specific — use as many measurements as possible: How much, of what, at what cost, of what quality, by when, under what circumstances?

_____
_____
_____
_____
_____
_____
_____
_____
_____
_____
_____

Section III — Performance Difficulties:

Review job functions; note "trouble spots" — things that made you less effective. Note any support you need. List training or experience needed to achieve better results.
What changes in plans, objectives, projects, occurred unexpectedly?
What new assignments, directions, were assigned to you?
What constraints — time, resources, methods — limited your effectiveness, if any?

_____
_____
_____
_____
_____
_____
_____
_____
_____
_____
_____

EMPLOYEE'S PERFORMANCE IMPROVEMENT PLANNING WORKSHEET

Section IV — Improvement Plans: Thinking through your job functions, objectives, contributions, and performance difficulties of the past year allows sound action planning for next year. As you develop improvement plans, use the following guidelines. Also, improvement plans may become apparent from a review of next year's work objectives.

- Improvement plans should consist of things you can do to increase your effectiveness or remove performance difficulties.
- Improvement plans should be specific enough so that you know when they have been accomplished.
- Improvement plans should indicate whether training or education would be helpful.

You and your supervisor should spend enough time discussing these plans to assure they are realistic and in line with other objectives of your department.

_____

_____

_____

Section V — Growth and Development Goals: Describe your short and middle range development goals. What other jobs do you feel you are qualified to handle? Do you have any other job or location interests you would like to have communicated to your line management?

_____

_____

Section VI — Additional Comments: If there are further questions or points you would like discussed related to your performance improvement plans, note them here.

_____

_____

SUPERVISOR'S SUMMARY OF PERFORMANCE IMPROVEMENT PLAN

EMPLOYEE'S NAME _____ JOB TITLE: _____ DATE _____

Performance Improvement	Results Desired by Management	Action Management will take to help employee achieve improvement goals	Action Employee will take to achieve improvement goals	Completion Date

SIGNATURES:

Employee _____ Date _____ Title _____ date _____

Title _____ date _____

9
Case Study: General Motors Corporation

General Motors Corporation has developed both a supervisor's handbook and a supervisor's guide* describing its appraisal process for salaried employees. Special permission has been received to reproduce parts of these materials for this book. Minor excisions have been made of material that would be of no use to people outside the company.

The supervisor's handbook contains the GM Human Resources Management (HRM) System's standards and procedures for the GM appraisal process. It provides an on-the-job reference to the steps used in the appraisal of salaried employees of General Motors, and it contains samples of all forms used in the appraisal process.

The supervisor's guide is to be used with the supervisor's handbook to help supervisors quickly learn the standards and procedures contained in the handbook and understand their role in the appraisal process. The guide also provides self-instruction exercises and examples that supervisors at General Motors must complete before attending classroom training. These exercises have been omitted here.

Supervisor's Handbook

PERFORMANCE APPRAISAL PROCESS
FOR SALARIED EMPLOYES

Two of the overall goals of the performance appraisal process are to assure that salaried employes receive fair and consistent treatment in all personnel administration decisions relating to them, and to guide their development. To meet these goals, the HRM System sets forth Standards and Procedures encompassing various aspects of personnel administration and development.

The appraisal process, as established by these Standards and Procedures, makes a unique contribution to the achievement of the overall goals of the HRM System. It does this in several ways.

- First, the appraisal process is designed to enhance each employe's understanding of his or her current responsibilities, how his or her current performance is viewed by management, and how effectiveness in current position can be increased.
- Second, it provides each employe the opportunity to express long range career goals and interests, to have this information entered directly to the HRM Inventory for use in personnel administration decisions, and to receive guidance on how to increase his or her chances for fulfilling career interests and goals.
- Third, it assures that data describing each employe's performance, potential, interests, and readiness for other positions will be examined and updated at least annually.

STANDARDS AND PROCEDURES

401 Every employe in a classified salaried position is to be appraised at least annually.
    401.1 The Performance Appraisal Review for Salaried Employes is to be used for annual appraisals.
    401.2 The Corporate appraisal training program, or its equivalent, is to be used to train appraisers.

402 The Performance Appraisal Review is to be completed and signed by the employe's immediate supervisor, and reviewed and signed by the next level of supervision prior to the appraisal interview.
    402.1 As part of the regular annual appraisal process, the supervisor is to give the employe an opportunity to complete the Appraisal Worksheet for Salaried Employes. This is to be done prior to completing the Performance Appraisal Review.
    402.2 The appraiser is encouraged to solicit the judgments of others fa-

miliar with the performance of the employe while completing the Performance Appraisal Review. This may occur prior to, or in conjunction with, the review by the next level of supervision.

403   The appraisal is to be discussed with the employe with respect to job performance.

403.1   The appraisal interview is to be conducted by the employe's immediate supervisor.

403.2   The supervisor is to plan in advance for the interview and provide for suitable private arrangements.

403.3   The Appraisal Worksheet, if completed by the employe, and the Performance Appraisal Review, as completed by the supervisor, are to be available for use by the employe and the supervisor during the interview.

403.4   The employe is to have ample opportunity during the interview to raise questions and to comment on his or her work and working conditions.

403.5   The Overall Performance Description is to be specified for the employe during the appraisal interview.

403.6   The appraiser is to be prepared to discuss his or her views of the employe's career interests, fields of greatest potential, estimate of potential level, readiness for other positions and other such personnel administration questions that may be raised by the employe.

403.7   The employe is to be encouraged to enter comments on the Performance Appraisal Review.

403.8   A summary of the appraisal interview is to be recorded on the Performance Appraisal Review.

404   The employe is to be asked to acknowledge by signature that the appraisal interview was conducted.

404.1   The employe is to be told that the signature does not necessarily represent agreement with the appraisal, but is an indication that the appraisal interview was actually held.

405   The employe's overall performance description, career interests, fields of greatest potential, estimate of potential level, and readiness for other positions are to be identified by standard GM codes on the Appraisal Summary Form for inclusion in the HRM-EIS Inventory.

405.1   The second level supervisor, in consultation with the appraiser and other members of management familiar with the work and background of the employe, is responsible for completing the Appraisal Summary Form.

405.2   Employe interests as specified by the employe are to be entered on the Appraisal Summary Form.

405.3   The employe's fields of greatest potential, estimate of potential level and readiness for other positions may be discussed with the employe at the option of the unit.

405.4   Standard GM codes are found in Appendix B of the Human Resources Management Manual.

406   A probationary employe is to be appraised prior to the end of the third and fifth months of the probationary period. The Performance Appraisal Review is to be used for this appraisal.

407   An employe whose overall performance description is *Needs Much Improvement* is to be appraised using the Performance Improvement Plan until performance reaches a satisfactory level, the employe is placed in a position in which satisfactory performance can be attained, or action is taken to terminate the employe.

407.1   Plans for improving the performance of an employe described as *Needs Much Improvement* are to be discussed with a Personnel Department representative *prior to* the appraisal interview.

407.2   Plans for improving the performance of an employe described as *Needs Slight Improvement* are to be detailed on the Performance Appraisal Review.

408   All completed Performance Appraisal Reviews and Appraisal Summary Forms are to be reviewed and signed by a Personnel Department representative.

408.1   The signature indicates acceptance of the appraisal and that necessary follow-up requirements have been completed.

408.2   The Performance Appraisal Review, the Appraisal Worksheet, and, if used, the Performance Improvement Plan are to be included as part of the employe's permanent personnel records and are to be accessible to the employe upon request.

408.3   After all information from the Appraisal Summary Form has been entered into the HRM-EIS Inventory, the local unit may retain or dispose of form.

408.4   Data generated by special appraisals are to be maintained by the local unit.

408.5   Accumulated statistical data showing how ratings are distributed within a unit will be supplied from the HRM-EIS Inventory on a periodic basis.

STEPS IN THE APPRAISAL PROCESS

Now let's look at the specific steps of the appraisal process, and at your responsibilities in carrying it out.

The numbers shown below in the left hand margin correspond to the numbers on the Appraisal Flow Chart at the end of this Handbook.

(1)   The process begins when you are notified that an employe is due for an appraisal. Local practice will determine how and when such notification is given. You will receive copies of the Appraisal Worksheet for Salaried Employes, shown in Exhibit A, and the Performance Appraisal Review for Salaried Employes, shown in Exhibit B. Examine these documents before proceeding further.

(2) (2A)   The employe's involvement in the process begins when you give the employe the opportunity to complete the Appraisal Worksheet for Salaried Employes. Be sure to provide a copy of the Codes for Fields of Work (Exhibit C) with the Worksheet.

(3) (3A)   The employe returns the Worksheet to you whether or not he or she elected to complete it. Worksheet information will serve as input to you as you complete the Performance Appraisal Review. Every effort should be made to meet with the employe before completing the Performance Appraisal Review to discuss any differences that exist in the definitions of key job elements. If this discussion does not occur before completing the Performance Appraisal Review, it should take place in the appraisal interview.

(4)   You then complete the Performance Appraisal Review according to the instructions in Exhibit D. It is recommended that you consult others at your level who are familiar with the performance of the employe as you complete the appraisal. This is a particularly useful technique to use when appraising higher level employes. Read Exhibit D before continuing further.

(5)   You are now ready to discuss the employe's Performance Appraisal Review with your supervisor if you have not already done so as you completed the form. If you and your supervisor agree the appraisal is an accurate reflection of the employe's performance, each of you signs the form. If the appraisal is not acceptable to your supervisor, the disagreement must be resolved; then the appraisal form is signed.

For employes whose overall job performance is described as *Needs Slight Improvement,* follow the special instructions in Exhibit D for completing the Action Plans section of the Performance Appraisal Review.

(6) (6A)   If an employee's overall job performance is described as *Needs Much Improvement,* the Personnel Department is contacted and a Performance Improvement Plan shown in Exhibit E is completed prior to the appraisal interview. Examine Exhibit E. The complete procedure for dealing with employes needing much improvement is found in Exhibit F.

(7)   You then inform the employe of the upcoming appraisal interview, and arrange for a time and location for the interview. Additionally, you should let the employe know generally what will be discussed in the interview. Sufficient advance notice should be allowed to permit the employe to prepare for the interview.

(8)   You are now ready to plan the appraisal interview. You should outline the significant points to be discussed and gather information or illustrations that help explain the appraisal.

(9)   You and employe meet at the designated time and place for the appraisal interview. During the interview you should:
- Explain the purpose of the interview (an appraisal of the employe's job performance).
- Discuss the employe's key job elements if this was not done previously.
- Discuss the comments you have entered in the Performance Summary section for each key job element. As you do so, be sure the employe understands your performance standards or expectations for each key job element and the reasons why you appraised his or her performance as you did.
- Discuss Action Plans for both the supervisor and the employe.
- Discuss training needs of the employe.
- Obtain information about the employe's job interests and/or career objectives for subsequent inclusion on the Appraisal Summary Form.
- Answer any questions the employe may have.

The interview should be conducted in a relaxed atmosphere. If the employe has completed the Appraisal Worksheet, every entry should be thoroughly discussed. The appraisal interview should be a two way discussion about the job, current performance, and career interests. The employe should feel free to ask questions, make comments, and agree or disagree during the entire interview.

(10)   The employe should be encouraged to write comments on the Performance Appraisal Review and asked to sign the form. As Appraisal Standard 404.1 states, this is an acknowledgment by the employe that an appraisal interview was conducted. It should be made clear that the signature does not necessarily imply agreement with the appraisal.

(10A)   If the employe believes the appraisal does not accurately reflect his or her performance and the two of you cannot resolve the disagreement, the employe should be encouraged to initiate the open door policy in his or her line organization. If the disagreement cannot be resolved in the line organization via the open door policy, the employe can request that the Personnel Department review the appraisal. If the employe wishes to appeal the appraisal, a representative of the Personnel Department will review the appraisal and the situation surrounding it. If the Personnel representative finds justification for the employe's point of view, the supervisor will be asked to re-appraise the employe and conduct another appraisal interview.

(11)   Based on the information obtained during the interview and your personal knowledge of the employe, summarize the major points discussed in the interview, the employe's feelings about his or her job objectives, preferred areas of work, and related matters. This summary is to be written on the Performance Appraisal Review in the space provided.

(12)   Next, your supervisor in consultation with you and other members of management familiar with the performance, background, and experience of the employe are to complete the Appraisal Summary Form shown in Exhibit G. Experience in a number of units suggests that ratings of Fields of Greatest Potential, Estimate of Potential Level, and Readiness for Other Positions can be substantially improved if multiple judgments are obtained.

(13)   The Performance Appraisal Review, Appraisal Summary Form, and Appraisal Worksheet are sent to the Personnel Department, where they are reviewed to ensure that the appraisal was conducted according to HRM Standards and Procedures. The forms are then signed by a Personnel representative to indicate acceptance of the appraisal and to confirm that the Personnel review has been completed.

(14)   The completed forms are then filed by the Personnel Department.

(15)   It is the Personnel Department's responsibility to assure that all data from the Appraisal Summary Form is placed in the HRM Inventory.

General Motors Corporation

APPRAISAL WORKSHEET FOR SALARIED EMPLOYES

GM

NAME:_____ JOB TITLE:_____

The appraisal process is intended to help both you and the organization. Completing this worksheet and returning it to your supervisor will contribute to your appraisal in two ways:

- It will assure your viewpoints are considered as your performance is appraised.
- It will help make your appraisal interview more productive.

If you need more space for any item, please use a separate sheet of paper and attach it to this form.

Section I – Key Job Elements: Describe your job as you see it in terms of key elements. Other words meaning about the same are: major responsibilities, primary duties, or important functions. Here are some questions to help you identify the key elements of your job: What important results are expected of you? What does your supervisor emphasize? On what things do you spend a lot of time and effort? What important things wouldn't get done if your job didn't exist? If you supervise others, include the following job elements: Organize and Plan, Communicate Information, Work with Others, Meet EEO Responsibilities, and Develop Subordinates. Even if you do not supervise others, you may use these elements if they apply to your job.

_____

_____

_____

Section II – Major Contributions: Review each job element and note any contributions you have made. These may include an important problem solved, an idea successfully implemented, an improvement in your job, the accomplishment of a work goal, or the successful completion of a difficult assignment.

_____

_____

_____

Section III – Performance Difficulties: Review each job element and note "trouble spots" – things that happened that made you less effective than you could be. Note any support you need to remove these difficulties.

_____

_____

_____

Section IV – Action Plans: Thinking through your job elements, contributions, and performance difficulties allows sound action planning. As you develop plans, use these guidelines.

- Action plans should consist of things you can do to increase your effectiveness or remove performance difficulties.
- Action plans should be specific enough so that you know when they have been accomplished.
- Action plans should indicate whether training or education would be helpful.

You and your supervisor should spend enough time discussing these plans to assure they are realistic and in line with other goals of your department.

_____

_____

_____

Section V – Career Goals: Describe your short and long range career goals.

_____

_____

_____

Now you have an opportunity to enter your career interests in the General Motors Employe Information System. This will assure that management is aware of your interests when job openings occur. From the codes for fields of work accompanying this worksheet, select the two fields in which you are most interested and enter the codes below. You may express your interests by indicating, either a major field of work heading such as 001 for Engineering, or a specific heading within a major field such as 031 for Emissions Engineering. Also, indicate whether you would be most interested in supervisory (S) or non-supervisory (N) positions in those fields by placing an S or N in the space provided.

	Enter S or N
Primary field of interest	
Secondary field of interest	

Section VI – Additional Comments: If there are further questions or points you would like discussed in your appraisal interview, note them here.

_____

_____

_____

Signature _____ Date _____

General Motors Corporation

PERFORMANCE APPRAISAL REVIEW FOR SALARIED EMPLOYES

NAME: _____

TYPE OF APPRAISAL: □ REGULAR ANNUAL   □ SPECIAL

S.S. # _____   JOB TITLE: _____   APPRAISAL DATE: _____   POSITION CODE: _____

KEY JOB ELEMENTS:

PERFORMANCE SUMMARY:

Review each key element and note major contributions. Also note where effectiveness could be increased or where improvements are needed. Then check the column on the right which best describes the employe's performance on each of these key elements.

Major responsibilities, primary duties, important functions of this employe.	Outstanding performance. far exceeds standard. achievable but seldom attained performance.	Highly effective performance. exceeds standard.	Good competent performance. meets standard. the level of performance most often achieved.	Needs slight improvement to meet standard.	Needs much improvement to meet standard.

SUPPLEMENTAL KEY JOB ELEMENTS: These elements are to be used when appraising supervisory employes. They may be used where applicable for non-supervisory employes. Summarize performance in the space provided. Note that the description accompanying each element contains only a few examples of the possible areas to be considered in evaluating performance on that element.

Job Element	Outstanding performance. far exceeds standard. achievable but seldom attained performance.	Highly effective performance. exceeds standard.	Good competent performance. meets standard. the level of performance most often achieved.	Needs slight improvement to meet standard.	Needs much improvement to meet standard.
ORGANIZE AND PLAN: Organizing the job; planning ahead, making efficient use of time; establishing appropriate and effective follow-up procedures.					
COMMUNICATE INFORMATION: Expression in both oral and written communication; organization of communication; appropriate use of language.					
WORK WITH OTHERS: Getting along with others; understanding of others; awareness and consideration of others' viewpoints.					
MEET EEO RESPONSIBILITIES: Achievement of organizational EEO objectives and timetables; demonstrating sensitivity in EEO areas; active implementation of management responsibilities in this area.					
DEVELOP SUBORDINATES: Training subordinates; giving instructions; coaching and counseling; appraising performance.					

OVERALL PERFORMANCE DESCRIPTION: Check the description which best matches your estimate of the employe's overall performance. If the description is "needs much improvement", consult with the Personnel Department before conducting the appraisal interview.

☐ Outstanding performance; far exceeds standard for this job; achievable but seldom attained performance.

☐ Highly effective performance; exceeds standard for this job.

☐ Good competent performance; meets standard for this job; the level of performance most often achieved.

☐ Needs slight improvement to meet standard for this job.

☐ Needs much improvement to meet standard for this job.

ACTION PLANS

What can the employe do to increase his/her effectiveness or make needed improvements? Note where training would be helpful.

What can management do to support the employe in his/her efforts to increase effectiveness or make improvements?

EMPLOYE COMMENTS:

Were you given an opportunity to complete the appraisal worksheet? ☐ Yes ☐ No

Did you complete it? ☐ Yes ☐ No

Enter below any comments you wish to make about your appraisal.

_____

Employe Signature _____ Date _____

Your signature does not necessarily signify your agreement with the appraisal; it simply means the appraisal has been discussed with you.

APPRAISER COMMENTS:

Enter summary of the appraisal interview in the space below.

_____

SIGNATURES:

Appraiser _____ Date _____

Personnel _____ Date _____

Other _____ Date _____

Appraiser's Supv. _____ Date _____

Other _____ Date _____

Other _____ Date _____

EXHIBIT C
CODES FOR FIELDS OF WORK

001 **ENGINEERING** (General, Misc.)	088 Vehicle Dynamics	124 Layout
	089 Ventilation	125 Machine Repair
002 Accessories	090 Wheels & Tires	126 Machine Tool Set-Up
003 Administration	091 Industrial Hygiene	127 Maintenance
004 Aerodynamics	092 Materials Engrg.	128 Mfg. Coordination
005 Aerodesign	093 Welding Engrg.	129 Mfg. Development
006 Aeronautical	094 Electrical Machinery-	130 Mfg. Services
007 Applied Mechanics	Motor and Generator	131 Mfg. Engineering
008 Architectural	Design	132 Master Mechanic
009 Brakes	095 Electrical Insulation	133 Material Control
010 Body	Systems	134 Material Handling
011 Chassis	096 Vibration Analysis	135 General Stores
012 Checking	097 Product Application	136 Tools
013 Chemical Engrg.	850 Analytical Services	137 Warehouse
014 Civil	851 Assembly Engrg.	138 Materials
015 Computer Technology	852 Ceramic	139 Mechanical Handling
016 Construction	853 Control Systems Engrg.	140 Numerical Control
017 Contact (Liaison)	854 Corrosion	141 Packaging
018 Cooling Systems	855 Electrical Component	142 Paint
019 Damageability	Testing and	143 Plant Engineering
020 Design	Evaluation	144 Powerhouse (Power
021 Detailing	856 Electrical Control	Plant Engine)
022 Development	Engrg.	145 Press
023 Diesel Engines	857 Electrical Facility	146 Process Engineering
024 Piston	Engrg.	147 Production Control
025 Rotary	858 Electrical Repair	148 Production Engineering
026 Drafting	859 Engrg. Computation	149 Repair
027 Drive Train	860 Engrg. Services	150 Salvage
028 Electrical	861 Engrg. Systems	151 Sanitation
029 Electrical Systems	862 Facilities Control	152 Scheduling
030 Electronics	863 Facilities Planning	153 Scrap
031 Emissions	864 Ferrous	154 Sheet Metal
032 Fuel System	865 Gage Engrg.	155 Tool & Die
033 Exhaust System	866 Gear Design	156 Tool Design
034 Combustion	867 Graphic Illustration	157 Tool Grinding
035 Energy Conversion	868 Laboratory Equipment	158 Tool, Equip., and
Systems (Other)	Design and Develop.	Die Estimating
036 Engrg. Mechanics	869 Material Properties	159 Tool Grinding
037 Engrg. Shop	and Specifications	160 Tool Inspection
038 Engrg. Specifications	870 Metals	161 Value Analysis
039 Engrg. Standards	871 Methods Engrg.	162 Waste Control
040 Environmental Engrg.	872 Non-Ferrous	163 Welder Maintenance
041 Fabrication	873 Plastics Engrg.	164 Welding
042 Field Service	874 Plant and Production	165 Work Standards
043 Fluid Dynamics	Process	166 Application Engrg.
044 Forward Planning	875 Polymer	167 Architectural and
045 Gasoline Engines	876 Procedure Writing	Construction Design
046 Piston	and Development	168 Budget Control
047 Rotary	877 Product Evaluation	169 Carpentry
048 Heating & Air Cond.	878 Product Inspection	170 Cold Extrusion
049 Heat Transfer	879 Reproductions	171 Conveyor and Mat'l.
050 Hydraulic Systems	880 Thermal Treatment	Handling Design
051 Hydrostatics	881 Automotive Engineering	172 Die Design
052 Induction Systems	882 Automotive Technology	173 Estimating
053 Instrumentation	883 Basic Engineering	174 Expense Control
054 Layout	884 Biomedical	175 Gauge Control-
055 Mass Transportation	885 Diesel Engineering	Reliability
056 Mechanical	886 Engineering Science	176 Heat Treat
057 Mechanical Devices	887 Engineering Technology	177 Machining
058 Model Shop	888 Heat Power	178 Machine/Equipment
059 Noise Abatement	889 Metallurgical Engineering	Design
060 Non-Automotive	890 Stress and Design	179 Metal Casting
061 Off-Highway Vehicles	891 Systems Engineering	180 Metal Finishing
062 Parts	892 Weight Analysis	181 Millwright
063 Petroleum Engrg.		182 Pattern Making
064 Pneumatics		183 Physical Metallurgical
065 Product Assurance	101 **MANUFACTURING** (General, Misc.)	and Spectrographic
066 Human Factors		Testing
067 Quality Control	102 Assembly	184 Plant Layout
068 Reliability	103 Engine	185 Plastics Mould Design
069 Serviceability	104 Metal	186 Plumbing
070 Radiation	105 Vehicle	187 Pressed Metal
071 Real Estate	106 Assurance	188 Processing (Paint,
072 Rear Axle	107 Inspection	Plating, etc.)
073 Refrigeration	108 Quality Control	189 Procurement Engrg.
074 Research	109 Reliability	190 Reliability Engrg.
075 Safety	110 Cut & Sew	191 Statistical Quality
076 Site Planning	111 Die Engineering	Control
077 Spectrographic	112 Fabrication	192 Time Study
078 Stress Analysis	113 Forge	193 Tinsmith
079 Structural	114 Foundary	194 Tool Planning
080 Suspension Systems	115 Cleaning	195 Utilities
081 Testing	116 Core Room	
082 Thermal Design	117 Die Casting	
083 Thermodynamics	118 Melting	201 **COMMUNICATIONS**
084 Transmissions	119 Molding	
085 Trucks	120 Pattern Shop	202 Communication
086 Turbine Engine	121 Gauge Design	Engineering
087 Vehicle (Complete)	122 Industrial Engrg.	203 Equipment Operation
	123 Jigs & Fixtures	204 Radio Dispatching

EXHIBIT C—continued

225 DATA PROCESSING	441 Human Resources Planning & Develop.	612 Applied Psychology
	442 Organization Develop.	613 Biological Sciences
226 Hardware Design	443 Nurse	614 Biochemistry
227 Operations	444 Physician	615 Toxicology
228 Operating Systems		616 Analytical Chemistry
229 Programming		617 Electrochemistry
230 Software	**501 PUBLIC RELATIONS**	619 Inorganic Chemistry
231 Systems Design		620 Organic Chemistry
232 Computer Application Programming	502 News Media	621 Physical Chemistry
233 Computer Systems Programming	503 Field Relations	622 Polymer Chemistry
234 Key Punching	504 Institutional Relations	623 Economics
235 Process Control Computer Activity	505 Community Relations	624 Electronics Technology
236 Tape Library	506 Newspaper Editor	625 Applied Math
		626 Mechanical Technology
	525 PURCHASING AND TRAFFIC	627 Medicine
251 FINANCIAL		628 Social Science
	526 Buying - Product	629 Sociology
252 Accounting - Cost	527 Buying - Non-Product	630 Statistics
253 Accounting - General	528 Expediting & Follow-up	631 Transportation
254 Accounting - Payroll	529 Traffic	632 Urban Planning
255 Analysis	530 Shipping & Receiving	633 Veterinary Medicine
256 Auditing	531 Warehouse	634 Computer Science
257 Banking & Exchange	532 Inventory Control	
258 Contract Admin.	533 Material Planning	
259 Insurance	534 New Model Tooling- Purchasing	**651 PHOTOGRAPHIC**
260 Methods & Procedures	535 Operations - Transp./ Traffic	
261 Stock Transfer	536 Pkg./Mat'l. Handling- Transp./Traffic	652 Artistic
262 Tax	537 Procurement - Purch.	653 Equipment Operation
263 Accounts Payable	538 Rate Analysis Transp./Traffic	654 Exhibit
264 Accounts Receivable	539 Schedules - Production Control	655 Film Processing
265 Billing	540 Steel & Raw Products Purchasing	656 Graphics
266 Budget & Forecast	541 Vendor Evaluation	657 Illustrating
267 Financial Systems		658 Offset Printing
268 Operation Analysis		659 Photography
269 Product Program	**550 SALES (General, Miscellaneous)**	660 Publications
270 Property Records		
271 Timekeeping	551 Advertising	**675 DESIGN**
	552 Credit	
	553 Collections	676 Creative Design
301 INSURANCE	554 Dealer Organization	677 Sculpture
	555 Distribution	678 Technical Styling
302 Claims Adjusting	556 Fleet	
303 Underwriting	557 Market Research & Analysis	**700 INDUSTRY-GOVERNMENT RELATIONS**
	558 Merchandising	
325 LEGAL	559 Order Department	701 Government Relations
	560 Owner Relations	702 Highway & Traffic Safety
326 Attorney	561 Parts	703 Urban Affairs
327 Para-legal	562 Retail	704 Government Liaison
	563 Sales Engineering	705 Legislative Analyst
	564 Service	706 Reporter - Legislative
351 LIBRARY	565 Service Engineering	707 Research Librarian- Non-Technical
	566 Training Center Admin.	708 Transportation Specialist
352 Legal Library	567 Wholesale	709 Urban Affairs Specialist
	568 Catalog Department	710 Writer - Non-Technical
	569 Central Office Admin. and Service	
375 OFFICE SERVICES	570 Charts & Display	
	571 Customer Relations	**751 MISCELLANEOUS**
376 Blueprint Operations	572 Dealer Sales	
377 Mailroom	573 Field Management	752 Administration
378 Multilith	574 Marketing Planning	753 Analysis
379 Stationary Stock	575 National Accounts	754 Business Management
380 Record Retention	576 Pricing	755 Clerical - Secretarial
	577 Product Marketing	756 Copywriting
	578 Sales Analysis	757 Driving
401 PATENT	579 Sales Management	758 Technical Writing
	580 Sales Promotion	759 Interpreting (Language)
	581 Sales Training	760 German
425 PERSONNEL (General, Misc.)	582 Service Management	761 French
	583 Service Training	762 Spanish
426 Coordinator-EEO, OD, Affirmative Action, etc.	584 Zone Sales	763 Laboratory
427 Education & Training (excl. teachers, instructors, GMI)	585 Zone Service	764 Office Management
428 Employe Benefits		765 Present Field (not specified)
429 Employe Services		766 Statistical Analysis
430* Employment	**601 SCIENTIFIC (General, Misc.)**	767 Technical (not specified)
431 Labor Relations		768 Business Machines
432 Medical	602 Acoustics	769 Flexowriting
433 Personnel Research	603 Chemistry	770 Janitorial Services
434 Plant Protection	604 Mathematics	771 Physical Testing
435 Safety	605 Metallurgy	772 Receptionist
436 Salaried Personnel Administration	606 Metrology	773 Stenographic
437 Suggestion Plan	607 Nuclear Engrg.	774 Telephone Operating
438 Teaching, Instructing	608 Optics	775 Teletype Operating
439 Alcohol & Substance Abuse	609 Physics	776 Typing
440 College Relations & Placement (Co-op)	610 Waste Treat-Research	
	611 Applied Science	**801 ENERGY MANAGEMENT**
		802 Energy Systems
		803 Energy Conservation
		804 Energy Resources
		805 Utility Relations

INSTRUCTIONS FOR USE OF
THE PERFORMANCE APPRAISAL REVIEW
FOR SALARIED EMPLOYES

The Performance Appraisal Review for Salaried Employes is a multi-purpose form. It is used for the regular annual appraisal and the special appraisal of probationary employes.

The Regular Annual Appraisal

1. When notified that an appraisal is due, encourage the employe to complete an Appraisal Worksheet for Salaried Employees. While the employe is not required to complete the Appraisal Worksheet, it should be thoroughly explained to ensure that the employe understands its purpose. If the employe wants to complete the Appraisal Worksheet, allow about a week for it to be returned.

2. To complete the Performance Appraisal Review, begin with the column titled Key Job Elements. If the employe has completed the Worksheet, consider his or her description of key job elements. Your description of key job elements will not always correspond to the employe's and you should be prepared to discuss, clarify, and resolve differences during the appraisal interview. If *major* differences exist, they should be clarified with the employe *before* completing other sections of the Performance Appraisal Review.

3. Next, complete the Performance Summary section. As you do so, consider what the employe has written about contributions and difficulties on the Appraisal Worksheet. Again, you may or may not agree. Some differences are to be expected, and should be used as a basis for discussion during the interview. It is important that you clearly specify where effectiveness can be increased or where improvements are needed. As you prepare to summarize performance, consult others at your level who know the employe's work. Experience shows this to be helpful in arriving at a balanced and accurate summary. For some Key Job Elements, you may find there is very little to summarize; on others, you may wish to make a number of points. It will depend on the situation and performance of the individual as you see it.

    For each Key Job Element, use the point on the rating scale which best describes the employe's performance on that element. When appraising a supervisory employe, performance must be summarized for each of the Supplemental Key Job Elements. These elements may also be used for non-supervisory employes where applicable.

4. After performance has been summarized and rated for each Key Job Element, check the Overall Performance Description which best describes the employe's performance. Standards of performance should be sufficiently high so that *Outstanding Performance* is seldom attained. *Highly Effective Performance* might be attained somewhat more frequently, though it would not be commonplace. The most commonly used description is *Good, Competent Performance.* At the same time it is not unusual to observe performance for which the best description is *Needs Slight Improvement.* When the best de-

scription is *Needs Much Improvement,* do not hesitate to use it. In fairness to the employe, you must acknowledge this level of performance when it exists. In all such cases, contact the Personnel Department before conducting the appraisal interview.

5. The Action Plans section of the Performance Appraisal Review is used to describe what the employe and you can do to bring about improvements or to increase effectiveness. Once again, consider any plans suggested by the employe on the Appraisal Worksheet. Be sure to indicate who is responsible for seeing that these action plans are implemented.

   Important: If the Overall Performance Description is *Needs Slight Improvement,* set target dates for each major part of the Action Plans and establish a schedule of special appraisals to review employe progress in making the needed improvements. Involve your supervisor when preparing for these special appraisals. When conducting these special appraisals, use the Performance Appraisal Review and check the "Special Appraisal" box on the face of the form. Completed special appraisals are to become a part of the employe's personnel file.

6. Prior to the appraisal interview, the Performance Appraisal Review is to be reviewed and signed by your supervisor. The Employe Comments section is to be completed at the time of the appraisal interview. Complete the Appraiser Comments section when the interview is over. When completing this section, indicate whether the employe completed the Appraisal Worksheet for Salaried Employes.

Special Appraisal of Probationary Employes

New employes are appraised prior to the end of the third and fifth months of employment. The Appraisal Worksheet for Salaried Employes is *not* intended to be a part of these special appraisals.

The objectives of these appraisals are to:

1. Provide a new employe with direction and guidance during the probationary period, and,
2. To review the selection decision and determine whether the employe has been properly placed.

The Key Job Elements column of the Performance Appraisal Review is used to describe the job and the initial assignments given to the employe. Use the Performance Summary section to record observations of performance. Rate the employe on those parts of the job and initial assignments where you have had an opportunity to observe performance.

An Overall Performance Description should then be checked. In addition, enter a comment in the Appraiser Comments section stating whether the employe should be retained.

If there are actions the employe should take to improve performance, note these in the Actions Plan section. Prior to the appraisal interview, the Performance Appraisal Review is reviewed and signed by your immediate supervisor.

Other parts of the form are completed in the same manner as a regular annual appraisal.

GM

General Motors Corporation

PERFORMANCE IMPROVEMENT PLAN

NAME: _____

DATE: _____

1. Performance Deficiencies	2. Behavior or Results Desired By Management	3. Action Management Will Take to Help Employe Correct Deficiencies	4. Action Employe Will Take to Correct Deficiencies	Completion Date

SIGNATURES:

Appraiser _____ Date _____   Employe _____ Date _____

Appraiser's Supv. _____ Date _____   Personnel _____ Date _____

Other _____ Date _____   Other _____ Date _____

APPRAISAL OF PROGRESS

Evaluate the employe's progress to date on the plan for improvement detailed on the reverse side.

SIGNATURES:

Appraiser _____ Date _____   *Employe _____ Date _____

Appraiser's Supv. _____ Date _____   Personnel _____ Date _____

Other _____ Date _____   Other _____ Date _____

*Your signature does not necessarily mean that you agree with the appraisal of progress; it simply means that you have had the opportunity to review it with your supervisor.

PROCEDURE COVERING EXPLOYES RATED AS
NEEDS MUCH IMPROVEMENT

The purposes of HRM Appraisal Standard 407 are:

1. To assure that management takes prompt and appropriate action in working with employes whose overall performance is rated as *Needs Much Improvement.*
2. To assure that every such case is carried to one of the following conclusions:
   - The employe's performance meets standard. (*Good, Competent Performance,* as defined on the rating scale contained in the Performance Appraisal Review.)
   - The employe is reassigned to a position in which standard performance can be attained.
   - The employe is terminated.

   To accomplish these objectives, the appraiser and the appraiser's supervisor are to meet with a Personnel representative prior to the appraisal interview in all such cases and complete a Performance Improvement Plan.

A. At this meeting, the Personnel representative will assist the appraiser in:
   1. *Specifying the performance deficiencies of the employe.* Performance deficiencies are specific statements describing results not accomplished or work habits or methods that are unacceptable and/or inappropriate. These statements should include examples of behavior which occurred or failed to occur resulting in a negative impact on performance.
   2. *Describing the results and behavior management wants; the results and behavior needed to meet standard (Good Competent Performance).* Once again, specific statements of results expected and behavior desired are to be entered.
   3. *Determining what management will do to assist the employe in making needed improvements.* While the specific causes of performance deficiencies are many and varied, they usually fall in three broad categories. Each of these should be considered in determining the causes of deficiencies and deciding what action management will take to assist the employe in making needed improvements.
      - *Deficiencies resulting from lack of technical and/or supervisory skill.* In some instances, employes simply don't know how to do what is expected of them. On-the-job coaching or formal training may have been inadequate, inappropriate, or non-existent. When this is the case, necessary coaching and/or training is to be provided. Management should be specific as to how the coaching or training will be provided, who will be responsible, and when it will be accomplished.
      - *Deficiencies resulting from problems in the performance environment.* In some cases, performance deficiencies are the result of unclear

performance standards. When this is so, it is necessary to clarify management expectations and to clearly communicate these to the employe.

Other deficiencies in the performance environment may be found in the job design. Poor job design should be suspected whenever there is a history of sub-standard performance from a succession of individuals on the same job, or whenever there is a disproportionate number of problem performance cases within a given job classification. In such cases, the job design should be investigated and modified as needed.

Inappropriate "feedback" processes are very common. Information given to the employe about job performance may be so infrequent, unspecific, late, or in such negative terms that it does not function in a constructive way to guide performance on a day-to-day basis.

The power to correct these three causes of performance deficiencies (unclear standards, poor design, and inappropriate feedback) lies with management. When such conditions exist, management should assist the performer by correcting these conditions.

- *Deficiencies resulting from personal problems.* If there is reason to believe that the performance deficiencies are caused by such things as alcohol or drug abuse, emotional disturbances, or other personal problems, special assistance will be provided by the Personnel Department in accordance with established policy.

4. *Specifying a timetable for special performance reviews.* The timetable is to be a function of the nature and seriousness of the performance deficiencies. In some cases, it may be desirable to schedule reviews as often as every two weeks; in others, monthly or bi-monthly reviews may be more appropriate. In any event, a timetable is to be established and followed. Within the timetable, a point is to be designated as the time when efforts at improvement in the current position will yield to the options of reassignment or termination.

5. *Preparing for the first interview.* This interview will be based on the completed Performance Appraisal Review for Salaried Employes and the Performance Improvement Plan. The interview should cover all relevant performance subject matter, such as:
- The key job elements.
- The specific deficiencies requiring improvement.
- The nature and extent of the deficiencies.
- The overall performance rating.
- The specific behavior that management wants; the behavior that will be necessary for the employe to be viewed as meeting the standard of the job.
- What management will do to assist the employe in making needed improvements.
- Any action the employe can suggest for bringing about the improve-

ment (to be documented in column four of the Performance Improvement Plan).

- Management's desire to see improvement and to be helpful in bringing it about.
- The date of the next special appraisal as established by the schedule. Depending on the circumstances surrounding the case, the second level supervisor and/or Personnel Department representative may be party to the appraisal interview.

B. Following the first interview, the employe's job performance is to be observed on a day-to-day basis. Specific improvements should be recognized, and constructive counsel provided regarding areas of continued sub-standard performance.

C. Prior to each scheduled interview, a Personnel representative will counsel the appraiser on conducting the interview. The reverse side of the Performance Improvement Plan is to be used to appraise progress. In doing so, each deficiency and desired behavior listed on the Performance Improvement Plan should be examined. Note what progress has occurred and whether overall performance meets standard (Good Competent Performance).

   1. If overall performance meets standard (Good Competent Performance), the process is terminated and the employe so informed. The employe's performance should be carefully observed for any indication that performance is declining; if there is a decline, the process is to begin again, and the employe is to be made aware of this continuing review.
   2. If substantial progress has occurred but further improvement is still necessary, a new Performance Improvement Plan is to be completed and reviewed with the employe.
   3. If progress has been minimal or non-existent, it should be made clear to the employe that he or she is on probation, that his or her job is in jeopardy, and that performance must meet standard (Good Competent Performance) within an established schedule or the employe will be removed from the job. Each appraisal of progress is to be documented on a separate Performance Improvement Plan.

D. This process continues until overall performance meets standard (Good Competent Performance) or the pre-designated point in time is reached when efforts at further improvement will be discontinued.

E. If performance has not reached desired levels within the time period established, it must be determined whether the employe is to be placed in another assignment or separated. The determination to transfer or separate the employe is to be made only after a review of the case by the employe's supervisor and department management in consultation with the Personnel Department.

EXHIBIT G

General Motors Corporation
APPRAISAL SUMMARY FORM

Employe's
Name:_____ Position Code:_____ CISCO_____ Dept. _____

S.S. #_____ Appraisal Date: _____

A. OVERALL PERFORMANCE (From Performance Appraisal Review-GM 1427.) Please circle one:

| 1 | Outstanding Performance | 2 | Highly Effective Performance | 3 | Good Competent Performance | 4 | Needs Slight Improvement | 5 | Needs Much Improvement |

	Primary	S/N	Secondary	S/N

B. EMPLOYE INTERESTS (From Appraisal Worksheet-GM 1426)............

	Primary	S/N	Secondary	S/N

C. FIELDS OF GREATEST POTENTIAL ....
   (See Codes for Fields of Work)

D. ESTIMATE OF POTENTIAL LEVEL
   Current estimate of highest level employe might attain within the next five years.
   (Mandatory for employes through 6th level; optional for others.) Please circle one:

   | 3 | rd Level | 4 | th Level | 5 | th Level | 6 | th Level | 7 | th Level | 8 | th Level | 0 | Unclassified |

   Current estimate of highest level employe might attain by end of career.
   (Mandatory for 7th and 8th level employes; optional for others.) Please circle one:

   | 3 | rd Level | 4 | th Level | 5 | th Level | 6 | th Level | 7 | th Level | 8 | th Level | 0 | Unclassified |

E. READINESS FOR OTHER POSITIONS

Considering the Overall Performance Rating, Employe Interests, Fields of Greatest Potential, and Estimate of Potential Level, list up to three positions, identified by GM position codes, that represent logical next assignments in the employe's career. These may be promotional or lateral moves. For each position code, indicate the employe's readiness for movement by checking the box best describing when the employe will be ready for that move.

Position Code	Readiness (in months)			
	(1) 0-6	(2) 6-12	(3) 12-24	(4) More than 24

SIGNATURES:

First level
supervisor: _____ _____ Second level supervisor: _____ _____
                                              Date   Date

Personnel:_____ _____ Other: _____ _____
                                           Date   Date

Other:_____ _____ Other: _____ _____
                                       Date   Date

APPRAISAL FLOW CHART

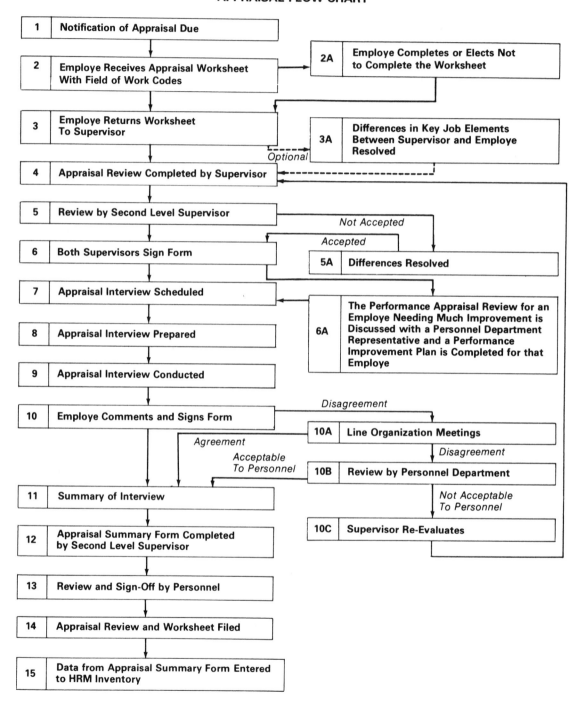

Supervisor's Guide

1. DETERMINING KEY ELEMENTS

One of the best ways of getting a handle on Key Job Elements is by thinking of those parts of the job in which the employe is expected to achieve results. As noted on the Appraisal Worksheet, other phrases that mean about the same thing are "major responsibilities," "primary duties," or "important functions." They are those things that contribute significantly to the accomplishment of the job.

Some examples of key elements might include:

Job	Key Elements
Manufacturing Supervisor:	Quality parts fabricated
	Costs controlled
	Safe operation maintained
	Etc.
Secretary:	Letters typed
	Dictation taken
	Files maintained
	Etc.
Design Engineer:	Eng. spec's interpreted
	Design completed and tested
	Reports written
	Etc.

As you can see from the examples, key elements are brief statements—no more than a few words or a short sentence. Most jobs can be adequately described with five to ten key elements.

The first time you develop key elements for a job, you may find it difficult to express each element in two or three words. After a little experience, this difficulty will disappear. The important thing to remember is that you are trying to describe the job in its key elements or key outputs.

Where Can You Find Key Element Information?

Key elements for a job can be developed using a variety of resources. These include:

1. The position description.
2. Selection requisitions.
3. Job studies, if they have been conducted in your unit.
4. Employes presently performing in the job.
5. Other supervisors who have done the job or supervise the job.

When developing key elements, it is important to describe the job rather than the special skills or abilities of the person currently filling it. Define the job, rather than the qualifications for the job.

Here are several useful guidelines for helping you write key elements.
- They should be as *objective* as possible
  Example: Position—Supervisor Production: "Production schedules followed and implemented" as opposed to "takes initiative."
- They should be stated in *clear and concise* terms
  Example: Position—Draftsman: "Drawings completed" as opposed to "be able to draw."
- They should be *job-centered*
  Example: Position—Supervisor Maintenance: "Safety rules implemented" as opposed to traits like "trustworthy," "dependable," etc.
- They should be *results-oriented*
  Example: Position—Plant Security Officer: "Movement of people and materials controlled" as opposed to "guards the gate."
  Example: Position—Salaried Supervisor: "Employes trained" as opposed to "able to train employes."

2. COMPLETING THE PERFORMANCE SUMMARY

After you have developed the key elements for a given job, the next step is to review each element, noting major contributions and areas for improvement under the Performance Summary section of the Performance Appraisal Review form.

Your next step is to check the performance description which best describes the employe's performance on each key element.

First, let's review the descriptors.

Outstanding performance; far exceeds standard; achievable but seldom-attained performance.	Highly effective performance; exceeds standard.	Good competent performance; meets standard; the level of performance most often achieved.	Needs slight improvement to meet standard.	Needs much improvement to meet standard.

Several final points about your standards of performance:

1. The employe must know what your standards are before you sit down to complete an appraisal.
2. Your standards and expectations should be a frequent topic of discussion—not just at appraisal time.

3. Sometimes standards can be expressed in measurable terms—percents, numbers, dates, costs, etc. When this can be done, it is very helpful.

You will be given practice in developing standards as part of your classroom training.

3. COMPLETING THE APPRAISAL WORKSHEET

Proper introduction and explanation of the Appraisal Worksheet is an important supervisory responsibility. The employes must know the benefits of completing the worksheet, that you will use the information constructively, and that it is an opportunity for them rather than a requirement.

When giving the Worksheet to the employe, do the following:

1. Call attention to information at the top of the Worksheet, emphasizing the benefits to the employe.
2. Review each section of the Worksheet, answering all questions, and provide the Codes for Fields of Work.
3. If this is the first time the employe has seen the Worksheet, take enough time to explain it in whatever detail is necessary.
4. Give the employe sufficient time to return it to you—about a week is reasonable.

When your employe is prepared in this manner and involved through completion of the Worksheet, then in most situations a more productive performance appraisal interview may be anticipated.

Note: Employes are not to be required to complete the Worksheet. If one of your employes does not want to complete it:

1. Be sure the employe understands the purposes of the Worksheet; particularly with respect to having his or her career interests recorded in the inventory.
2. Be sure the employe understands that he or she may complete any portion of the Worksheet.
3. Respect the employe's decision.

4. OBSERVING PERFORMANCE

During the course of the year we must observe job performance and compare it to our standards and expectations. Observing your employe's job performance obviously is not something you do between the time you receive notice an appraisal is due and the time you fill out the form. Performance observation is an on-going task, with information and examples being accumulated and discussed with the employe on a continuous basis.

Job performance observations should be objective and comprehensive. Since it is not possible to observe all performance, you have to rely on sampling. This opens the door to errors. Here are some tips on how you can avoid errors and improve objectivity and comprehensiveness.

1. Periodically discuss the employee's job and your standards of perform-ance with the employee. Your employee's understanding of what you ex-pect and what's important to you is developed in your day-to-day con-tacts. Make the most of these opportunities to assure mutual understanding.

2. Make sufficient observations of performance. Insufficient information re-sulting from too few observations is fair to neither the employe nor you.

3. Guard against observing only those key elements on which the employe is having difficulty. These elements do require more attention, but don't let this bias your appraisal of the employe's total performance.

4. Observe all key elements, avoiding the following:
   - *Location errors:* These result from observing the handiest elements, such as those closest to your work station, those where the employe interfaces with you or those performed inside your department.
   - *Time errors.* These occur from observing only the latest or temporarily most convenient samples. Make and record your observations period-ically throughout the year.
   - *Convenience errors.* These occur from observing only the key ele-ments which are easiest to assess, such as written documents, inter-department relationships, computer data, etc.

5. Observe for results not methods. Often an employee's methods will differ from yours. If the desired results are obtained and the employe's meth-ods cause no other difficulties, don't let the employe's method bias your appraisal.

While your observations and records are the principal source of data from which you will appraise your employe, you are encouraged to obtain the obser-vations and judgments of others at your level or above who have been in a po-sition to observe the employe's performance. Following such a practice has proven to make appraisals far more accurate and complete. Many GM units form appraisal teams to carry out this function. Whether your unit does this is a matter to be decided locally.

Another source of performance information to consider is the Appraisal Worksheet filled out by the employe. This does not mean that employees should appraise themselves; rather, it means that by considering their inputs you may be reminded of important employe contributions and difficulties (or cause of dif-ficulties) which would otherwise go unnoticed.

Rating Errors

After you have compiled the key elements, made your observations, and written the Performance Summary, your next step is to select the description on the five point scale which best represents performance as compared to standard. There are four errors that you should keep in mind as you make the selection.

1. *Leniency* is a tendency for supervisors to consistently appraise toward the high end of the scale. This may be the result of:
   - A desire to make your employees look good.
   - Reluctance to face up to substandard performance.
   - Concern that the appraisal may affect the employee's career.
   - Concern that the low appraisal will reflect on you, as the supervisor.
2. *Harshness* is a tendency to consistently appraise at lower end of the ratings.
3. *Central Tendency* occurs when supervisors avoid appraising employes either very high or very low, and cluster their ratings around the average.
4. Halo Effect is the tendency to appraise employes higher in all key elements because they are nice people, easy to supervise, don't cause any problems, etc.

These four appraisal errors can be minimized by assuring you have standards of performance for each key element, and by forthrightly acknowledging both high and low performance.

5. SETTING ACTION PLANS

This unit will explain how to complete the Action Plans section of the Performance Appraisal Review form.

Action Plan Guidelines
- Prepare for the appraisal interview by noting in the Action Plans section anything you would like to see the employe do to improve performance or increase effectiveness. Review the Performance Summary section of the Performance Appraisal Review to identify needs for such action.
- Review the employe's Appraisal Worksheet and prepare to discuss any action plans the employe has suggested.
- Keep in mind that "Rome wasn't built in a day"—if the employe's overall performance description is "Good Competent Performance" or higher, concentrate action plans on a few really important needs. This is usually more productive than trying to improve everything at once.
- Encourage the employe to participate, to take the lead in this discussion and to develop commitment. If you cannot support a plan the employe suggests, be sure to acknowledge this and explain why.
- Ask the employe how you can help. If you can provide the help requested, note it in the Action Plans section.
- If you feel there are certain actions the employe must take (you feel strongly about it), make your position known. Don't hide under the cover of "participation."
- Don't feel compelled to fill up all the space just for the sake of making the

form look complete—Action Plans should be only as detailed as they need to be—you and the employe are the final judge of this.

6. REVIEWING THE APPRAISAL WITH YOUR SUPERVISOR

After completing the Performance Appraisal Review form and prior to conducting the appraisal discussion, discuss your Performance Appraisal with your supervisor.

If there is agreement, each of you signs the form. If there is disagreement, it must be resolved and the Performance Appraisal Review form signed prior to the appraisal interview.

Your supervisor's review of the Performance Appraisal Review is an important step in the appraisal process. The purpose of the review with your supervisor is to:

1. Provide you with a broader view of your employe's performance based on the observations of your supervisor.
2. Facilitate consistency and uniformity in the appraisal process across the organization and to prevent unilateral judgments about employes.

Two special notes to be kept in mind during the preinterview review with your supervisor:

1. For the employe whose *Overall Job Performance* is described as Needs Slight Improvement, an Action Plan must be completed as described in Unit 5 of this Supervisor's Guide and Exhibit E of the Supervisor's Handbook.
2. For the employe whose *Overall Job Performance* is described as Needs Much Improvement, the appraisal is to be reviewed with the Personnel Department prior to the appraisal interview.

7. CONDUCTING THE INTERVIEW

Like any other interview, an appraisal interview consists of three parts: preparation, body of the interview, and its close. HRM Standards 403 and 404, found near the beginning of the Handbook, briefly describe what is to happen during these three parts.

In the previous units of this Guide, you have learned how to carry out the bulk of the preparation. You have only to review the employee's personnel file for past experience, education, training, special skills and past performance to complete your preparation.

You will be attending a workshop in Appraisal Discussion Skills in the near future. During this workshop you will sharpen your Discussion Skills and practice dealing with various situations that may occur during an appraisal discussion. But there are several basic points we should discuss now.

- Schedule a comfortable, quiet place to conduct the interview, free from distractions and interruptions, and allow sufficient time for the discussion. Try to establish and maintain a relaxed and friendly atmosphere throughout your discussion.

- Remember, the appraisal interview is for the benefit of the employe. It is a "shoulder-to-shoulder" discussion rather than a "nose-to-nose" encounter. The two of you want to jointly and objectively look at past performance and future plans.

- Your comments on performance are most useful if you keep them objective. They should be based on facts you have entered on the Appraisal form and on specific examples. They are to be performance-oriented. By focusing on performance rather than personality you will avoid the impression of "attacking" the employe as a person.

- In the event that a disagreement occurs, attempt to resolve it during the interview. If additional information is needed or if you find yourself or the employe becoming angry, agree to continue the discussion at a specific time in the very near future. If the two of you still cannot resolve the difference, assist the employe in implementing the "open door" policy within your department.

- The Action Plans section of the appraisal concerns itself with the development plans you've formulated with the employe. During this discussion you will detail the actions to be taken to bring performance up to standard in areas needing improvement and to build new knowledge and skills in areas where standards are raised, or added. The employe's commitment to these plans evolves through the observed inclusion of inputs from the completed Worksheet, the sense of management's commitment to the plans, and through the opportunity you provide during the interview to comment and contribute to their refinement and finalization. Unit 5 describes this section in more detail.

- During the interview, this is also the place to discuss the employe's views on career interests, fields of greatest potential or other such personnel administration questions that may be raised. If you are unfamiliar with the career interests as expressed by the employe's Codes for Fields of Work, then assure the employe that you will find someone who can explain the career field in more detail. Help can generally be obtained from Personnel or someone now working the career field.

- The close of the appraisal interview begins with a summation of the major points discussed, commitments made, and differences unresolved, if any. The employe is then encouraged to complete the employe comment block on the Appraisal form, and to acknowledge by signature that the appraisal interview was conducted. Note particularly the sentence below the employe signature line.

- The lower portion of the back page of the appraisal form is used to summarize your comments on the appraisal interview. Keep your summary

factual, noting major points of agreement and disagreement, and any commitments made.
- Finally, sign the form, then make an appointment with your supervisor to review the appraisal and complete the Appraisal Summary Form as described in the next unit of this Guide.

8. COMPLETING THE APPRAISAL SUMMARY FORM

The next step in the process is to review with your supervisor the results of the employe's appraisal interview and complete the Appraisal Summary Form (Exhibit G in the Handbook). First, the Overall Performance and Employe Interests sections are completed using the data as it appears on the Performance Appraisal Review and Appraisal Worksheet.

Your inputs and observations are particularly useful as your supervisor completes sections C, D and E. Your knowledge of the employe will be blended with your supervisor's experience and knowledge of GM operations and opportunities as the sections are completed. In this way a better, more objective assessment can be made of the employe's Fields of Greatest Potential, Estimate of Potential Level, and Readiness for Other Positions.

You and your supervisor sign the Appraisal Summary Form; then it and the Appraisal Review and Appraisal Worksheet forms are sent to Personnel.

Personnel will do three things with the appraisal forms:
- First, they will review them to assure they are complete and in compliance with Appraisal Standards and Procedures.
- Next, they will enter the information from the Appraisal Summary Form into the HRM Employe Information System so that your employe may have maximum visibility and opportunity to be considered for movement when openings occur in your plant, division, or in the Corporation.
- Finally, Personnel will file the forms in the employe's permanent personnel record jacket.

9. COACHING AND COUNSELING

Well, maybe the formal documentation for this year is over for the employe with overall "Good Competent Performance." But the on-going part of the process is not. You and your employe will be carrying on the Action Plans you've both agreed to. You will also be giving your employe feedback on his or her performance on a day-to-day basis.

If your employe "Needs Slight Improvement" overall, you will have established an action plan with a schedule of special appraisals. The process used for these is essentially the same as that for the annual appraisal, except for the frequency and for the fact that you have checked the "Special" box on the Review form indicating you are focusing on the specific areas needing improvement as specified on the regular annual appraisal.

If your employe "Needs Much Improvement" overall, you will be working more closely with the employe, your supervisor, and the Personnel Department. You will be providing coaching and counseling to help the employe to achieve a good, competent level of performance.

10. FORMS USED IN THE APPRAISAL PROCESS

This matrix summarizes the procedural aspects of the forms used in the GM Appraisal Process:

	Name of Form			
	Appraisal Worksheet for Salaried Employes	*Performance Appraisal Review for Salaried Employes**	*Performance Improvement Plan*	*Appraisal Summary Form*
Who completes the form?	Employe	You	You and your supervisor with guidance from Personnel.	Your supervisor with you and other appropriate members of management.
When is the form completed?	Before *you* complete the Performance Appraisal Review.	Before the appraisal interview.	After you and your supervisor decide employe needs much improvement and before the appraisal interview.	After the appraisal interview.
Who signs the form?	Employe	Employe, you, your supervisor, Personnel, and others as desired.	Employe, you, your supervisor, Personnel.	You, your supervisor, Personnel, and others as desired.

*This form is to be reviewed by Personnel prior to the appraisal interview. For employes rated "Needs Much Improvement."

10
Case Study: Kimberly-Clark Corporation

The forms and procedures described here are not required but are used in most Kimberly-Clark divisions and units. They have the endorsement of the chief executive officer and the human resources staff. Regardless of what form is used, there is one requirement: the subordinate must sign the form indicating that a performance appraisal discussion has been held.

This case study begins with a diagnostic look at the performance appraisal system at Kimberly-Clark. The word *system* is used here to mean all the methods by which the company evaluates employee performance, for whatever purpose.

What objectives are or could be served by evaluation of individual performance in Kimberly-Clark?

A. *To Strengthen Principal-Deputy Relationships*
    The questions "What is expected of me?" and "How am I doing?" emerge consistently as questions employees expect to have answered by a "fully communicating" supervisor. Implicit in both questions is an evaluation of performance. Whether principal-deputy relationships are in fact strengthened by an evaluation is a judgment that simply cannot be made without taking into account *how* the evaluation is communicated. There is ample evidence to support the motivational value of recognition, achievement, responsibility, and growth potential of a job. The principal is the major "provider," and the act of providing ought to strengthen the relationship. Yet, the "providing" cannot be done effectively without appraising performance; which suggests, indirectly at least, that strengthened relationships *can* be an objective served by performance evaluation.

B. *To Achieve Results in Accordance with Goals*
Whether or not a company has formally adopted MBO as a corporate program, if it believes and supports the idea of managing to previously agreed-
to goals/targets/objectives, it follows that such an approach to managing
requires periodic evaluation of progress toward those goals. Certainly one
objective of an appraisal system can be to stimulate goal setting and provide
a reading of where employees stand in relation to identified business and behavioral objectives. However, if the system merely "monitors" and does not
give feedback to the employee, it fails to provide any stimulus to continue to
manage by objectives in the true sense of the meaning of that expression.

C. *To Assist in Individual Development Planning*
A performance appraisal system *can* be concerned with developing the individual employee. Most managers are at least intellectually committed to the
idea that it *should* be. "Development" suggests that the appraisal does not
merely look at past performance, but also deals with how to improve future
performance. To do this kind of development *it is necessary to have a face-
to-face meeting between principal and deputy.* . . or, as we have come to
call it, an appraisal interview or performance review.

   Note: If any one, or combination of A, B, and C above were the *only* objectives to be served by reviewing performance, there would be no need to attach
a rating label to the employee's performance.

D. *To Provide Data for Human Resource Planning*
One objective in evaluating performance can be to do an audit of management talent, i.e., to evaluate the present supply of human resources for replacement planning and identify candidates for promotion. Corporate inven-
tories used to plan hiring, promotions, transfers, etc., are only as good as
their answers to the questions (1) Who's capable of doing what? (2) How capable? and (3) With what potential for growth? There is no denying the fact
that submitting data to a corporate human resources inventory involves "evaluation of performance" and, as such, is an integral part of a company's total
performance appraisal system. If, however, this were the only purpose for the
system, there would be no necessity for a face-to-face review.

E. *To Serve as a Basis for Compensation Decisions*
A compensation program in which merit handling—by definition—requires
that the principal determine a performance rating for each deputy makes
such a program part of the total appraisal system of the company. As with
human resource planning decisions (above), judgments on employee ratings
could be made by principals to satisfy salary administration needs without requiring face-to-face performance reviews.

F. *To Assure Documentation for Action to Change an Employee's Status*
Company practices with regard to performance evaluation have become the
subject of discrimination lawsuits. While documented data to support dis-
missal action should have been a normal part of good supervision, it has now
become a legal necessity. Simply recording performance is not enough.
Face-to-face discussions with the employee must have occurred.

G. *To Influence the Amount of Company Dollars Available Annually to the Employee for Self-Development (Kim-Ed Allotment)*
A performance appraisal objective unique to Kimberly-Clark is the need for
an individual performance rating of all exempt salaried personnel for the purpose of factoring it into the formula for allotting Kim-Ed dollars. It is unlikely
that this factor would have been built into the Educational Opportunities Plan
had not some other reason for rating performance (salary handling) already
existed. In any event, it is now a procedural requirement for the formula cal-
culation and, as such, becomes an objective served by evaluating performance.

EMPLOYEE PERFORMANCE REVIEW

 KIMBERLY-CLARK CORPORATION

PERSONAL EVALUATION GUIDE

Items listed on the Personal Evaluation Guide, are to help the supervisor determine those factors which influenced the deputy's results either positively or negatively during the review period. While use of this tool is optional, supervisors will find it particularly valuable as an aid to completing Part IV of the Performance Evaluation Summary. Completion of the Personal Evaluation Guide independently by the principal and the deputy prior to the evaluation discussion should provide a basis for meaningful communication between them.

PERFORMANCE EVALUATION SUMMARY

I   ANALYSIS OF JOB PERFORMANCE

Primary consideration when reviewing performance (at least annually) should focus on the information called for in Section I of the report: _results achieved_. Part A provides space for an abbreviated listing of principal accountabilities and on-going responsibilities and documentation of results achieved for the items listed. Similarly, Part B is based on the **_specific objectives_** previously agreed to for this review period. The level of performance (commendable, unsatisfactory, etc.) represented by the achieved results for each item listed is recorded (√) in the columns on the right. Previously agreed to standards for each performance level should eliminate evaluation surprises.

II   ADDITIONAL CONTRIBUTIONS

This section provides an opportunity for the supervisor to record performance "extras" of the employee, unplanned and unexpected accomplishments which represented significant added value to the unit, division or company.

III   OVERALL PERFORMANCE

Before making a summary judgment of the employee's overall performance, the supervisor needs to consider the following important questions:

—— What was the level of difficulty experienced in attaining these results? (considering external circumstances, uniqueness of assignments, resources available, competing priorities, etc.)

—— What was the individual's direct contribution to the results?

—— How much assistance was required from me? Others?

—— What impact did the achievement have on other employees' performance?

—— To what extent did the achieved results contribute to unit and company objectives?

After determining whether the value of the results achieved was enhanced, diminished or unchanged by the above considerations, the Overall Performance rating should be checked in Section III.

IV   PERSONAL DEVELOPMENT

Record both the strengths and areas for needed growth that were apparent during the review period. The Personal Evaluation Guide can be very useful in arriving at conclusions for this section. Again, the deputy's own evaluation should be part of this discussion and his/her input to the action plan in particular, is essential for gaining commitment.

V   OTHER COMMENTS

This section of the Performance Evaluation Summary might be used for any of the following:

(a)   Remarks about performance during the review period which are not reflected in other parts of this Summary and which the deputy would like "on the record."

(b)   Strategies agreed to regarding how principal-deputy relationships can be strengthened during the next period.

(c)   Preliminary thoughts on business and managing objectives to be developed for the next period.

(d)   Targeted dates for future discussions on objective setting, progress reviews, career planning, etc.

NOTE:

Expanded definitions for Performance Evaluation terms "competent, provisional, unsatisfactory, commendable, outstanding" are available from your personnel representative.

PERSONAL EVALUATION GUIDE

		Exceeds Require-ments	Meets Require-ments (Fully Satisfactory)	Requires Improvement	Not Applicable
EMPLOYEE NAME _____ DATE _____ REVIEW PERIOD FROM _____ TO _____	**CHECK APPROPRIATE COLUMN**				
A. JOB KNOWLEDGE AND APPLICATION					
1. DEPTH OF UNDERSTANDING OF POSITION					
2. BREADTH OF UNDERSTANDING OF FUNCTION					
3. APPLICATION OF THESE UNDERSTANDINGS ON THE JOB.					
B. JOB ADMINISTRATION/MANAGEMENT					
1. SETTING REALISTIC GOALS/OBJECTIVES					
2. DEVELOPING PRACTICAL WORKABLE PLANS					
3. PLANNING WORK DETAIL					
4. ORIGINATING NEW OR IMPROVED CONCEPTS, METHODS, TECHNIQUES					
5. AWARENESS AND ADHERENCE TO INTERNAL POLICIES, PRACTICES, CONTROLS					
6. UNDERSTANDING OF EXTERNAL REQUIREMENTS (LAWS, REGULATIONS, ETC.)					
7. UTILIZING PERSONNEL EFFECTIVELY (ORGANIZATION, DELEGATION)					
8. KEEPING SUPERVISOR INFORMED					
9. KEEPING ASSOCIATES AND/OR DEPUTIES INFORMED					
10. EXERCISING ECONOMY IN USE OF AVAILABLE RESOURCES					
11. MEETING DEADLINES					
12. ANTICIPATING AND TAKING APPROPRIATE ACTION					
13. ANALYZING PROBLEMS AND DEVELOPING LOGICAL CONCLUSIONS					
C. COMMUNICATION					
1. EFFECTIVENESS OF ORAL EXPRESSION					
a. INFORMAL DISCUSSION (SUCCINCTNESS AND DIRECTNESS)					
b. FORMAL PRESENTATION (EXPRESSION, PROJECTION, ORGANIZATION)					
2. EFFECTIVENESS OF WRITTEN EXPRESSION					
a. LOGICAL ORGANIZATION, READABILITY, GRAMMATICAL CORRECTNESS					
b. ACCURACY, COMPLETENESS, CONCISENESS					
3. LISTENING EFFECTIVENESS					
D. PERSONAL QUALIFICATIONS THAT MAY AFFECT JOB PERFORMANCE					
1. WINNING CONFIDENCE AND RESPECT					
2. DEMONSTRATED LEADERSHIP CAPABILITY					
3. EFFECTIVE INTERPERSONAL RELATIONSHIPS					
4. WORKING AS A PART OF A TEAM					
5. DEMONSTRATED INITIATIVE					
6. EFFECTIVE MANAGEMENT OF TIME					
7. PERFORMING UNDER PRESSURE					
8. ADAPTING TO REQUIRED CHANGES IN THE WORK ENVIRONMENT					
9. AMOUNT OF SUPERVISION REQUIRED					
10. DEVELOPMENT OF OTHERS					
11. CONTINUING SELF DEVELOPMENT					
E. OTHER					
_____					
_____					

PERFORMANCE EVALUATION SUMMARY

GENERAL INFORMATION	REVIEW PERIOD FROM _____ TO _____	CHECK APPROPRIATE COLUMN				
	TIME IN	Outstanding	Commendable	Competent	Provisional	Unsatisfactory
NAME _____	PRESENT POSITION _____					
TITLE _____	EVALUATED BY _____					
DEPT. _____	DATE _____					

I ANALYSIS OF JOB PERFORMANCE

A. PRINCIPAL ACCOUNTABILITIES AND ONGOING RESPONSIBILITIES FOR THIS REVIEW PERIOD	RESULTS ACHIEVED					

B. SPECIFIC OBJECTIVES FOR THIS REVIEW PERIOD	RESULTS ACHIEVED					

II ADDITIONAL CONTRIBUTIONS _____

_____

_____

_____

III OVERALL PERFORMANCE

Fulfills Expectations   **Is Below Expectations**   **Exceeds Expectations**

☐ Competent   ☐ Unsatisfactory   ☐ Provisional   ☐ Commendable   ☐ Outstanding

IV PERSONAL DEVELOPMENT

STRENGTHS _____

_____

_____

_____

_____

_____

_____

SPECIFIC DEVELOPMENT NEEDS _____

_____

_____

_____

_____

_____

ACTION PLAN _____

_____

_____

_____

_____

_____

_____

_____

_____

V OTHER COMMENTS _____

_____

_____

_____

_____

_____

_____

_____

_____

_____

_____

_____

_____

_____

Employee's Signature   Date   Supervisor's Signature   Date

Signatures indicate that the Performance Evaluation Discussion has been held

KC 1687

NON-EXEMPT EMPLOYEE PERFORMANCE REVIEW

KIMBERLY-CLARK CORPORATION

Name	
Title	
Evaluated By	Date / /
Review Period From / / To / /	

Part I   Accomplishments

In evaluating accomplishments for the review period, consider whether work assignment objectives and responsibilities were satisfied; deadlines met; work done accurately and completely; and, the extent to which assistance from others was required.

General Job Responsibilities	Comments	EVALUATION					
		O	Cm	Cp	Pr	Un	N/A

Specific Assignments Given	Results						

Part 2   Personal Effectiveness

In evaluating personal effectiveness, only rate those factors which influenced the individual's accomplishments during the review period

	Exceeds Requirements	Meets Requirements	Needs Improvement	Unacceptable	Not Applicable		Exceeds Requirements	Meets Requirements	Needs Improvement	Unacceptable	Not Applicable
Cooperation Interacting constructively with co-workers and associates						**Dependability** Reliability - seeing things through to conclusion					
Organization Proper planning of work, knowing priorities						**Attitude** Identification with company/unit goals and objectives; acceptance of directions, criticism					
Independent Judgment Ability to work with minimal direction						**Initiative** Anticipate problems, and take action					
Oral Expression Ability to communicate with co-workers and supervisors in an effective and understandable manner											
Observance of Office Schedule Attendance, lunch, breaks, etc											

ADDITIONAL CONTRIBUTIONS: _____

_____

_____

_____

_____

OVERALL PERFORMANCE RATING:

Fulfills Expectations   **Is Below Expectations**   **Exceeds Expectations**

☐ Competent   ☐ Unsatisfactory   ☐ Provisional   ☐ Commendable   ☐ Outstanding

PERSONAL DEVELOPMENT:

STRENGTHS: _____

DEVELOPMENT AREAS: _____	ACTION PLANS: _____

OTHER COMMENTS BY PRINCIPAL AND/OR DEPUTY: _____

_____

_____

_____

_____

_____

_____   _____   _____   _____
Employee's Signature   Date   Supervisor's Signature   Date

Signatures indicate that the Performance Evaluation Discussion has been held

Definitions of Rating Factors

O - Outstanding — Job performance is exceptional. Results consistently exceed expectations.

Cm - Commendable — Exceeds standard performance requirements to a noticeable degree. Results are substantially above required performance for the position.

Cp - Competent — Level of performance fulfills essential requirements. Results are normally expected. Encompasses good performance.

Pr - Provisional — Shows need for further improvement; not fully satisfactory. Some results are acceptable, others fall short.

Un - Unsatisfactory — Poor performance; requires early improvement to justify retention.

N/A - Not Applicable — Either no basis for judgment or judgment can not be made because assignment is not completed at time of review, or no need to carry out responsibility existed during review period.

KC 2140 Back

Explanation of Column Headings in Performance Evaluation Summary Section

Outstanding
- Demonstrates a knowledge that normally can be gained only through long periods of experience in his/her particular type of work.
- Recognized by all as a real expert in particular job area.
- This employee is a number one candidate for promotion when a higher-level position becomes open in his/her own or related field.
- Actions show an understanding of more than his/her own work. Outsiders seek him/her out because of knowledge of *many* facets of the department's work.
- Requires little or no supervision or follow-up.
- Shows unusual initiative and is a self-starter.
- Almost invariably takes the best approach to getting the job done.

Note: This level of performance must be looked at in terms of both *quantity* and *quality.* Use of this category shows that you are recognizing really outstanding worth to the unit and company within the level of his/her position.

Commendable
- This employee exceeds position requirements on some of the more difficult and complex parts of the job. Seizes the initiative in development and in implementation of challenging work goals. Normally, this individual will be considered for promotion.
- You are getting *more* than you bargained for.
- You find the employee accomplishing *more* that you expect.
- Is able to take on extra projects and tasks without defaulting in other activity fields.
- Each project or job he/she tackles is done thoroughly and completely.
- The employee's decisions and actions have paid off to a higher degree than would be expected.
- Continually provides "extras."
- Requires only occasional supervision and follow-up.
- You find the employee does his/her own advance planning, anticipates problems and takes appropriate action.
- Shows a good grasp of the "big picture." Thinks beyond the details of the job, works toward the overall objectives of the department.
- "If you had four like him/her you would only need three."

Competent
- The employee is doing a complete and satisfactory job. Performance is what is expected of a fully qualified and experienced person in the assigned position.

- You would not *require* the employee to improve significantly. *If* there is improvement, it's a plus factor for your unit's effectiveness. If *not,* you have no reason to complain.
- If all your employees performed at this level, your unit's overall perform-ance would be completely satisfactory, in your judgment and that of your manager.
- You get few complaints from others with whom the employee's work interfaces.
- Errors are few and seldom repeated.
- The employee demonstrates a sound balance between quality and quan-tity of work.
- The employee does not spend undue time on unimportant items, neg-lecting problems or projects that should have priority.
- You feel reasonably secure in quoting or utilizing his/her input or recommendations.
- Requires only normal supervision and follow-up and almost always com-pletes the work assignments or projects on schedule.
- Has proven capable of handling all elements of the job.
- You consider this employee a good, solid member of your team and feel reasonably secure in giving him/her any kind of an assignment within the scope of his/her position.

Provisional
- This employee is doing the job reasonably well. Performance definitely meets the minimum requirements for the position and many of the normal performance requirements.
- Performance is not really poor, but if *all* your people were at this perform-ance level you would be in trouble.
- You definitely would like to see him/her improve, but in the meantime he/she is doing you some good.
- There's room for improvement, but it looks like he/she is headed in the right direction.
- This kind of employee needs some pushing and follow-through, but does the job under close guidance.
- If you didn't have to keep such a close watch on him/her you would con-sider a competent rating.
- Effort could qualify him/her for fully competent rating but needs to acquire more know-how to go with his/her drive.
- You have to plan his/her programs or assignments step by step. After that, usually gets the job done.
- Some of your people have to "carry" him/her on occasion.

Inexperienced Employees
- Doing quite well for being fairly new on the job.
- Making progress on the job, momentarily at provisional level, on way to-ward being fully competent.

- Has not been on the job long enough to have encountered all its aspects. Performance has been satisfactory on those he/she has handled.

Unsatisfactory
- The employee has been on the job long enough to have shown better performance. Should let the employee know he's/she's running out of time.
- Work is holding up that of the other positions with which it interrelates.
- The employee is creating problems with those who have to help carry his/her load (including yourself).
- Just doesn't seem to have the drive or the know-how to do the job. Would be better off on some other job for which qualified.
- It is more than likely the employee recognizes that the job is not getting done.
- If performance continues at this level, employee should be replaced.
- No matter how many times you explain things, he/she doesn't seem to grasp the situation.
- Just doesn't seem to get things accomplished.
- Work keeps falling behind. If you keep the employee much longer you will be in real trouble.
- Performance is losing a lot of credibility for your unit.
- You have been put on the spot yourself because of his/her lack of performance.
- Seems to make one mistake after another, some of them are repeats.
- Apparently does not have the background or ability to grasp the work.

SOME SELF-APPRAISAL THOUGHTS

1. What have my major achievements been in the past year, and how have they related to my objectives?

2. What major dissatisfactions do I have with my performance during the past year?

3. What are the most important assets I bring to the job I am currently performing?

4. What are the personal development areas in which I most need to improve?

5. What have I learned in my work during the past year which will help me most in the future?

6. What can my immediate principal do to help me improve my effectiveness on the job?

7. What would I most like to see changed in the way our department is currently operating?

Note: This form is optional and may be given to subordinates in preparation for the appraisal interview. The form is generally not given to the boss.

11
Research at
General Electric Company

General Electric has conducted continuous research to determine the effectiveness of the various approaches to performance appraisal that have been used in different divisions of the organization. Some of the approaches and results of this research are described here. It is important to note that the research described in this chapter is more than 15 years old.

Current research is being conducted under the direction of Selig Danzig, who emphasizes that more research is needed.

> The issues raised here involve important questions that have not been asked in past research. They represent opportunities for new knowledge about, and insights into, the dynamics of the performance appraisal process that are needed if we want to make this system work.
>
> We should not permit major changes in human resource systems to be introduced without a clear picture of what we expect such changes to accomplish for the organization. Moreover, we should have a clear plan for monitoring and evaluating such changes to ensure that they fulfill the expectations their designers predicted.
>
> If we apply the same disciplined approach to our personnel management systems as we do to other investment decisions, our performance appraisal systems will be more likely to meet the real needs of subordinates, managers, and administrators.[1]

Meyer and Walker's 1961 Study[2]

The subjects of this study were 31 managers in several manufacturing components of the General Electric Company and 31 specialists whose status (position levels) in the organizations was approximately the same as the managers'.

253

All the company components included in the study had formal performance appraisal programs. One of the primary purposes of these programs was to provide the measure of merit for determining pay level under a merit-pay type of salary plan. Appraisals were generally based on the responsibilities assigned to each employee as described in his position guide. The appraisal forms used also included sections for identifying development needs and for suggesting remedial actions.

During the interviews conducted as a part of this research study, each subject was questioned about his experience with the performance appraisal program and was asked to give an especially detailed description of the last performance appraisal discussion with his boss.

Of the 62 men interviewed in this study, 49 (23 of the managers and 26 of the specialists) reported that they had had performance appraisal discussions with their managers within the last year or two, which they could describe in some detail. Of the 49, there were 21 who reported that they had taken some specific constructive action to improve performance, on the basis of suggestions made or topics discussed in the feedback interview.

The results of this study suggest that the skill with which a supervisor handles the appraisal feedback discussion with subordinates is a key factor in determining whether or not the performance appraisal program is effective in motivating behavioral changes. The supervisor's skill in handling the appraisal discussion also seemed to have an important influence on how well the subordinate understood the philosophy of the pay-for-performance salary plan. This in turn might influence his attitude toward the plan. Moreover, a favorable attitude toward the salary plan was found to be significantly correlated with whether or not the employee took constructive action on the basis of performance appraisal.

Kay, French, and Meyer's 1962 Study[3]

The general purpose of this study was to examine some of the psychological effects of performance appraisal interviews and performance improvement planning discussions between managers and their subordinates. Eighty-four manager-subordinate pairs were observed in performance appraisal and goal planning discussions. The subordinates were interviewed before and after these discussions in order to obtain reports of their reactions and other before-and-after measures. For half the subjects, managers were instructed to permit a high level of subordinate participation in performance improvement planning, while for the other half, managers were instructed to use a nonparticipative approach. A follow-up check was made 12 to 14 weeks after the performance appraisal and goal planning discussions to determine the degree to which performance improvement had been achieved.

Briefly stated, the findings of the study were:

1. Most subordinates felt they deserved more favorable appraisals and greater salary increases than they actually received.

2. Criticisms of performance typically resulted in defensiveness on the part of subordinates. The more criticisms or improvement needs the manager cited in an appraisal discussion, the more likely the subordinate was to be defensive.

3. The more criticism and defensiveness were observed in the appraisal discussion, the less performance improvement was achieved 12 to 14 weeks later.

4. The use of praise had no measurable effect on employee reactions to criticism or on subsequent job performance.

5. Appreciable improvements in performance were realized only when specific goals were established with time deadlines set and measurement of results agreed upon. Regardless of how much emphasis the manager gave to an improvement need in the appraisal discussion, if this did not get translated into a specific goal, very little performance improvement was achieved.

6. Subordinate participation in goal planning resulted in improved subordinate attitudes and subordinate-manager relations, but it resulted in little difference in the degree to which goals were achieved. Actually, more substantial differences in attitudes and goal achievement were associated with the subordinates' ratings of the usual level of participation they experienced in day-to-day work-planning activities with their managers.

On the basis of this study's results, the following recommendations regarding practical applications relating to performance appraisal programs appear to be warranted:

1. Summary appraisals for salary administration should be separated from goal planning discussions.
2. Goal planning discussions should yield greater returns than comprehensive appraisal discussions.
3. Subordinate participation in goal planning should result in improved performance and attitudes.

Bassett, Meyer, and Kay's 1965 Study[4]

Which kind of performance review is more effective, one prepared by the subordinate or one prepared by the manager? This study was carried out to compare the results obtained in appraisal discussions using these two kinds of reviews. Some of the specific questions to answer were:

How do the two parties react to the subordinate-prepared appraisal?
Are subordinates more likely to be more constructive, rather than defensive, if the discussion is based on a self-appraisal?
Under what conditions is one approach superior to the other?

What effect does either approach have on subsequent subordinate-manager relations? On subsequent performance?

Thirty-five managers in the Apollo Support Department at Daytona Beach, who had at least two appraisal discussions scheduled with subordinates within about a one-month period, agreed to participate in the study. Several had three or more scheduled, so there were 81 subordinate participants appraised in all.

Both manager and subordinate were interviewed prior to each appraisal discussion. Ratings of the subordinate's performance and a description of his or her opportunities for improvement were obtained from both. The subordinates also completed a questionnaire covering attitudes toward their managers, their jobs, the appraisal system, their past experience with appraisal, and the department's salary plan.

Following the appraisal discussion, both parties were interviewed again to determine their respective impressions of and reactions to the appraisal discussion. Each was asked to specify what improvement needs or criticisms had been brought out in the discussion. The subordinates also completed a second questionnaire designed to measure any changes in attitude that might have occurred and gave an estimate of how they thought their managers had rated them in the appraisal.

Near the close of each appraisal discussion, the manager asked the subordinate to prepare a list of job-related goals. Two weeks later they met again to discuss, modify, and agree upon a final list of goals the subordinate would work toward in the ensuing months.

Twelve weeks after the appraisal discussion, manager and subordinate were interviewed again to obtain estimates of how well the goals set had actually been achieved. The experimenter recorded three goal achievement estimates: the manager's, the subordinate's, and his own, based on the evidence of performance accomplishments cited by both people interviewed.

Here are the results of the study:

1. The majority of managers (23 out of 35) preferred the subordinate-prepared appraisal approach.
2. Performance was less likely to fall short of expectations following the discussion based on subordinate-prepared appraisal.
3. The subordinate-prepared appraisal approach had the most beneficial effect on low-rated employees.
4. Subordinates who had had no previous appraisal discussion with their present managers reacted best to the manager-prepared appraisal approach.
5. Frequent informal discussion of performance result in improved subordinate-manager relations.

The New Approach: Work Planning and Review

On the basis of the research described above, a new approach was developed. The Work Planning and Review (WP&R) process consists of periodic meetings between an employee and his or her supervisor. The meetings are oriented toward the daily work and result in mutual planning of the work, a review of progress, and mutual solving of problems that arise in the course of getting the job done. The process does not involve formal ratings. Rather, it provides the basis for the subordinate and the manager to sit down informally, discuss the job to be done, and then agree on a plan and review progress. Marion Kellogg describes this program in detail in her book *What to Do About Performance Appraisals*.[5] Two other studies on Work Planning and Review are summarized here.

Behavioral Research Service's 1964 Study[6]

In an intensive study of the performance appraisal interview completed in the Small Aircraft Engine Department early in 1962, work planning and goal setting discussions between subordinate and manager were found to be far more effective in improving job performance than was the typical performance appraisal discussion in which needs for improvement were considered.

Following that study, approximately half of the department switched to a Work Planning and Review approach. The other half stayed with the annual comprehensive performance appraisal discussion as a means for motivating performance improvement. This provided an opportunity to compare the two approaches under normal operating circumstances. The researchers carried out a before-and-after survey of attitudes toward the phases of job performance and subordinate-manager relationships that they felt should be affected by work planning and performance appraisal activities.

Generally, the results show positive and significant gains by the WP&R group in five of the six areas measured by the questionnaire:

> Help received from manager in doing present job better
> Mutual agreement on job goals
> Future improvement and development
> Participation in job-related decisions
> Attitudes toward performance and appraisal discussions

The performance appraisal groups showed no change in any of the areas measured. In the sixth area, which covered attitudes toward salary practices, both groups were at the same level in 1962.

Kay and Hastman's 1966 Study[7]

In this study, 56 subordinate-manager WP&R discussions were observed, and the activities that occurred in these discussions were recorded. Follow-up performance evaluations were then obtained three months later for the subordinates in each discussion. The purpose was to determine how the manner in which the WP&R interviews were conducted seemed to affect subsequent job performance.

The study found that maximum improvement in job performance was realized by those employees whose WP&R interviews consisted predominantly of problem-solving discussion—that is, the review of problems encountered in achieving job goals and the discussion of alternate solutions to those problems and anticipated future problems. The least performance improvement was noted for employees whose WP&R interviews had been conducted like a performance appraisal interview. The same pattern found in a previous study of the performance appraisal process was observed in this study: criticism of the manager followed by defensiveness on the part of the subordinate and lack of improvement in subsequent job performance.

The subordinate played a significant role in most WP&R interviews. It was a highly participative process. Managers were observed to adapt their approach to WP&R interviews to fit individual subordinates' needs. These WP&R interviews were carried out in a much less standardized manner than were performance appraisal interviews observed in a previous study.

It is important to note that work planning and review discussions are not meant to cover everything.

> Some managers have attempted to use the WP&R program as a substitute for the performance appraisal program. There were, however, several objectives which performance appraisal programs are designed to achieve which were not achieved in most of the WP&R discussions observed in this study.
>
> For one thing, these discussions generally did not include a *summary judgment* on the part of the manager as to the subordinate's overall performance. Some subordinates expressed a need for this. The WP&R discussions were focused almost entirely on relatively short-term plans and goals and on problems associated with the accomplishment of these goals.
>
> A second topic of interest to the subordinate seldom mentioned in WP&R discussions was *salary*. This was according to design, for it had been found in previous research that the consideration of salary frequently had an emotional effect which left the employee in a poor frame of mind for considering job problems constructively. Needless to say, however, this is a topic which should be discussed with each employee periodically. Salary discussions, held separately from WP&R discussions, should provide an excellent opportunity for the manager to communicate to the subordinate his summary appraisal of the subordinate's overall job performance.

A third topic which seldom was discussed in WP&R interviews was *career planning* for the subordinate. This was of special interest to those employees who had aspirations to advance in the Company. Some provision should be made by the manager to meet this need. As in the case of communications regarding salary, a separate discussion focusing on career plans and development needs should serve the purpose in this area better than the traditional annual comprehensive performance appraisal discussion.

Based on the additional knowledge and understanding of the WP&R process which this study has provided, the following conclusions seem warranted with regard to practical implications:

1. Most employees will respond best if allowed to contribute heavily to the discussion of job plans, goals, and the solution to problems. In other words, the manager who uses a nondirective, participative approach will probably get the best results from WP&R discussions.

2. The manager should avoid turning the WP&R discussion into a performance appraisal interview. The evidence from both this study and a past study of the performance appraisal process indicates that attempts to motivate employees to improve by criticizing their past performance are not likely to be successful.

3. The WP&R process does appear to have a positive and constructive effect on the performance of employees in most jobs. Based on the observers' reports (not on the analysis of data), this process seems to be better adapted to some kinds of jobs than to others. More research is needed to determine the types of jobs, or perhaps the types of managerial styles, that are best suited to the constructive use of a systematic work planning and goal setting procedure.

References

1. Selig M. Danzig, "What We Need to Know About Performance Appraisals." *Management Review*, February 1980.
2. Herbert H. Meyer and William B. Walker, "A Study of Factors Relating to the Effectiveness of a Performance Appraisal Program." *Personnel Psychology*, Autumn 1961.
3. E. Kay, J. P. French, Jr., and H. H. Meyer, "A Study of the Performance Appraisal Interview." Lynn, Mass.: Behavioral Research Service at General Electric, 1962.
4. G. A. Bassett, H. H. Meyer, and E. Kay, "Performance Appraisal Based on Self-Review." Daytona Beach, Fla.: Behavioral Research Service at General Electric, 1965.
5. Marion Kellogg, *What to Do About Performance Appraisals.* New York: AMACOM, 1975.
6. "A Comparison of a Work Planning Program with the Annual Performance Appraisal Interview Approach." Lynn, Mass.: Behavioral Research Service at General Electric, 1964.
7. E. Kay and Roy Hastman, "An Evaluation of Work Planning and Goal Setting Discussions." Lynn, Mass.: Behavioral Research Service at General Electric, 1966.

Index

Affirmative Action Plan, 24
agreement, in appraisal
    interview, 58
Allhiser, Norman, 65
American Management
    Associations, 9, 44
analyst, job description of, 29–30
    in marketing, 29–30
    in systems, 27
Appley, Lawrence A., 9
appraisal form, *see* forms
appraisal interview
    approach in, 52
    checklist for, 58–59
    conducting the, 55–59
    critical incidents method and,
        47–48
    definition of, 18
    evaluation of, 59
    guidelines for, 55–57
    objectives of, 51
    preparation for, 51–55
    self-appraisal and, 50–51
    setting for, *see* climate
    techniques for, 57–58
appraisal, job performance
    categories and scales in, 48–49
    communication of, 12
    data for, collecting, 47–48
    definition of, 18, 45
    forms in, use of, 22
    frequency of, 23
    program objectives for, 19–20
    see also self-appraisal,
        appraisal interview
argument, avoiding, in appraisal
    interview, 56
athletics, coaching in, 73–81

behavior change, requirements
    for, 63

blind-spot effect, 46
boss, *see* supervisor
Broyles, J. Frank, 74, 80
Bryant, Bear, 75

career counseling, 15–16
career planning and develop-
    ment, factors in, 12–15
Chaddock, Paul, 67
checklist, in appraisal interview,
    58–59
climate
    in appraisal interview, 52, 55
    as requirement for behavior
        change, 63
coach
    approaches and techniques of,
        81–91
    characteristics of, 73–81
compatibility, and halo effect, 46
confrontation, avoiding, 56
consultants, in performance
    improvement plan, 64
contrariness, and horns effect,
    46
coordinator of management
    development, performance
    standards for, 42
counseling, characteristics of, 82
Coverdale, Dave, 9
critical incident method, 47–48
Crocker National Bank of
    California, 15

data, for performance appraisal,
    47–48
data processing manager, job
    description of, 31
Dayton-Hudson Corporation, 67
Delco-Remy Division of General
    Motors, 47

department head, performance
    standards for, 43
desire, as requirement in
    behavior change, 63
Dietzel, Paul F., 74
discrimination, and personnel
    policies, 24
division manager, performance
    standards for, 43–44
dramatic incident effect, and
    horns effect, 47

Education Exchange, 97
emotions, handling of, 85–86
employee(s)
    measuring coaching practises
        and, 86, 90
    motivation of, 7–8, 64, 80–81
    on-the-job coaching and, 82–
        90
    performance improvement
        plan and, 62, 66, 72
    performance problems and,
        64–65
    potential of, 9, 13
    preparation by, for appraisal
        interview, 54
    promotion of, 19
    self-appraisal by, 50–51
    setting performance standards
        for, 44
    strengths of, in appraisal
        interview, 57, 60
employment supervisor
    performance standards for, 40
equal employment opportunity,
    23–24
Erickson, John, 74, 80
evaluation, of appraisal
    interview, 59
expectations, clarification of, 9

Flanagan, J.C., 47–48
foreman, production, performance standards for, 39–40
forms
    "Individual Development
        Plan," and, 67, 70–71
    performance improvement
        plan and, 87–89
    use of, in performance
        appraisal, 22, 52, 57–58, 60
    future, in appraisal interview, 57,
        60

General Electric, 15, 21
General Motors, 47
guidelines, for appraisal
    interview, 55–57
guilt-by-association effect, and
    horns effect, 47

halo effect, 46
Hayes, James L., *v-vi*, 44
Hayes, Woody, 74
Herzberg, Frederick, 8
high-potential effect, and halo
    effect, 46
Hirsch, Elroy, 74–75
horns effect, 46–47

IDP ("Individual Development
    Plan"), 67
improvement of performance, 20
    in appraisal interview, 60
    see also performance
        improvement plan
"Individual Development Plan"
    (IDP), 67
    forms for, 70–71

job descriptions, samples of
    27–32, 38–43
job performance, *see*
    performance
job segments, *see* significant job
    segments
job training, 11

Kellogg, Marion, 20–21
Kirkpatrick, Donald L., 9
Knight, Bob, 75
knowledge, in behavior change,
    63

Landry, Tom, 75
Levy, Seymour, 59, 60
listening, in appraisal interview,
    56

machine-shop supervisor, job
    description of, 29
Mahler, Walter, 58, 86, 90–91
Management by Objectives
    (Odiorne), 46
management development
    coordinator, performance
    standards for, 42
Management Institute,
    University of Wisconsin—
    Extension, 65
management, philosophies of,
    98–99
manager(s)
    of data processing, job
        description of, 31
    of division, performance
        standards for, 43–44
    of manufacturing, job
        description of, 32
    of sales, *see* sales manager
    see also supervisor(s)
manufacturing manager, job
    description of, 32
maximum job performance
    conditions for, 8
    and effective coaching, 80
    rewarding, 16, 64, 80–81
McClain, Dave, 75
McGlocklin, Jon, 79
McGuire, Al, 75
McKay, John, 74
Meyer, Ray, 76
Meyer, Tom, 76
Miller, Ralph, 76
Morrissey, George L., 64
motivation, of employees, 7–8,
    64, 80–81

no-complaints bias, and halo
    effect, 46
nurse, job description of, 30

oddball effect, and horns effect, 46
Odiorne, George, 46, 82
OFCP (Office of Federal
    Contract Compliance
    Programs), Department of
    Labor, 23

office supervisor, performance
    standards for, 40
off-the-job activities, and
    performance improvement
    plan, 65–66
Olsen-Tjensvold, Reynolds, 9
one-asset person, and halo
    effect, 46
on-the-job coaching
    approaches and techniques of,
        81–91
    characteristics of and, 73–81
    definition of, 18
    performance improvement
        plan and, 72, 86–69
openness, in appraisal
    interview, 58, 60
Osborne, Tom, 77

Parseghian, Ara, 77, 84
Paterno, Joseph, 77
payroll supervisor, job
    description of, 28–29
perfectionism, and horns effect,
    46
performance appraisal, *see*
    appraisal, job performance
performance
    improvement of, *see*
        improvement of
        performance
    maximum job, *see* maximum
        job performance
    plan for improving, *see*
        performance improvement
        plan
    problems in, *see* problems,
        performance
    record of, *see* record,
        performance
    review of, program for, *see*
        performance review program
    standards of, *see* standards of
        performance
performance improvement plan,
    61–72
    Dayton-Hudson approach to,
        67
    definition of, 61–63
    development of, 64–65
    example of, 68
    finalization of, 67
    forms for, 70–71, 87–89

performance *(continued)*
  implementation of, 69
  off-the-job activities in, 66
  on-the-job coaching and, 72,
    86–89
  secondary, 69
  training professionals for, 64
  as written, 72
performance review interview,
  see appraisal interview
performance review program,
  controls on, 98–99
  definition of, 17–18
  forms, use of in, 22
  objectives of, 19–20
  pilot program of, 99
  requirements of, 92–99
personality, in appraisal
  interview, 57, 60
personality-trait effect, and
  horns effect, 47
Peter Principle, 8
Phelps, Richard "Digger," 77
philosophies of management,
  98–99
Planty, Earl, 85–86
positive reinforcement, and on-
  the-job coaching, 84
present job, form for
  improvement of, 70
problems, performance
  categories of, 64–65
  solutions to, 65–67
promotion
  of employees, 12–17, 19
  form for, preparation for, 70
psychologists, in appraisal
  process, 53

rapport
  in appraisal interview, 55–56
  building of, 12
  performance improvement
    plan and, 69
record, past, and halo effect, 46
record of performance,
  critical incident method and,
    47–48
  focus on, in appraisal
    interview, 57
reinforcement, positive, and on-
  the-job coaching, 84
requirements, for performance
  review program, 92–99

resentment
  on-the-job coaching and, 83
  performance improvement
    plan and, 69
reviewers, skills required for, 94
rewards, in behavior change, 64,
  80–81

salary administration, 19–22
sales representative, job
  description of, 28
sales manager
  job description of, 31–32
  performance standards for, 41
"sandwich" approach, on-the-
  job coaching and, 83–84
scales, in appraisal process,
  48–49
Schembechler, Bo, 74
secondary performance
  improvement plan, 69
secretary
  job description of, 27
  performance standards for,
    38–39
*Selecting and Training First-Line
  Supervisors,* (Kirkpatrick,
  Coverdale, Olsen-
  Tjensvold), 9
self-appraisal, 18, 50–51
  in appraisal interview, 59
self-comparison effect, and horns
  effect, 47
setting, *see* climate
significant job segments
  in appraisal interview, 57
  definition of, 18
  lists of, 27–32, 38–43
  performance improvement
    plan and, 61–62
  selection of, 26, 32–33
Simpson, William, 97
situation, as category of
  performance problems, 64–65
skills, for reviewers, 94
Smith, Dean E., 77
Stagg, Amos Alonzo, 78
standards of performance
  in appraisal interview, 57
  definition of, 18, 33–38, 44
  workshop outlining, 97–98
Starr, Bart, 78
Storey, Walter, 15
strategy, for performance

  improvement plan, 62–63
subordinate, *see* employee
supervisor (s)
  behavior changes by, require-
    ments for, 63–64
  as coach, 73–91
  coaching practises of,
    measurement of, 86, 90
  conducting appraisal interview
    by, 56–59
  emotional situations and,
    85–86
  employee self-appraisal and,
    50–51
  of employment, performance
    standards for, 40
  example of, 66–67
  expectations of, 9,
  gathering information for
    appraisal by, 47–50
  job segments, determined by,
    32–33
  of machine-shop, job
    description of, 29
  of office, performance
    standards for, 40
  of payroll, job description of,
    28–29
  performance improvement
    plan and, 62, 69
  performance problems and, 64
  preparation for appraisal
    interview by, 51–54
  selection and training of, 9
survey of coaching practises, 86,
  90

team, weak, and horns effect, 47
termination, of appraisal
  interview, 57, 60
They Call Me Coach (Wooden),
  78
time management, form for
  improvement of, 71
training professionals, and
  performance improvement
  plan, 64, 72
training program for performance
  reviewers, 94–98

Wisconsin—Extension,
  University of, Management
  Institute at, 65
Wooden, John, 78, 80, 84